MUTINY
AT SALERNO 1943

MUTINY

AT SALERNO 1943
AN INJUSTICE EXPOSED

Saul David

CONWAY

Saul David is an acclaimed historian and broadcaster. He is the author of *Churchill's Sacrifice of the Highland Division: France 1940*, as well as *Military Blunders: The How and Why of Military Failure*, *The Indian Mutiny: 1857* and *Zulu: The Heroism and Tragedy of the Zulu War of 1879*.

Copyright © 1995 Saul David

First published in 1995 by Brassey's

This edition published in 2005 by
Conway
The Chrysalis Building
Bramley Road
London W10 6SP
www.chrysalisbooks.co.uk

An imprint of **Chrysalis** Books Group plc

Distributed in North America by
Casemate Publishing
2114 Darby Road
2nd Floor
Havertown, PA 19083, USA

ISBN 1 84486 019 1

Printed and bound in Great Britain.

For Robin and Cherry

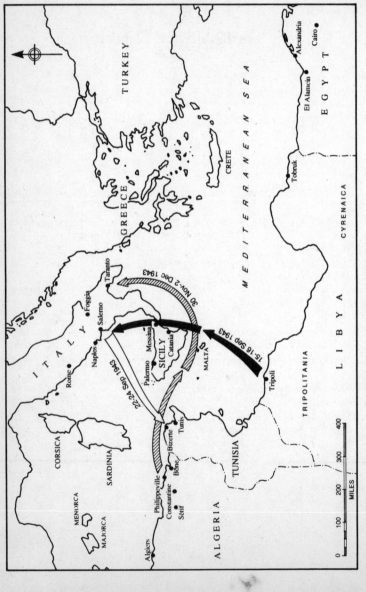

The three voyages taken by the mutineers between September and December 1943.

Contents

Acknowledgements

I first heard about the little-known mutiny at Salerno during an interview for my first book, *Churchill's Sacrifice of the Highland Division: France 1940*, with a man who had been captured at St Valéry, escaped and went on to fight the remainder of the war with the reformed 51st (Highland) Division. When he mentioned that members of his own unit were involved, my interest was immediately aroused: firstly, because I was not aware of *any* large-scale mutiny by front-line British troops during the Second World War; secondly, because I knew that at the time of the Salerno landings, September 1943, the 51st was resting in Sicily.

Anxious to learn more, I scanned the history books and found only an occasional brief reference to a mutiny at Salerno. The basic facts, however, were not in doubt: almost 200 veterans of the illustrious Eighth Army, mostly from the 50th (Tyne Tees) and 51st (Highland) Divisions, were convicted of mutiny for refusing to join units of the US Fifth Army fighting at the beachhead. How these men found themselves at Salerno, why they disobeyed orders and what happened to them after conviction were all questions left largely unanswered. I was determined to flesh out the bones by writing the first book to concentrate solely on the events surrounding the mutiny; I did not imagine for a moment that in the course of my research I would expose the trail of official incompetence, deceit, injustice and insensitivity contained in these pages that caused so many veterans to risk their lives for the sake of principle.

The most serious obstacle to uncovering the truth was the absurd 75-year closure that applies to court martial papers. I was able to surmount this with the assistance of Bill Murgatroyd, the only defending officer from the trial still alive, who provided me with a large chunk of the court martial transcript and crucial defence documents. It may well have been due to his intervention that the Ministry of Defence mysteriously agreed to release the trial papers 25 years early, and I owe him my gratitude.

A big thank you must also go to the many other participants in the tragic events of 1943 who consented to be interviewed. Without their testimony this book could not have been written; they are all named in Appendix 1. In particular, I am indebted to the seven mutineers who received me into their homes. All were visibly upset at having to relive the terrible events of 1943, even the ones who claimed to have led relatively normal lives since the war. Sadly, two of them – Percy Aveyard and Robert Thompson – did not live to see the publication of this book. Alexander McMichael, a Highland reinforcement who did not mutiny, also died recently. I hope this book is a fitting memorial.

Most of the mutineers are long since dead. Some did not survive the war, others died prematurely of causes which cannot be dissociated from the trauma of their convictions. The voices of many, however, live on in these pages. For this I am particularly grateful to Hannah Innes and Colin and Ian McFarlane.

Archie Newmarch, Hugh Fraser, Dr Molly Main and William Harris gave me access to unpublished documents, letters and personal accounts. I thank them.

Of the institutions that assisted me, I am again grateful to the staff of the Public Record Office, the British Library and the Imperial War Museum.

The following publications kindly ran free of charge my appeal to find eye-witnesses: *Bedfordshire Magazine*; *Birmingham Post*; *The Courier and Advertiser* (Dundee); *Daily Record*; *Daily Star*; *Evening Chronicle* (Newcastle); *The Mail on Sunday*; *Scotland on Sunday*; *Yorkshire Post.*

Acknowledgements for permission to include quotations from documents held at the Public Record Office (Crown copyright) and from editions of *Hansard* (Parliamentary copyright) are made to the Controller of HM Stationery Office; from *The Montgomery Papers* by Field Marshal Montgomery, to Viscount Montgomery of Alamein; from *Scottish Soldier* by Major General D N Wimberley, to the Trustees of the Imperial War Museum and the Controller of HM Stationery Office; from *Psychiatry in the British Army in the Second World War* by Robert H Ahrenfeldt, to Routledge & Kegan Paul; from *That Reminds Me* by Lord Russell of Liverpool, to Macmillan, Inc; from *Through The Waters: A Gunnery Officer in HMS Scylla 1942–3* by Robert Hughes, to Harper Collins; from the programmes *The Secret Mutiny, Mutiny* and *Newsnight* to the BBC; from a March 1982 issue of the *Blackpool Evening Gazette* to Reed Regional Newspapers; and from the 21 April 1945 issue of the *Daily Express* to Express Newspapers.

Once again I would like to thank everyone at Brassey's for the support and advice they have given me during the preparation of this work: in particular Jenny Shaw, Bryan Watkins and the indefatigable Caroline Bolton.

If this book achieves its aim – a royal pardon for all those convicted of mutiny at Salerno in 1943 – it will in no small part be due to my legal consultant, Adrian Clarke. A brilliant criminal lawyer, he has spent much of his valuable time advising me on the legal issues involved. I am extremely grateful.

My thanks are also due to Sir Ludovic Kennedy. As narrator of the 1981 radio programme *The Salerno Mutiny* and author of *10 Rillington Place*, the book that led to Timothy Evans being awarded a posthumous free pardon for murder, he was the obvious person to write the foreword.

Finally, I owe much to my family and to Louise. Anyone who is close to a young author trying to forge a career for himself will know how much.

Callow, January 1995   SAUL DAVID

Foreword
by
Sir Ludovic Kennedy

Ever since 1943, accounts of the so-called Salerno Mutiny have come to us in dribs and drabs in newspaper articles and radio broadcasts. However, it wasn't until the 75 year ban on the official papers was prematurely lifted in 1993 that Mr Saul David had access to them as source material for his book.

The full story, which he presents so admirably here, is truly shocking, with all the elements of a Greek tragedy; a tale in which a body of brave, decent men were treated as cattle and in which a gross early injustice, instead of being at once corrected, led to and was compounded by others.

In the summer of 1943, the bridgehead which the Allies had established at Salerno on Italy's west coast was in danger of collapsing. Reinforcements being urgently required, arrangements were made for 1,500 men to be shipped to Salerno in three cruisers from a base camp in Tripoli. Many were battle-hardened men of Montgomery's Eighth Army, who had fought their way across the desert, some still recovering from wounds or laid low with dysentery or malaria, others fresh from training camps in England.

Monty always believed in taking soldiers into his confidence with the result that Eighth Army morale was outstanding and the men ready to follow him anywhere. Because he made them feel a part of one big family, he stressed the importance, after any period of enforced separation, of soldiers being returned to their own units. That way you kept *esprit de corps*.

Afraid that the Eighth Army men would not take kindly to being told they were being sent to join Fifth Army men and would have to live and fight alongside soldiers who were complete strangers, the camp commandant lied to them, spread word around the base camp that they were being returned to their own units. When some of the less fit heard the good news, they at once presented themselves for embarkation, happy to be given this opportunity of rejoining their comrades. So rushed and chaotic was the embarkation that some men sailed with rifles but no ammunition and others with ammunition but no rifles.

On arrival at Salerno they found that the emergency had passed and there was no immediate call for their services. No officer came to put them in the picture, and for two days they were left to cool their heels in a field near the beach, stewing in the heat by day, bedding down on the bare earth by night, without medical attention and with time to brood.

Eventually orders came for them to be moved north. The bulk of the 1,500 obeyed, fearful of the consequences if they refused. But just under 200, mostly from the Tyne-Tees and Highland Divisions, stood firm. It was a spontaneous reaction from men who felt they had been messed about enough and, because there were no ringleaders and no conspiracy, hardly worth the name of mutiny. They were put into a prisoner of war cage next to some German prisoners who jeered at them. They were fed on hard tack and water and denied their cigarette ration, though the Germans were given theirs. Worst of all was their acute sense of having been deceived.

Shipped back to North Africa, they were taken in cattle trucks to Bizerte where a court martial awaited them – altogether three sergeants, 16 corporals or lance corporals and some 170 men, one of whom, John McFarlane, had won the Military Medal for bravery in the desert. All but a handful had clean records.

From the start everything was stacked against them. The charge should have been the lesser one of disobeying the orders of a superior officer, but the court simply could not accept that such a large body of men *could* have acted spontaneously and therefore the mutiny charge, though without a scintilla of evidence to support it, was correct. The prosecution were given five weeks to prepare their case, the defence six days; and of the 14 officers appointed to the defence, only four had had legal training. Although the charge against the men was of acting individually, no individual statements were taken from them, and those who had lied to them at Tripoli naturally refused to help the defence by admitting it.

If the guilty verdicts were predictable, the sentences were not. Despite the guidelines in King's Regulations that first offenders be given light sentences, the court condemned the three sergeants to be shot without any recommendation to mercy and the others to between five and ten years penal servitude. Yet if, as was said at the time, such draconian measures were intended to deter others, they entirely failed; for until the end of the war the whole affair was kept secret.

Soon after the trial the Adjutant General of the Army, General Sir Ronald Adam, arrived in North Africa on other business and having studied the papers on the case, declared the trial and sentences to be 'the worst thing we have ever done'. Consequently, the sentences were suspended.

But this was by no means the end of the affair. The men were returned to Italy and sent to the front, their reputations not only as mutineers but as cowards unwilling to fight going ahead of them. Hearing of a plan to keep them in the front line when others were relieved, in the hope they might be killed, no less than 40 per cent deserted. After capture or having given themselves up, their suspended sentences were activated and they found themselves in prisons in the company of robbers and rapists.

The final degradations came later. Those who had fought so bravely with the Eighth Army were denied the general war medal and the prized Africa Star with Eighth Army clasp. Private McFarlane was ordered to return his Military Medal of which he was proud, and only did so for fear of his suspended sentence also being activated. The wives of married men were told to return their army allowance book which entitled them to the few pathetic shillings a week they could draw from their husband's pay. After the war and the return of the men to their homes, some families were ostracised and forced to move to another area. Bitterness was widespread and understandable.

Although both Montgomery and the Fifth Army commander Alexander said that had they known about it, they would never have authorised the embarkation of the 1,500 men, post war petitions for pardons or a review of the case failed. Even as late as 1982, a Ministry of Defence inquiry during the Secretaryship of John Nott found that the men had not been deceived and there had been no miscarriage of justice.

Mr David's book gives the lie to this and more besides. Most of the participants in the 'mutiny' are now dead and the diminishing band of survivors are into their late 60s and 70s. To them, as much as for the widows, sons and daughters of their fellow convicted, it is surely time – indeed way past time – to put the record straight. In the last chapter of his book, Mr David makes a powerful plea for a pardon for all those involved. Whoever is the Secretary of State for Defence when this book is published, should not lose a moment's time in implementing it. Until then the stain on the British Army's record will remain.

Prologue

'No recommendation to mercy'

They came for them, like thieves, in the early hours of a cold and damp November morning. An NCO of the camp guard entered their spartan tent and rudely awakened the three sergeants, instructing them to dress and bring their kit. The most senior of the trio, Wally Innes, a veteran who had survived Dunkirk to take part in the Eighth Army's victorious advance across North Africa and Sicily, felt anger tinged with fear. 'What about the other lads? We've been through a lot with them, we can't just sneak out now,' he implored.

Anxious to complete his unpleasant task but struck with sympathy for the sergeants, the guard chose to defer to his officer. Innes was taken to see the camp commandant, Lieutenant Ted Everett, a decent, moustachioed officer whose respect for the prisoners had steadily grown since their arrival five weeks earlier. Permission was granted for the sergeants to say goodbye to their comrades and it was some time before they had visited all 30 or so tents, black shapes silhouetted against the moonlit African sky.

Their consciences clear, the three men marched out of the compound and were directed towards the back of a large truck, waiting with its engine running. First in, Innes felt his initial apprehension return as he identified, with eyes now accustomed to the gloom, four NCOs carrying Thompson sub-machine guns. 'What's going on?' he asked, nervously.

'It's not our idea, it's orders,' one of their heavily armed escort replied. Before the conversation could continue, the back doors were slammed shut and the truck moved off.

Lost in thought and filled with trepidation, Innes was only aware that the truck had come to a halt when the doors were flung open and he was ordered to step down, alone. Nearby he could just make out what appeared to be a long Nissen hut, divided into three. It was to the nearest end room he was taken, and ordered to strip. After a thorough search of his clothes he was allowed to dress again, but the only personal possession returned was his handkerchief. He was then directed into the second room, and as he closed the door he could hear one of the other sergeants enter the first. Inside, the room was bare apart from a stern-faced officer sitting at a table, faced by an empty chair.

'I've got a job I don't like to do, but it's my orders,' said the officer.

'Orders,' thought Innes, alarmed. 'That's the excuse the guard in the truck had used.'

'Sit down,' invited the officer, interrupting Innes' uneasy contemplation.

'No, sir, I'll stand.'

'Sit down!'

Innes complied. The officer handed him a sealed, unmarked envelope. Suspecting something was very wrong, Innes tried to postpone the awful moment by making to put the envelope in his pocket.

'No, I want you to read it,' insisted the officer.

His hands trembling, Innes opened the envelope and pulled out a single sheet marked 'Army Form A3996'. Scarcely breathing, he began to read.

To: 4452346 Sgt W Innes.

The Court have found you guilty of the following charge: Mutiny. The Court have passed a sentence of death upon you . . .

His eyes blurred; if he had not been sitting he would have fallen. Through his tears, and with racing heart, he read on.

The Court have made no recommendation to mercy.

This was too much. With a lump in his throat he asked the officer to finish reading it for him.

'Can't you read?' came the incredulous reply.

'Of course I can read, but I can't read any more.'

'All right, put it in your pocket and finish it when you get to your destination,' said the officer, sympathetically.

In a state of shock, Innes was hardly aware of being shepherded out of the room. Back in the truck, the words '*upon you . . . upon you . . . upon you*' kept echoing in his mind. And they had made *no* recommendation to mercy. He could not believe it; after all he had done for the army. The world had gone mad, he had only wanted to be sent back to his own unit. Such dark thoughts were interrupted by a figure climbing in beside him. It was his pal, Sergeant George Middleton. To the newcomer's whispered enquiry, Innes recounted the bad news. 'The same happened to me,' Middleton muttered, adding a stream of invective against the men he held responsible. They lapsed into silence and before long Sergeant Joe Pettit appeared, considerably shaken. As the truck moved off a faint glow to the east heralded the coming dawn, and it occurred to a bitter Innes then that, with a firing squad awaiting him, he might not see many more.

The day before, the three sergeants – all from the Durham Light

Infantry – had been found guilty of mutiny by a field general court martial in Constantine, Algeria. They had been arrested six weeks earlier after refusing repeated orders to join battalions of the 46th Division fighting at the Salerno beachhead in Italy. Also found guilty were five corporals, 11 lance corporals and 162 privates. Like the sergeants, all but two were battle-hardened veterans of the crack 50th Tyne Tees and 51st (Highland) Divisions. It was the largest-ever mutiny by British troops at war.

Chapter 1

Operation AVALANCHE

The Second World War, like so many wars, started badly for the British. In the west the German *blitzkrieg* tore through France, forcing the evacuation of the British Expeditionary Force from Dunkirk by June 1940 and the capitulation of our only notable ally. In the east the yellow tide from Japan gradually washed away many of our imperial outposts, including Hong Kong, Malaya and the key naval base of Singapore; by May 1943, following the conquest of Burma, it was threatening to submerge the jewel in our imperial crown – India.

Only in the Middle East was there a ray of hope, as the Desert Army under Lieutenant General Sir Richard O'Connor annihilated superior Italian forces in Egypt and Libya in the winter of 1940–41. But even there the glint soon dimmed when General Erwin Rommel, at the head of the first elements of what would later become his famous Afrika Korps, made a lightning strike at El Agheila in February 1941. Driving the Commonwealth forces before him, he advanced to Tobruk and threatened the whole position of the British in the Middle East. Though forced to withdraw in December by General Sir Claude Auchinleck, Rommel bounced back to take Tobruk the following June before continuing his thrust towards the Nile delta. Checked by Auchinleck at the first battle of El Alamein, he withdrew behind the extensive minefield to the west and began to build up for another attack. When that blow fell in August, Lieutenant General Sir Bernard Montgomery had taken command of the Eighth Army and was waiting for him on the Alam Halfa feature.

Montgomery's stunning success in a defensive battle convinced his troops that no more morale-sapping withdrawals were necessary. Here was a dynamic new commander in whom the men could place their trust. Confirmation of the newly-born 'Montgomery cult' was given in October with his seminal victory in the second, and this time offensive, battle of El Alamein, in which both the 50th (Tyne Tees) and 51st (Highland) Divisions fought with distinction. After 13 days of bitter fighting, the Axis front collapsed and Rommel was lucky to escape with the remnants of his army. The tide had turned. Churchill brilliantly summed up the significance of this success with the words: 'This is not the end. It is not even the beginning of the end. But it is, perhaps, the end of the beginning'.[1]

When the Anglo-American First Army landed at Algeria in November, the writing was on the wall for Rommel. Forced to fight on two fronts, he was handicapped further by Hitler's decision to give the Russian front absolute priority. Even so, the attempt to snuff out the Axis presence in North Africa by a link-up between the two Allied armies did not quite go according to plan. While the Eighth Army was winning a string of hard-fought victories and advancing more than 2,500 miles, the First Army suffered a humiliating defeat at the Kasserine Pass and remained bogged down in the mud of Tunisia. When the remnants of the Axis forces surrendered in May 1943, the Eighth Army had become the hammer and the First Army the anvil. Inevitably, the lion's share of the victory laurels went to Montgomery's troops, strengthening their *esprit de corps* and belief that no other formation was comparable, particularly the unheralded First Army. Such thinking was a major factor in the tragedy that lay ahead.

With only a minor pause to rest and regroup, the Allies – comprising the British Eighth Army and the American Seventh Army – landed at Sicily on 10 July 1943. With a full-scale invasion of mainland Europe from Britain not due until 1944, it was seen as a way of drawing resources away from the Russian front while also securing the Mediterranean shipping lanes. The final decision to extend the campaign to mainland Italy was only taken after Mussolini, the Italian dictator, had been toppled by a *coup d'état* on 25 July and the new head of government, Marshal Badoglio, had initiated secret peace negotiations. On 3 September, a couple of weeks after the last Axis troops had evacuated Sicily, the armistice was signed at the Sicilian headquarters of General Sir Harold Alexander, commander of the Allied 15th Army Group.

That same day, the first phase in the invasion of the Italian mainland began, when Montgomery's Eighth Army – without its spearhead divisions, the 50th and 51st, which were resting in Sicily – crossed the short Straits of Messina and landed unopposed at Reggio. This assault, code-named Operation BAYTOWN, was intended to secure the sea short cut through the Straits, while at the same time providing a diversion for the main landing by the American Fifth Army further north at the Gulf of Salerno six days later.

The choice of Salerno, 35 miles south of Naples, for the northern assault – code-named Operation AVALANCHE – was not ideal, but the alternatives were even less attractive. The Bay of Naples was too heavily defended, while the plain of Campania to the north was protected by offshore sandbars and, more importantly, was well beyond effective fighter cover from Sicily. Salerno, on the other hand, offered 20 miles of sandy beaches with open approaches and gradients ideal for landing craft. Coastal defences were patchy and the Montecorvino airfield, just three miles inland, was big enough for four fighter squadrons.

There were disadvantages, though, particularly once the troops were ashore. The prospective battlefield was a triangular plain – the beaches forming its 20 mile base, its apex 12 miles inland – fringed with rugged high ground. The defenders, dug in on the heights, would have a bird's-eye view of the plain and beaches below. Criss-crossing the heavily-cultivated plain were rivers and streams, the biggest of which, the Sele, cut through the centre and spanned 500 yards in places. Farm buildings were plentiful, as were olive and fruit trees, and although the corn had been cut, vines and tobacco plants stood higher than a man. In effect, the Salerno plain was a dead end, cluttered with obstacles and overlooked from above. Yet, in the minds of the planners, these drawbacks were outweighed by the advantages for an amphibious assault and the fact that Salerno was the furthest north the Allies could land while retaining land-based fighter cover.

At the request of the Allies, the Italians agreed to delay announcing the armistice until the evening of 8 September, only a matter of hours before the Salerno landings were under way. Eisenhower had ordered that his BBC broadcast should be relayed to the Fifth Army troops, nervously awaiting zero hour aboard ships, and their reaction was one of euphoria tinged with relief – most imagining, erroneously, that their task had been made immeasurably easier. Less ecstatic was Italy's erstwhile ally. The German commander-in-chief in the southern half of Italy, Field Marshal Albert Kesselring, had anticipated such an event and on hearing the news signalled to his commands the codeword 'Axis' – the prearranged sign to disarm Italian troops. Rome was sealed off, but not before King Victor Emmanuel and his government had fled to Allied-held Brindisi in southern Italy. The Italian fleet, too, managed to evade German clutches and by the morning of 11 September it, with the exception of the flagship *Roma*, sunk by a German bomber, had arrived at Malta, as laid out in the terms of the armistice. More successful was the German action against Italian troops, the majority of whom were disarmed by the morning of 9 September.

The task of the Fifth Army, as laid out in the instructions to its American commander, Lieutenant General Mark Clark, was 'to seize the port of Naples and to secure the airfields in the Naples area with a view to preparing a firm base for further operations'.[2] To achieve this, Clark had been allotted a bi-national force comprising the American VI Corps of the 36th and 45th Divisions (with the 3rd and 34th Divisions in reserve) under Major General Ernest Dawley, and the British X Corps of the 46th and 56th Divisions, a Commando brigade and a US Ranger force (with the 7th Armoured Division in reserve) under Lieutenant General Sir Richard McCreery. Clark was also able to call on the American 82nd Airborne Division. Strangely, given the onerous nature of the task, not one of these three generals had previously commanded such large formations in action. Only two of the assault divisions (the 45th and the 46th) had been extensively battle-hardened, while only one (again the 45th) had previously taken part in an amphibious landing. If events turned against the invaders, there would be little experience to fall back on.

The nomination of the untried Clark as army commander was aided by his close friendship with the Supreme Commander, Eisenhower. They had met while cadets at West Point, both had gone on to serve in the First World War, and since the outbreak of the Second World War both their careers had prospered. In June 1942, aged 51 and still only a major general, Eisenhower had been chosen over the heads of 366 senior generals to command the American forces fighting in Europe. His responsibility was expanded at the Casablanca Conference when, in an attempt to streamline the war effort, he was put in charge of all Allied troops in the Mediterranean theatre.

Clark, six years Eisenhower's junior, had thrust to the fore in 1941 when, as a lieutenant colonel, he was allotted the task of reorganising and expanding the American ground forces. With success came rapid promotion, and in May 1942 he accompanied Eisenhower across to Europe with the rank of major general. When he was given the Fifth Army in 1943, Clark's staff abilities were well recognised; his ability to command a large formation in a tough fight was untested and, consequently, more in doubt.

The plan of invasion was for X Corps – designated the Northern Attack Force – to land close to the port of Salerno and, once established, advance from there to capture Naples. The 56th Division would land with two of its three brigades on four beaches on the right of X Corps, while the 46th Division would be deployed with one brigade in the middle, just to the right of Salerno. The most important task, though, was to seize the road corridors through the Sorrento peninsula – the rugged neck of land separating the Gulf of Salerno from the Bay of Naples – and this was reserved for the special forces: the Commandos and the Rangers, who would land to the left of Salerno at the villages of Vietri and Maiori respectively. Once ashore, the 46th Division was instructed to link up with the Commandos on its left and the 56th

Division on its right, and then push inland as one to take Montecorvino airfield (six miles), the road and rail junction at the town of Battipaglia (six miles), and, if possible, Ponte Sele (12 miles).

VI Corps, or the Southern Attack Force, was given the job of protecting X Corps' right flank. To achieve this it would land two brigades of the 36th Division to the right of the River Sele, which was selected as the boundary between the two corps. Its D-Day objective was to link up with the 56th Division and advance to the high ground between Ponte Sele and Magliano – a full 13 miles from the coast.

German opposition to a landing was potentially fierce; both in terms of numbers and, more importantly, quality. Stationed near Battipaglia, directly opposite the invasion beaches, was the 16th Panzer Division. The Hermann Goering Panzer Division was near Naples, while the 15th Panzer Grenadier Division was only a couple of hours' drive further north at Gaeta. Five more divisions were within striking distance, including a parachute formation, two panzer grenadier divisions and a panzer division.

Shortly after 3.30am on 9 September the advance elements of the Fifth Army clambered down the ramps of their landing crafts and splashed ashore. They were at the sharp end of a vast invasion armada of more than 600 boats – including warships and merchant vessels – that had approached the Gulf of Salerno in the ideal conditions of a calm sea and a clear, moonlit night.

Although by nightfall on the first day the Fifth Army had not gained all its objectives, its landing was deemed a success. X Corps had met the stiffest resistance, but the 56th Division had still managed to occupy Battipaglia, while the Ranger force had advanced six miles across the Sorrento peninsula and was in sight of the Naples plain beyond. The 46th Division had failed to take Montecorvino airfield, but had advanced past Pontecagnano and reached the high ground to the north. The 36th Division of VI Corps had also fallen well short of its goal, and was held on high ground about five miles from the beaches. Even so, the beachhead seemed to have been firmly established, around 40,000 men had come ashore, and the commanders were reasonably confident.

Yet landing on the beaches was one thing, securing them and breaking out quite another. The race was now on to bring in reinforcements. If the Germans could hurry their crack troops to the area quicker than the Allies could land back-up, even the survival of the beachhead was by no means certain. Eisenhower's headquarters had anticipated the dilemma of reinforcements a week before the invasion began. On 2 September, Major General Whitely, Eisenhower's deputy chief of staff, wrote to the War Office in London stating:

> The follow-up problem is perhaps more complicated than anything we
> have met hitherto. Apart from using the North African ports and Tripoli,
> ferry services must be run from the two ports in Sicily.[3]

The main difficulty was availability of transport rather than manpower,
complicated by the fact that reserve divisions and replacements for the
assault formations were based as far apart as Sicily, Libya, Tunisia and
Algeria.

Between 10 and 12 September the Allies fought desperately to extend
their beachhead. But German forces were pouring into the area and,
after a series of punches and counter-punches, the Germans had
retaken Battipaglia from the 56th Division and were still in control of
the village of Altavilla, a key objective of VI Corps. The 46th Division was
well established at Salerno and Vietri, but the Germans were still too
close to allow the harbours to be opened. General McCreery was far
from happy and, fearing increased German pressure on the 46th
Division, he asked General Clark to shift elements of VI Corps across the
River Sele to take over the right section of the 56th Division's front, so
units of that division could be freed to shorten the 46th Division's front.
Clark agreed.

Yet his fears that the Fifth Army was becoming overstretched were
growing. At 1.10pm on 12 September, he sent a signal to his immediate
superior, General Alexander, commanding the 15th Army Group,
which comprised the Fifth and Eighth Armies on the Italian mainland
and the Seventh Army in Sicily:

> Will appreciate your assistance in expediting shipment of follow up
> convoys especially Seventh Armoured Division. Our build-up rate all
> important. Largest air raid yet now in progress.[4]

Under the circumstances, it was perhaps fortunate that Alexander's
high reputation as a commander was based largely on his ability to make
the best of a bad lot. Born in 1891, the third son of a Northern Irish earl,
Alexander had shown early promise as an artist and for a time it seemed
that he would seek to make a living by painting. But the militaristic
fervour of the pre-1914 days proved too much for this most unlikely
army officer and he joined the Irish Guards as a regular in 1911. Any
desire to redirect his career back to a more aesthetic bent was expunged
by the 1914–18 war, which quickly exposed his outstanding martial
talents. In 1915, aged just 23, he was already a major with acting
command of his battalion, and for a time in 1918 he was an acting

brigadier. Twice decorated for gallantry and twice wounded, his only respite from four years in the front line, other than the occasional training course, was for convalescence.

Unlike many other outstanding fighting soldiers, Alexander's career prospered between the wars. In 1937, aged just 45, he became the youngest major general in the British Army. When war broke out again, he was in command of the 1st Division. His skilful handling of it during the retreat from Belgium resulted in his appointment as corps commander of the rearguard at Dunkirk, from where he refused to leave until he was certain that no British troops remained. From one military disaster he was pitched into another. In early 1942, with the Japanese pouring through South East Asia, he was given the unenviable task of commanding the Anglo-Indian army in Burma. Again, his composure in a tight spot was displayed when he narrowly evaded the encircling enemy and supervised a masterly withdrawal back to India. By August 1942, with the reputation of the man who had helped to save two armies, he was appointed Commander-in-Chief Middle East with the task of saving another, and, in conjunction with his subordinate General Montgomery, he managed this and more. If any man could stay cool in a crisis, especially one that involved a bi-national force, it was Alexander.

The problem he faced at Salerno was how to find a way to accelerate the build-up. All available sea and air transport was accounted for as part of an inflexible timetable. The next infantry replacements were not due to arrive until 15 September, while the advance elements of the American 3rd Infantry Division and the British 7th Armoured Division were not expected until later still.

The crisis came to a head on 13 September. By now, battle groups from six German divisions had arrived at the beachhead, and shortly after midday elements of the 16th Panzer and 29th Panzer Grenadier Divisions attacked VI Corps down each side of the River Sele. Within hours, four American battalions had been overrun and German armour had arrived at the junction of the Sele and Calore rivers, about three miles from the coast. For a time it seemed that the enemy would reach the sea and split the bridgehead in half. Only desperate action by two artillery battalions firing over open sights, backed up by drivers, cooks and clerks from army headquarters, prevented this. That evening General Dawley shortened his line, enabling him to move an infantry battalion across to the trouble spot, and in the early hours of 14 September, at General Clark's request, two parachute battalions from the 82nd Airborne Division were dropped into VI Corps' sector.

Disaster had been narrowly averted, but such had been the precariousness of the situation on 13 September that Clark had gone to the extreme of instructing his staff to draw up two contingency plans for evacuation: each involving the withdrawal of one corps before relanding it to reinforce the other. The subsequent opposition of General McCreery and the naval chiefs implies that such plans were impractical, and it was lucky for Clark that they were never needed.

Despite the apparent stabilisation of VI Corps' line during the night of 13–14 September, the top brass were still acutely aware that the very existence of the beachhead was in danger. At a morning conference on 14 September attended by Generals Eisenhower and Alexander – at the latter's tactical headquarters in Bizerte, Tunisia – the conversation centred, not surprisingly, on reinforcements for the Fifth Army. To help alleviate the crisis it was agreed that fast-moving cruisers would be used to rush troops to Salerno, while another battalion of paratroops from the 82nd Airborne Division would be dropped into the beachhead that night.[5]

The task of transporting the parachutists posed few problems; from their base in Sicily they were a short plane ride from Salerno. The cruiser-borne reinforcements were a different matter. As VI Corps had already been, and was due to be, bolstered by airborne troops, it was only natural that any other replacements would go to X Corps. After all, X Corps had also been heavily attacked, and by nightfall on 12 September had suffered over 1,300 casualties. The generals were aware that the corps was due to receive 2,000 men on 15 September, as part of the planned build-up of troops, but less than half of these would be infantry. It was decided, therefore, that all the emergency reinforcements would be infantrymen – the front-line foot-sloggers whose battle expenditure was inevitably the highest.

The question now was which troops. There were various options open. If speed was of the essence then the obvious choice would be men based in Sicily: either elements of the American 3rd Division, which was already destined for Salerno, or battalions from the illustrious British 50th and 51st Divisions. That none of these formations was used is probably explained by the desire to reinforce existing X Corps battalions, rather than to back them up with separate units. Furthermore, the 3rd Division was already part of VI Corps, while both British divisions were under consideration by the War Office for a move back home to train for the Normandy landings planned for 1944. Even so, given the supplementation of VI Corps with separate units of paratroops and the proximity of Sicily to the crisis at the beachhead, it is strange that neither of these expedients was used on a temporary basis.

Instead, it was decided to scrape up infantry reinforcements from base camps in North Africa – a 14-hour journey by ship from Salerno.

A clue may lie in the administration instruction concerning British reinforcements for the Italian campaign, issued by General Alexander's staff on 29 August. It stated that the 'main reinforcement depots' in North Africa 'are located' at the Algerian port of 'Philippeville'.[6] Indeed, all the planned reinforcements for X Corps were being handled by the Advanced Reinforcements Section at Philippeville, and it is not surprising that the initial effort to find more men was directed there. At 12.27pm on 14 September, Alexander's 15th Army Group tactical headquarters in Bizerte sent a signal to Clark's headquarters at Salerno, and repeated the message to Allied Force Headquarters (AFHQ) in Algiers:

> 1,000 infantry reinforcements for each 46th and 56th Divisions, total 2,000 are embarking in 3 cruisers from Philippeville 1900 hours today 14 September. Signal most immediate your acceptance.[7]

Yet at 1.25pm Eisenhower's staff at AFHQ sent a contradictory signal to Tripolitania district headquarters in Tripoli, stating that 1,500 infantry reinforcements for Salerno were 'required immediately', and that they were to 'stand by at two hours' notice for embarkation by Royal Navy probably today'.[8]

So why did AFHQ contradict 15th Army Group's notification that 2,000 reinforcements would be coming from Philippeville? The answer lies in the lengthy time it took to encode, send and then decode important signals. According to AFHQ's signal log, the message from 15th Army Group was not received until 2.40pm – long after its own message was sent. In other words, Eisenhower's staff had not contradicted it because when they sent their own signal they were not yet aware of it.

This bizarre overlapping of signals was to continue throughout the day. A full 40 minutes before Alexander's staff at Bizerte became aware of AFHQ's signal to Tripoli, they, mysteriously, had also decided to bring the men from the Libyan port. At 2.45pm, 15th Army Group tactical headquarters signalled to Clark that 1,500 infantry reinforcements for Salerno would embark from Tripoli at 7am the following morning aboard Royal Navy cruisers.[9] Although this message was an implicit revision of the earlier signal, there was no specific mention that the 2,000 men from Philippeville had been cancelled, and this was to cause some confusion.

At the same time, Alexander's staff sent a signal to AFHQ asking them to disregard the earlier 12.27pm message in favour of the updated version that had just been sent to Clark (further evidence that they were not yet aware of AFHQ's signal).[10] Acting on this information, AFHQ then sent a second signal to Tripolitania district headquarters at 6pm, giving the definite time of departure as defined by 15th Army Group – 7am the following morning.[11]

This extraordinary sequence of signals tends to confuse who was taking what decision. The administrative instruction relating to reinforcements, issued on 29 August, defined the roles of the two headquarters: 15th Army Group headquarters was 'responsible for co-ordinating, confirming and passing all firm demands for personnel and shipping to AFHQ', which in turn was 'responsible for meeting these demands and for making and notifying shipping arrangements'.[12] So in theory, the subordinate headquarters would tell AFHQ what it needed, leaving the latter to make the arrangements. In practice, Alexander's staff would interfere throughout the process, resulting in a morass of orders and counterorders.

The minutes of the morning conference make no reference to where the reinforcements were to come from, probably because AFHQ, the responsible party, still had to make enquiries as to the most suitable place. By midday, assuming the men would be collected from Philippeville, Alexander's staff contacted Clark accordingly. Yet within hours they had changed their minds. In the meantime, unknown to Alexander's staff but possibly for the same reason, AFHQ had set in motion the collection of the reinforcements from Tripoli. So why did both headquarters decide on Tripoli when they should have known that most of the reinforcements allocated to X Corps were based in and around Philippeville? The obvious inference is that there were not enough reinforcements readily available at Philippeville. But there were.

The main replacement centre for X Corps was 1 Infantry Reinforcement Training Depot (1 IRTD), located just outside the port of Philippeville. Its war diary states that during the month of September 1943 there were never fewer than 121 officers and 3,196 men in its holding battalions.[13] Given that only 1,500 officers and men were needed for Salerno, even this minimum figure would have been more than adequate. In any case, an alternative source of reinforcements had been mentioned in 15 Army Group's administrative instruction of 29 August: 'if base depots are exhausted' the main policy was 'to take reinforcements from 4th Division in North Africa'.[14]

Although a regular formation, the British 4th Division had unofficially been designated a replacement pool because it was under strength – two brigades instead of three – and because it had only arrived in Africa two months earlier. Already, by 14 September, it had lost its commander to the 46th Division and almost 1,800 of its infantrymen had been posted to the infantry reinforcement depot at Philippeville.

Of these, 730 had been sent on as reinforcements for X Corps as part of the planned build-up, and more would go before the campaign was over. Between 21 September and 2 October a further 1,200 infantrymen would be sent to Philippeville to await posting.[15] So with over 3,000 men at the infantry reinforcement depot on 14 September, and many more with the 4th Division at Bougie, why did the higher commands not ask for them?

Distance cannot have been a factor, as Tripoli and Philippeville are virtually equidistant from the Salerno beaches where all three cruisers were on anti-aircraft duty when they received orders to proceed to Tripoli.

It is just possible that AFHQ made a mistake. After all, 56th Division and other X Corps' troops had embarked from Tripoli *en route* to Salerno, and it may well be that AFHQ staff officers assumed that their reinforcements were based there. This confusion could have come about because, while Philippeville was in an area directly controlled by AFHQ in Algiers, Tripoli came under the authority of the British Middle East Force Headquarters in Cairo.

But if AFHQ was originally unaware that Tripoli contained mainly Eighth Army men, a signal sent by Tripolitania district on the evening of 14 September soon disabused it of this fact. The 1,500 reinforcements ready for despatch, the signal pointed out, were 'Husky' men as there were 'none for Avalanche' at Tripoli.[16] As 'Husky' was the codename for the Sicilian campaign, in which the Eighth Army was the sole British formation, Tripoli left no doubt as to the type of troops it was about to send. AFHQ's failure to act on this information by cancelling the draft can be seen in two ways: either it knew the true state of affairs all along, or, given the emergency, it was too late to look for an alternative.

There is also some reason to suspect that Alexander's staff genuinely believed that there were enough reinforcements for X Corps at Tripoli. Admittedly, his staff had issued the administrative instruction that outlined Philippeville as the main centre for British reinforcements, but they too might have been confused by the embarkation of part of X Corps from Tripoli. Also, according to the war diary of the No 6 Advanced Reinforcements Section in Tripoli, a staff captain from the 15th Army Group arrived on 2 September to ascertain the number of reinforcements available for both the Eighth Army and X Corps.[17] Furthermore, although in theory all X Corps men had left Tripoli by the time of the Salerno landings, a few were still left there after this date in 155 Camp.

On the other hand, the switch to Tripoli could have been a calculated move. Given the apparent seriousness of the situation at Salerno, the quality of troops might have been considered crucial. The 4th Division had yet to see action in the theatre, and many X Corps' replacements at Philippeville had a similar lack of battle experience. Tripoli, on the other hand, could boast a large transit camp full of Eighth Army veterans – men who had seen it all and who, to staff officers oblivious of their fierce regimental and divisional ties, must have seemed ideal for the situation.

There is a second mystery, though. Who were the officers who ordered the switch? The obvious candidate at 15th Army Group tactical headquarters is the commander, General Alexander. Certainly General Sir Ronald Adam, the adjutant general, later thought so. He became involved in the course of events by chance when on a routine visit to North Africa in November, and in April of the following year he wrote to General Montgomery (by then in Britain commanding the 21st Army Group), admitting that he had 'put a good deal of the blame' for sending Eighth Army men to reinforce Fifth Army units on Alexander and his lack of a 'proper administrative staff'.[18] Montgomery, on the other hand, thought Major General Charles Miller, Alexander's administrative chief, was to blame. In a letter to Adam, also sent in April, Montgomery set out the facts as he knew them:

(a)   Reinforcements were urgently required for British Divisions in the 5th Army on the Naples front.

(b)   Charles Miller could not find enough men from their own reinforcements, so he ordered up certain men of the Eighth Army from my depots in Tripoli.

(c)   Before taking action as in (b) he did not consult me, nor did he consult Alexander.
       If I had known what was to be done I would have said 'No'. Alexander would also have said 'No'; I am sure of this as we discussed it together afterwards.[19]

If Montgomery is to be believed, and there is no reason to doubt him, then the switch was made by an insensitive – and, in Montgomery's eyes, incompetent – staff officer. The fact that he and Alexander, the two most senior and experienced British generals in the Mediterranean, would not have agreed to the change of plan proves that such a move was asking for trouble.

There is other evidence to back up Montgomery's assertion that Alexander was not aware of the switch to Tripoli. In his memoirs, General Mark Clark insists that Alexander arrived at his Salerno headquarters in time for breakfast on the morning of 15 September, via a destroyer that had carried him from Bizerte.[20] Such a voyage would have taken well over 14 hours, and there is every reason to assume, therefore, that Alexander was absent from his tactical headquarters at Bizerte before the second signal, informing Fifth Army that reinforcements would arrive from Tripoli, was sent.

A number of signals sent on 15 September confirm that Alexander was unaware of the switch. Back at Clark's headquarters that evening, following a tour of the front-line sectors, Alexander despatched two messages – one to General Eisenhower at Algiers and one to Winston Churchill, the Prime Minister, who was aboard a cruiser in mid-Atlantic returning to Britain from the Quadrant Conferences in Canada. To Eisenhower, Alexander noted: 'I have asked for 1,500 British Infantry Reinforcements from Philippeville to come at earliest possible'.[21] To Churchill, he was even more specific: the 1,500 men from Philippeville would arrive in 'under 48 hours'.[22]

The true state of affairs was also lost on General Clark. His headquarters had been informed on 14 September that the 46th and 56th Divisions would be reinforced by 1,500 men from Tripoli, but he and his staff must have assumed that they were in addition to the 2,000 already promised from Philippeville. As late as the evening of 17 September, a full day after the 1,500 men from Tripoli had arrived at the beachhead, Clark sent a signal to AFHQ:

> When General Alexander visited this Headquarters on September 15th he offered to make available to Fifth Army by Naval vessels 2,000 replacements. General Alexander's cable through this Headquarters to Tac 15th Army Group requested these replacements should be forwarded ...[23]

Clearly, during his visit to the beachhead Alexander had signalled his own headquarters to make sure the 2,000 men were on their way. It cannot have been until he arrived back at Bizerte on 16 September that he was informed of the change of plan, and by then it was too late to do anything about it.

So was General Miller the main culprit, as Montgomery suggests? It would make sense. Miller was in command of 15 Army Group's administrative branch, and thus responsible for all forms of resupply, including manpower. Furthermore, all the signals relating to the reinforcements for Salerno sent from 15th Army Group's tactical headquarters on 14 September were classified with the prefix 'MGA', while the crucial signal informing Fifth Army that the men would be coming from Tripoli was signed by a major general. As Miller's official title was Major General, Administration, or MGA for short, it is reasonable to assume that he authorised the signals. Although his administrative branch was based in Cassibile, Sicily – with the rest of Alexander's main headquarters – he was at tactical headquarters, the nerve centre of the army group, at this early and crucial stage of the campaign.

The man at AFHQ who sanctioned the use of base camps at Tripoli for Salerno reinforcements must have been Lieutenant General Sir Humfrey Gale, the chief administrative officer and senior British rank. If this was so, it is ironic that Gale was later given the responsibility of confirming the harsh sentences meted out to those soldiers who subsequently refused to join units at Salerno.

By the evening of 14 September the cumbersome cogs of military resupply had been put in motion. When they ground to a halt two days later, 1,500 men, many of them veterans and under the illusion that they were returning to their own battalions, had been needlessly transported from an Eighth Army transit camp to join Fifth Army units fighting in the cauldron of Salerno.

Chapter 2

'You're going back to your units'

The urgent request for reinforcements on 14 September caused some consternation at the Tripoli headquarters of Tripolitania district, the army-controlled area covering the western half of Libya. Under the impression that they had only Eighth Army men available, the staff in Tripoli replied as such to AFHQ. But they also wasted no time in notifying their main base depot, 155 Reinforcement and Transit Camp, that men were required at short notice.

Situated by the sea on the edge of town, 155 Camp was a massive, tented metropolis that could house anything up to 12,000 troops, administered by a permanent staff of 20 officers and 200 men. Its purpose, as its full title suggests, was to house, temporarily, troops on their way to serving units. These men included raw recruits drafted from Britain, soldiers transferring from one unit to another, and, most importantly, veterans who had recovered from illness and wounds sustained in the front line. As the population of such a camp was constantly changing – individual soldiers rarely remained for longer than a few weeks before posting – discipline was lax, training unsystematic, and entertainment limited. With no guards and no wire surrounding the perimeter, the inhabitants were largely free to come and go as they pleased. In theory, all new arrivals had their particulars taken before being acquainted with camp routine: reveille at 6am, breakfast beginning 15 minutes later, and roll-call at 8.30am. For the rest of the morning the men were supposed to be allocated to fatigues or weapon training. The reality was very different, according to one man chosen for the draft to Salerno, Private Archie Newmarch of the 5th East Yorkshires:

> Everyone appeared to be left to their own devices, particularly within their own lines. The only bugle calls taken notice of were reveille, chow-up or fall-in. No passes were in evidence, nor were any guards on duty. The whole of the camp appeared very demilitarised: no one seemed to know who was who, where the different groups had come from, and no information was forthcoming, either verbally or otherwise.[1]

On 14 September the camp contained over 9,000 soldiers of all arms, including infantry, gunners, sappers and tankmen. To facilitate their administration, the men were assigned to specific areas. Not surprisingly, the infantry lines were the biggest. In a statement – or 'proof of evidence' – given to the defence prior to the trial of the mutineers, Company Sergeant Major R Green, the senior NCO in charge of the infantry, asserted that on the day in question there were 'approximately 1,700 men in the Infantry Lines available for posting to Eighth Army'. In addition there were 'other men ... of the X Corps also available for posting'. Given that in another statement Green says that 155 Camp was, to his knowledge, 'a Transit Camp only for the Eighth Army',[2] it is reasonable to assume that the X Corps infantrymen were few in number and could never have made up more than a fraction of the required draft. They were probably members of the 56th Division who had not been fit enough to take part in the invasion and had been left behind to recover. Certainly, their presence was the exception to the rule, which explains why district headquarters reported to AFHQ that it only had 'Husky' (Eighth Army) men available.

Shortly after 5.30pm on 14 September, the camp commandant, Lieutenant Colonel T R Richards, received word from district headquarters that 1,500 infantrymen were needed for Operation AVALANCHE. As district headquarters had yet to receive confirmation that Royal Navy cruisers would carry them, and as the shipping available at Tripoli was sufficient to transport just half the required total, only 750 men were initially requested to stand by. Major Carter, the officer in charge of the infantry lines, was informed, and he in turn instructed Sergeant Major Green to detail the 750. Green takes up the story:

> I paraded all available men in camp. As only certain units were designated, I detailed the 750 men from the units specified. To the best of my belief, no Highland Division reinforcements were called for; therefore I dismissed the Highland Division personnel on that parade.[3]

About an hour later, while Green was waiting for the first batch of 750 men to return to the parade ground with their kit, a member of the camp staff arrived with an updated order from the movements section at district headquarters. Definite news had by now been received that three cruisers, with a carrying capacity of 1,500, would arrive at Tripoli in the early hours of the following morning. A further 750 men were required. Green later stated:

> I sent runners, corporals and everybody I could get hold of who was in a responsible position to go round to the tents, the canteen, the beach and also to the dining rooms to get the men.

Once the men had been rounded up, Green called out the names of the second batch of 750. Many of them were Highlanders. He recalled:

> I cannot remember whether the order stated that Highland Division personnel were required, or that I was to obtain the 750 men from any and every source. I think, but cannot swear, that the Highland Division was specified, because, when all available men were called on parade so that I might detail the 750 men now called for, Highland Division men were among the first whom I ordered to stand by for the draft.[4]

One such man was Private Raymond Whitaker of the 7th Battalion, the Argyll & Sutherland Highlanders. He recalls that during the first parade the sergeant major in charge had said that all men from the 51st Division could stand down because they were not needed, but when the second parade was called the sergeant major said that men from this division were 'wanted as well' as its units were 'involved'.

The exact composition of the draft is unknown, but certain deductions can be drawn from the evidence. Given that the staff at district headquarters were aware that the destination of the men was Operation AVALANCHE, or Salerno, it is probable that the X Corps infantry mentioned by CSM Green were among the units specified in the first batch of 750. On the other hand, many of the men subsequently tried for mutiny claim they heard repeated rumours that for some reason these X Corps men were left behind.

There were two other groups of soldiers in the camp whose members – or at least those remaining – would almost certainly have been considered for the draft. The first was a collection of 18 officers and over 400 infantrymen – only nominally attached to certain regiments – who had arrived at the camp on 10 August. According to the camp's war diary, the 'intention' was to 'hold them' as 'free reinforcements after a period of training'. In other words, they were inexperienced troops who could be drafted to any unit. The fact that almost 90 of them were Royal Fusiliers, a regiment represented by two battalions in the 56th Division, is further reason for them to have been chosen on this particular detail.

The second group that might have been represented was a collection of over 700 raw recruits who had arrived in the camp between 16 and 22 August. Instead of the usual regimental affiliation, these 'rookies' were listed in the camp war diary as a drafts from the part of the country they had enlisted in. What sets these two groups apart was the fact that none of their members belonged to any specific battalions. So although they were intended as Eighth Army reinforcements, their drafting to X

Corps was unlikely to have been complicated by a keen sense of unit loyalty.[5]

Veterans who belonged to specific battalions and divisions within the Eighth Army were a different kettle of fish. It is difficult to know for certain how many members of the draft fell into this category, but a conservative estimate would be around 500, with most belonging to the illustrious 50th (Tyne Tees) and 51st (Highland) Divisions. After all, it is surely no coincidence that almost all the 192 men subsequently arrested for mutiny at Salerno were members of these two formations. Why Highland troops were excluded from the first batch but were, according to Green, included in the second is something of a mystery. It may well be that the staff at district headquarters appreciated the potentially dire consequences of sending such troops to units other than their own, but when a second 750 were needed they had no one else to send. On the other hand, there might have been a conscious decision to use such tried and tested fighting troops in what was apparently a desperate situation.

Whatever the reason behind the choice of veterans from these two divisions, there was no precedent. As CSM Green later stated, 'up to the time of this draft' 155 Transit Camp 'had sent reinforcements to the Eighth Army only'. In his estimation, '999 out of a 1,000 from our Camp returned to their own units', while this was the 'first time' in which 'any men from 50th or 51st Division were sent to units other than their own'.[6] Far from posting men out of the Highland Division, it was common practice among the camp staff to encourage suitable soldiers to join. Green remembered a conversation earlier in the year with Major General Douglas Wimberley, then commanding the 51st Division, on the subject of transfers:

> He said to me: 'I want to get all Scotsmen in the 51st Division. If you have any Scotsmen at the Camp who are not in the 51st Division, will you try and persuade them to transfer.' As a result, at several subsequent parades I called for volunteers from among the Scotsmen ... There were a number of transfers.
>
> There were also ... some applications to transfer out of the 51st Division. No such transfers were allowed. It was the general rule at the Camp that 50th or 51st Division men were only sent to their own Division. This rule was universally known in the Camp by all the men.[7]

As well as it being accepted routine always to return men to their own units, especially those from the Highland Division, there was a specific order to this effect. Green later testified at the trial that the order, issued by General Headquarters (GHQ) Middle East in Cairo and signed by the adjutant of 155 Camp, stated that 'men from Sicily who were ex-hospital would return to their own units'.[8] As most of the veterans involved had been evacuated during the Sicily campaign, either through wounds or illness, they should never have been sent to Salerno.

Ironically, the day before these reinforcements were detailed, an officers' conference at the Highland Division headquarters in Sicily had addressed the problem of ensuring that casualties were reunited with their units. The 'bad arrangements . . . for returning men from the base and from hospitals' were discussed. Such complaints had been made to 'higher authority' many times without result. It was decided, therefore, to send a liaison officer from divisional headquarters to the base to do all he could to return the division's personnel at transit camps to their units as speedily as possible. Sadly, for those members of the division sent to Salerno this initiative came too late.[9]

The real scandal of this draft, though, lies not so much in the decision to use Eighth Army veterans to reinforce Fifth Army units in action at Salerno – which, however contrary to common practice and current orders, the army had a legal right to do – but in the way the authorities in Tripoli, both at district headquarters and at the camp, let it be known that the men were returning to their own units. The truth was hidden even from the camp staff NCOs organising the draft. Sergeant Major Green testified at the court martial that he 'heard nothing official except the fact that they [the reinforcements] were going back to their own units'. Consequently, Green innocently passed on this misinformation to the men. When questioned at the trial what his answer would have been to any man who asked whether he was going back to his own unit, Green replied: 'It would have been "Yes".'[10] Following the departure of the draft, Green sent a copy of the nominal roll to Corporal Floodgate, whose job was to keep the particulars of the men in the camp. As Green later stated, Floodgate 'marked against the name of each man in the Draft the letters RTU [Returned to Unit]'.[11]

Certainly, operational security would have precluded informing the men of their exact destination, but they could and should have been told that they were going into action with units other than their own. By disseminating a lie, the district staff and camp officers were probably hoping to circumvent the inevitable opposition among veteran soldiers to such a posting. Only the higher-ranking officers on the draft were told the truth. One of them, Captain Albert Lee of the 1st Battalion, the York & Lancaster Regiment, recalls that he and another officer were told to report to the office of the camp commandant, Lieutenant Colonel Richards:

He told us that we were each being put in charge of 750 reinforcements that were destined for Salerno. Then he specifically ordered us not to tell the men where we were going. He said this was necessary for security reasons and we thought no more about it. It was not until I got to Salerno that I heard that the men had been told they were going back to their own units.

Corporal Hugh Fraser of the 5th Battalion, the Queen's Own Cameron Highlanders, was in bed when he heard the bugle sound the 'fall in'. A native of Inverness, the capital of the Highlands, he had been a swimming instructor in pre-war days, and had joined a Territorial battalion of the Camerons as an extra leisure activity. When war broke out he was under the minimum age of 19 years for overseas service and so fortunately missed sharing in the fate of his battalion – the 4th – when it was captured with the majority of the original 51st (Highland) Division at St Valéry, northern France, in June 1940. Instead, he was posted to the 5th Battalion in the 9th (Scottish) Division, which was soon renamed as the new 51st Division.

With this formation Fraser left for North Africa in July 1942. Laid low with desert sores, he missed the pivotal battle of El Alamein in which his division received its glorious baptism of fire. But he was soon fit again, and took part in the rest of the campaign, seeing action with the six-pounder anti-tank platoon at Wadi Zem Zem, the Mareth Line, and the bitter struggle at Wadi Akarit in which the Highland Division once again distinguished itself. It was not until halfway through the bloody fighting in Sicily that Fraser was again *hors de combat*, evacuated off the island with a recurrence of desert sores. After a spell in hospital in Tripoli he was transferred to a convalescent camp, and from there to 155 Camp. Just three days before the draft was detailed, he had celebrated his 22nd birthday.

Fully fit and raring to get back to the familiar surroundings of his unit, he was anxious to be assured of his destination. After the parade, Fraser approached the sergeant major in charge, Green, and asked him whether they were being sent back to their own units.

He said we were. That sticks out clearly in my own mind. Green said specifically that we were being returned to our own units. At that time I had no idea where the 51st Division was. I had left them in Sicily; where they were at the time I hadn't got a clue. I didn't care. I was going back to my mates and that was fine.

Other members of the draft back up Fraser's version of events. Years later, Charles Daley from Glasgow, then a young private in the Argyll &

Sutherland Highlanders, recalled that a member of the draft on parade asked the sergeant major if they were returning to their units. The reply was 'definitely yes'.[12]

Lance Corporal Percy Aveyard from Bradford also remembers an NCO assuring the men of this fact. Just 19 in 1943, he had already managed to serve two-and-a-half years by lying about his age. Although initially with his local regiment, the West Yorkshires, he was soon posted to the Durham Light Infantry and joined the 9th Battalion in time to see action in the latter stages of the North African campaign. His luck finally ran out during the battle for the Primo Sole Bridge in Sicily.

The men of the 1st Parachute Regiment had initially been given the task of taking this key bridge over the fast-flowing River Simeto, enemy possession of which barred the advance to the town of Catania on the east side of the island. Before the airborne troops could be relieved by a flying column of Aveyard's 9th Durhams, they were driven off the bridge by German paratroops. It was left to the 151 (Durham) Brigade of the 50th Division, comprising the 6th, 8th and 9th Durhams, to retake the bridge by frontal assault. The battle raged for two days and cost the Durhams over 500 killed, wounded and missing. For a time, the river literally ran red with blood, while many of the casualties were found in 'Stink Alley', a narrow gully 300 yards north of the bridge that at one point was enfiladed by machine-gun fire. It was here that Aveyard's entire section of 10 men was wiped out by a shell, while he was hit in the head by shrapnel and had to be dug out of the collapsed bank. From a Tripoli hospital he was eventually discharged to a convalescent depot and then on to a transit camp. By 14 September, like Fraser, he was eager to return to his mates:

> On parade we were told that those detailed on the draft would be going back to their own units, and that we were to check our kit and get any shortfall made up at the stores.

Privates Archie Newmarch, Fred Jowett and Charlie Smith – all members of the 5th Battalion, the East Yorkshire Regiment – were returning from their first visit into town when they heard the bugle sounding the fall in. Although both Newmarch and Jowett had been called up on the same day, 29 January 1942, and Newmarch and Smith had met during a train journey in June of that year, all were in different sections of the battalion and had not been mates before now. They had been thrown together by the loose organisation of the transit camp, which encouraged men from the same units to seek comfort in the familiar.

In appearance they could hardly have been more different: Jowett,

20, tall and muscular from hard manual labour at a Hull oil refinery, favoured a pencil moustache and slicked-back hair; Newmarch, a painter and decorator from Beverley, the home of the East Yorkshires, was small and slightly built with a sensitive, boyish face that made him seem even younger than his tender 19 years; Smith, 22, an agricultural labourer from near Doncaster, was a strong, handsome, freckled blonde of medium height. Yet they had shared experiences. Both Jowett and Newmarch had left Britain for North Africa on the same ship on the day the battle of El Alamein began. For all three, the war had begun in earnest at the Mareth Line, the most formidable German obstacle since El Alamein, where the 50th Division was initially repulsed before a flanking movement by New Zealand troops forced the Axis forces to retire.

All went on to fight in Sicily before being evacuated as casualties: Smith with mental and physical exhaustion, or 'shell-shock'; the other two with malaria. They were not the only ones. The marshy plains of Sicily are ideal breeding grounds for the infected mosquito, and in 50th Division alone 430 men went down with malaria during the five-week campaign. This was the first time that the Eighth Army had faced the problem, and it was hopelessly unprepared. After the campaign, the deputy director of medical services in XXX Corps – which included the 50th and 51st Divisions – came to a number of conclusions. The policy relating to malaria 'must be uniform throughout the force'. This had not been so in Sicily, where 'troops arriving from the Middle East were taking two tablets of mepacrine [anti-malarial treatment] on Mondays and Wednesdays; those from Tunisia were taking one tablet on Monday, Tuesday, Thursday and Friday'. What was needed was one tablet 'taken daily'. Another criticism was dress. The men had been still wearing their desert khaki drill – comprising shorts and a light shirt – whereas slacks were necessary to protect the legs from bites. Furthermore, 'many reinforcements arrived without their anti-malaria kit, nets, cream and mepacrine, and in consequence their sojourn in the forward areas was exceedingly brief'.[13]

Newmarch was one such, lasting a little over three weeks before evacuation to Tripoli, via a hospital in Syracuse, with a temperature of 104°F. The standard treatment for malaria at the time – given the need to return veterans to combat as quickly as possible – was only a two-week course of quinine, followed by a further two weeks convalescing. This was rarely enough time for the more serious cases to recover, and Newmarch, his recovery complicated by a non-related spinal injury, had already had one relapse at the convalescent depot before being sent, still far from fit, to the transit camp. Jowett, on the other hand, was fully recovered by 14 September, thanks to his sturdier constitution. He, like the others, was chosen for the draft and remembers hearing the 'lie'.

> I remember thinking that it was a strange time for a parade. Anyway, during it we were told by an NCO, a member of the permanent camp staff, that we were going back to our own units in Sicily. That was the cause of the trouble. Somewhere along the line this sergeant major must have been misinformed, because I think he passed the information on in all sincerity.

Newmarch's recollections differ on at least one important point. Instead of being detailed by name to join the draft, he recalls that the sergeant major instructed 'all those of the 50th and 51st Divisions wanting to return to their own units to parade at 0400 hours in the morning'.[14] Another source backs up Newmarch's assertion that a general offer to join the draft was made to members of these two divisions. Towards the end of 1944 the War Office instructed an army psychiatrist, Lieutenant Colonel Thomas Main, to interview a number of men involved in the mutiny who were still in prison. In his report, Main noted that 'the draft which set out from Tripoli was firm in the belief that it was formed to reinforce the 50th and 51st Divisions'. He went on to state that a sergeant major at the camp 'had sent runners round the camp in the early hours of the morning telling late arrivals that any man who wanted to join 50 or 51 Divisions should join the draft'.[15]

One possible explanation lies in Sergeant Major Green's 'proof of evidence'. When he detailed the second 750 men for the draft by calling the roll, 'a number of men were found not to be present'. These men 'were on Pass and could not be got back to Camp'.[16] Given that the first two parades took place in the early evening, and Jowett and Newmarch did not return to the camp until around 10pm, it is possible that a third parade – which Green omits to mention – was called later to detail the men who had been missing from the first. If there had still been some gaps in the draft after that, Green might well have put out a general call to men of the 50th and 51st Divisions to join the draft if they wanted to return to their units.

In response to convicted mutineers insisting that they were told they would be returning to their own units, it is tempting to conclude: 'They would say that, wouldn't they?' One man who was named on the draft, but who has no such axe to grind because he reluctantly agreed at the last minute to join a unit fighting at Salerno, is Andy Scott, then a private in the 5/7th Battalion, the Gordon Highlanders. He recalls that 'the NCOs definitely told us that we were going back to our own units in the 51st Division', and that following the news 'morale was high because we were going back to our mates'.

Newmarch's version of events – and that of a number of witnesses interviewed by Main – stating that Sergeant Major Green made an open offer to men of the 50th and 51st Divisions to join the draft because it would return them to their own units, may or may not be accurate. What is not in doubt is that Green believed the men were returning to their own units and passed on this information in all sincerity. Whether all the men heard it from his lips or not is irrelevant; he clearly told some, and they would have quickly told others until the news spread like bushfire. This probably explains why a number of men who should not have been on the draft joined it.

In two statements that made up part of his 'proof of evidence', Green recalled: 'The position regarding [the] drafts was chaotic from the beginning.' 'Everything was done in a rush. Three hurricane lamps & one candle was all the lighting available.'[17] Amid such confusion it is hardly surprising that the draft eventually left with a sizeable number of men not fully fit for combat, and without proper equipment.

During the two early evening parades, Green had called out the timetable of events: the men would collect their kit and sleep on the football field; a medical inspection would be held at 10pm, reveille at 2.30am, breakfast at 3am and a roll-call an hour later. For some reason, which Green later claimed not to be aware of, the medical inspection was cancelled. Later, the only probable explanation he could think of was 'that things were confused'.[18]

Two men who might have been put on a sick report if there had been an inspection were Archie Newmarch and Charlie Smith. Fred Jowett, who remained with these two men throughout this time, remembers that 'Archie was still getting attacks of malaria', while Charlie 'was obviously suffering from battle fatigue or shell-shock', a condition that deteriorated when he arrived at Salerno.

Private John McFarlane, a Scotsman from Lanarkshire serving with the 6th Durhams, was surprised to see a Seaforth Highlander called John Pepler being carried on to one of the cruisers with a back wound. Apparently, Pepler had heard a rumour that the 51st Division was returning to Britain and, anxious to go with it, he had joined the draft unofficially.

Another man who heard this rumour was Glaswegian Robert Thompson, a 24-year-old private in the 5th Battalion, the Seaforth Highlanders. A veteran of El Alamein, the Mareth Line and Wadi Akarit among other battles, he had caught severe malaria during the fighting in Sicily and, despite eight weeks trying to recover, was still unwell:

The information that I got was that the 50th and 51st Divisions were going home and they wanted us to join them before they went. I wasn't yet over the malaria – I still had the shakes at times, and headaches, but this wasn't going to stop me getting home.

Thompson also remembers one man on the draft – an acquaintance of his from home called Boyce – wearing a pair of sand-shoes because his wounded feet were still too tender for boots. This account of men wearing footwear hardly suitable for combat is confirmed by another witness. On BBC Radio in 1981, Peter Paterson of Edinburgh, then a private in the 7th Argylls, stated that the news that the draft would be returning men to their units caused many sick cases to join it:

> When we told the rest of the boys that we were going to join the battalion ... practically all of them volunteered, and they were all sick ... Whether they actually explained to the personnel that was giving them the kit that they were sick and they were going on a draft to rejoin the battalion, I don't know... When we walked down to the docks the next day... some of them ... were walking down in sand-shoes.[19]

On the same programme, *The Secret Mutiny*, Hugh Fraser recalled a similar incident:

> One of my companions was not fit enough to join the draft, his wound or illness had not completely cleared, but so keen was he to return to his own unit as he thought that he joined the draft, and there were many others who did the same thing.[20]

In a recent interview with me, Fraser named this man as Anderson, also of the Camerons. He was to share Fraser's fate.

A clue to why there were so many unfit men in 155 Camp at the time of the draft is provided by Private Edwin Scott of the 8th Durhams. Still suffering from malaria when he was named on the draft, he had transferred to 155 Camp before his period of convalescence was up because he was told his division – the 50th – was going home and he did not want to miss out:

> One day my adjutant turned up out of the blue at the convalescent depot and said to me and the other Durhams there: 'If you feel well enough to get back to your unit, get your things together. The Division's going home.' Obviously, everyone started to put in to transfer to the transit camp because you had to be there before you were posted back to your unit. It was only a couple of days later when we were named on the draft.

This practice of officers scouring the reinforcement and transit camps for their men was not unusual. After all, with battle casualties running at a high rate at this stage of the war, recuperated veterans who knew the ropes and could help assimilate the 'rookie' replacements were worth their weight in gold. Backing up Scott's story is the fact that – according to the 8th Durhams' war diary – his adjutant was wounded during the fighting in Sicily and may well have been on the mend in Tripoli.

Ray Whitaker of the Argylls, the man who at the second parade heard Green specifically ask for men from the 51st Division, was not surprised that many sick men went on the draft:

> It wasn't that unusual for men to get back to their units before they were fully fit; they would recover there. A lot of men who went on this draft weren't well. They'd only been out of hospital a short while and were still recovering from wounds and illness. Even I wasn't 100 per cent; I was still weak with jaundice.

Like Pepler, Sergeant Joe Pettit of the 9th Durhams' was still recovering from wounds. Given his third stripe at the age of 20, making him one of the youngest sergeants in the Eighth Army, Pettit was already a veteran of numerous battles since El Alamein. He had been close to death amidst the slaughter at Primo Sole Bridge in Sicily, when fragments from a grenade hit him in the chest and thigh. Convinced he was dying, the battalion padre gave him the last rites, but his medical officer assured him he would pull through, and he did. When the draft was detailed, Pettit still had two dressings on his wounds and only joined because, like Pepler and Thompson, he had heard that he would be returning to the 50th Division which was on its way back to Britain.

Another man on the draft with open wounds was Captain Albert Lee, the officer forbidden to tell the men of their true destination. From relatively humble Sussex origins – and so lacking the distinctive public-school accent of the traditional officer – Lee had done well at school and in 1938 had qualified as a chartered accountant. Called up in 1940 and directed to the Royal Sussex for basic training, Lee's professional status was noted and he was soon marked down as officer material. During his short time as an officer cadet, he had stated his preferred regiments as the Royal Sussex, the Royal West Kents and the Hampshires. Perversely, he was posted to the 1st Battalion, the York & Lancaster Regiment.

By September 1943, Lee had already been abroad for more than two years, passing through South Africa, India, Persia, Iraq, Syria and Egypt. But, surprisingly, he had had to wait until the Eighth Army's invasion of Sicily to see his first action. Just 10 days into the campaign, Lee and 11 other men were taking cover in a deep irrigation ditch in the foothills of Mount Etna when a shell landed amongst them. Ten were killed outright, one died of his wounds. Lee had a large piece of shrapnel lodged in his left thigh and smaller fragments in his back, but none were life threatening. Evacuated to Tripoli, he remained in hospital until 16 August when he was transferred to a convalescent depot. After three weeks there he was still far from fully recovered and was surprised to be discharged to 155 Camp. Although by 14 September he could walk, the serious wound on his thigh was still open and required daily dressings by the medical staff at the camp. Lee recalls:

> I think you could say that many of the people on the draft were cripples. We were all ex-hospital, and not everyone had been allowed enough time to recover from their wounds and illness. In civilian life we would certainly have got a day off work.

A good week after landing at Salerno, Lee was still in a bad way. This is confirmed by Lionel Daiches, the assistant prosecutor at the trial of the mutineers and later a prominent Scottish QC, who took a statement from Lee a few days after the arrest of the men at Salerno. In a recent interview, Daiches told me:

> Many of the chaps on this consignment of 1,500 reinforcements – from which the mutineers were eventually drawn – were scarcely fit for active service. Captain Lee himself had been very badly wounded and was still recovering from his wounds when I met him. He told me he was still undergoing some form of medical treatment.

The accusation that some men were literally taken from their sick-beds and sent on this draft has long been made by many of those subsequently convicted of mutiny. This has always been denied by the Ministry of Defence, but there is some evidence to support it. Alec McMichael from Dundee was then a private in the 5th Battalion, the Black Watch. A painter in civilian life, he had joined his battalion's Pioneer Platoon and, during the victorious advance through the desert, had helped daub the many HD (Highland Division) signs that led to the nickname 'Highway Decorators'. Like so many others, he had been evacuated back to Tripoli after contracting malaria in Sicily. After two weeks in hospital, McMichael had been transferred to a convalescent camp, but the staff had failed to warn him not to swim and he had suffered a relapse and was still recovering there by 14 September. He recalls:

> I was in the convalescent depot in Tripoli, still on medication for malaria,

when I and some others were told, by the usual army procedure, to get ready to go at such and such a time. We were then loaded on to trucks and taken to a transit camp to get rigged out. Normally you've an awful job getting anything replaced; they just said 'Help yourself'. Of course we'd lost everything except what we stood in. The next morning we were embarked on cruisers. I was put on the HMS *Euryalus*, but I was yet to get over my malaria and I wasn't feeling too well. I remember one of us was a sergeant whose thigh wounds were still weeping. We were, at this time, under the impression that we were being taken back to our own units.

If McMichael is telling the truth – and he has no reason to lie because, like Andy Scott, he later joined a unit at Salerno and was not arrested for mutiny – then not only did unfit men join the draft of their own free will in the mistaken belief that they were to be returned to their own units, but others were actually ordered to do so.

Sailors aboard the three cruisers that transported the draft to Salerno also remember that many of the men were not fully fit. Michael Winter, an able seaman training to be an officer aboard HMS *Euryalus*, recalls:

We were detached from Salerno and dashed like hell to pick up these troops at Tripoli. As they came on board they looked pale and sick, they didn't look like fit fighting troops. I think there were even some with bandages on their wounds. We were told that they'd come, more or less, from hospitals and that the reason they had been pulled out was because the situation at Salerno was so desperate. The only troops that were immediately available were these poor chaps who had been in hospital and who were just about capable of crawling on to the beaches with a rifle. We were surprised at their condition and felt very sorry for them.

David Royle was a gunner aboard HMS *Charybdis*. In 1975, on behalf of the Charybdis Association, he published a personal account of his time aboard the ship. The relevant passage relating to the draft of reinforcements reads:

Charybdis started to embark troops for further landings at Salerno. This was an obnoxious occasion, for whilst the ship's company... knew every sailing was for more 'action', the embarking troops thought they were on their way home. Many had fought right through the Desert Campaign ... They came aboard ... some with slight wounds although I saw several with head wounds, and indeed several with bandages over one eye. All looked extremely fatigued, but it appeared that if they could hold a rifle then they could fight on. WE ON *CHARYBDIS* WERE NOT PLEASED BY WHAT WE SAW... [Here] we were embarking men who were battle weary, wounded, and transporting them to, in all probability, their deaths.

John Eskdale, then an 18-year-old Royal Marine aboard the *Charybdis*, confirmed that some of the men were unfit:

> My station was manning one of the after-turret 4.5-inch guns, and I actually spoke to some of the troops grouped around. Some were still recovering from wounds and had bandages. The ones I spoke to around the turret told me that they had come straight from hospital and thought they were being taken home. I assumed that they sent these men into battle not fully fit because of the serious situation at Salerno.

Witnesses aboard *Charybdis*'s sister ship, HMS *Scylla*, relate a similar story. One of the ship's crew was Peter Rayner, a young Royal Marine like Eskdale. During a campaign to clear the mutineers in the early 1980s, Rayner contacted Alfred Morris, one of the MPs involved:

> My main reason for penning this letter is to emphasise and protest at the disgusting way the authorities have treated these men. I am sure all the facts have not come to light.

The reinforcements 'were only silhouettes of men', he explained:

> We, on the ship were completely amazed at the state of these troops and to a man we knew they would never be any good as a fighting force.[21]

Robert Hughes, then a lieutenant in the Royal Navy, wrote a book about his experiences on board the *Scylla* which was published in 1956. Although less impassioned than Rayner's, his account of this episode is no less sympathetic:

> The decks were cluttered with khaki figures from many regiments, each man equipped barely, with a rifle, some ammunition, and a lifebelt. They wolfed our sandwiches with relish, smoked the proffered cigarettes, and chewed the bars of chocolate given to them by the sailors, who always had a soft heart for the Army – the Pongoes or the Brown Jobs. They, in turn, were grateful, and high in their praise of the Navy, envying our life because we went into battle with our homes, our food, and our simple comforts. We felt a great pity for these men, many newly convalescent, who, in a few hours, would be hurled into the bloody struggle that was Salerno[22]

It is tempting to conclude from all this evidence that Sergeant Major Green's task of filling the emergency draft was proceeding relatively smoothly until the second batch of 750 men was asked for. This new request was complicated by the fact that Green was now ordered to use men specifically from the 51st Division, many of whom, as Green admitted, were away from camp visiting the town. As the hours ticked by, the camp staff must have begun to panic and were forced into desperate measures. The medical inspection was probably cancelled because it would have excluded too many of the men who were ultimately used to fill the draft. This 'panic' theory also helps to explain the reports that men were taken straight from the convalescent depot, and that Green's staff went round the camp in the early hours of the morning recruiting men of the 50th and 51st Divisions with the promise that they would be going back to their units. This promise, and the knowledge by some of the rumour that both these divisions would soon be returning home (the final decision had not yet been taken, but both did indeed sail within eight weeks), meant that virtually all those detailed were happy to co-operate. They were joined by a few not named on the draft who did not want to miss out.

As if the deception over the draft's destination and the inclusion on it of a number of men unfit for combat were not bad enough, another scandal was perpetrated on that balmy September evening: many were packed off from the transit camp without the proper kit.

In one of the statements that made up his 'proof of evidence', Sergeant Major Green pointed out the existence of an 'Order of GHQ Cairo that all deficiencies in kit according to Middle East Scale must be made up before a man is sent from 155 Transit Camp as a reinforcement'. Included in this scale of kit, according to Green, was a rifle, bayonet, water bottle and 50 rounds of small-arms ammunition. Such an order was particularly necessary because casualties from the front line would be evacuated without much of their kit. And yet, as Green admitted in the same statement, 'there was no kit inspection before the Draft left'. It was probably dispensed with for the same reason as the medical inspection: if it had been held, many of the draft would have failed it and there would have been a hold-up. Green conceded as much in a separate statement when he pointed out that 'there was a shortage of some kit at the Camp in September'. The end result, he conceded, was that 'some of the men detailed for the Draft went away deficient'. In another statement still he listed the kit in short supply as 'water bottles, bayonets and perhaps ammo. Also bayonet scabbards . . .'[23]

In fact, many were sent off without even rifles. Archie Newmarch insists that neither he nor his two mates, Fred Jowett and Charlie Smith, were issued with any form of firearm. Jowett confirms this. According to Newmarch, the necessary kit for battle – known as light fighting order – included small pack, pouches, steel helmet, ammunition, bayonet, rifle, water bottle and entrenching tool. Of these, he was only equipped with the first four:

We were never issued with the proper kit at the transit camp. Some got rifles and no ammo, I got ammo but no rifle. A lot of others didn't have rifles either, and some of the rifles that were issued were rusty and must have come off the battlefields. Some had helmets, some hadn't – Charlie Smith for one. Few of us had water bottles, bayonets or entrenching tools.

Robert Thompson of the Seaforths had a rifle but only five rounds of ammunition and remembers that 'a lot of other people didn't have the proper equipment'.

Even the officers were sent away deficient. Captain Lee departed with just a pistol, a blanket and a canvas bucket. Normally he would have taken a small pack into combat, containing the bare essentials of shaving and washing gear, towel and spare underclothes. 'The one thing we did grumble about was the lack of equipment', Lee recalls. 'The men were generally as poorly equipped as I was.'

John Eskdale, the Royal Marine aboard HMS *Charybdis*, remembers:

When the men came on board they were not kitted out in proper battle order. Some had rifles but they didn't have enough ammunition. When they went ashore we were only able to give them ten rounds each.

Of course, the fact that these men were despatched from Tripoli without the relevant fighting kit does not necessarily mean that they were destined to go into battle in such a state. Such shortfalls – especially in weapons and equipment – would inevitably have been made up at Salerno. But it does emphasise, once again, the fact that the staff of 155 Transit Camp were caught on the hop. The ensuing organisational chaos ultimately lead to many semi-fit, under-equipped men being sent unawares to Salerno.

Just two men from the original 1,500 detailed managed to avoid going. After hearing his name called, Rifleman Reilly of the Cameronians complained to Sergeant Major Green and refused to go. The substance of his complaint is unknown. Possibly he, like many others, was unfit and objected on these grounds. Possibly he had managed to get wind of the true destination of the draft. Whichever, he got his way. Put under close arrest, he was subsequently awarded 28 days field punishment by the camp commandant, Colonel Richards. If later he became aware of the fate of many of those who did go, he must have considered this punishment a small price to pay.

The other man got off scot-free. Private William White of the Argyll & Sutherland Highlanders accompanied the draft as far as Tripoli harbour when the sight of its transport – three Royal Navy cruisers –

made him suspicious about its destination. If they were being taken home, as he had been led to believe, surely they would not assign warships for such a job, he mused. Their presence could only mean an emergency. Aware from the casualties coming back that the Allies were having a rough time at Salerno, White rightly concluded that they were being sent there. On a radio programme in 1981, he recalled his near escape:

> I voiced my fears to some of the men and they said, oh no, they couldn't think about going back into action again. When I saw the [warship] out in the bay I thought, 'Well, this ship's not going to Blighty' . . . So I just fell out, jumped over onto the beach and walked home. The next morning when I came out onto the parade ground, I was all on my own there, the sergeant major says: 'Where was you last night?' I says: 'Well I was down having a swim, it was so warm.' He said: 'Well, you've missed the boat. I'm sorry. All the other men are on their way home.' Even he didn't know.[24]

Chapter 3

'We've been shanghai-ed!'

A little after 7am on 15 September, the three Dido-class light cruisers sent to collect the reinforcements – HMS *Euryalus, Scylla* and *Charybdis* – steamed out of Tripoli harbour, leaving behind the stark sight of a blackened, burnt-out Italian passenger liner still moored to the quay, highlighted by the whitewashed buildings on the seafront.

From a distance the deck of each cruiser seemed thick with ants – in reality 500 khaki-clad men, all eager for their last glimpse of the Libyan capital, some anxiously unaware of their destination, others convinced they would soon be back with their units, a few certain they were on their way home. Only the ships' crews and the senior reinforcement officers knew the truth.

On the bridge of the *Scylla*, the navigator calculated the speed necessary to reach Salerno by the following morning and informed Captain Macintyre, who in turn spoke to the officer of the watch. 'Revolutions for 30 knots!'

'Aye, aye, sir!'

The required speed was then repeated down the voice pipe to the quartermaster, and almost immediately the roar of the turbines increased and the ship seemed to rise imperceptibly from the water. Within minutes, a strange tremor shook the 5,200-ton ship and she began to vibrate. News quickly arrived from the engine room that the starboard turbines of both engines were quivering on their beddings. The revolutions were decreased and then increased again, until the critical speed at which the vibrations began was ascertained. At this reduced speed, *Scylla* continued on towards Salerno with her precious cargo. She was escorted by *Charybdis*, but *Euryalus*, the flagship of Rear Admiral Sir Philip Vian, went on ahead.

The three cruisers sent to collect the reinforcements were part of Force V, an aircraft carrier group that had been providing aerial cover for the Salerno beachhead since day one. This force comprised five converted carriers – each equipped with Seafires, the naval version of a Spitfire – and an escort of 10 destroyers. The job of the cruisers, bristling with high-angle anti-aircraft guns, was to protect the force from air attack.

On its way to Salerno late on 8 September, Force V had passed through the Straits of Messina, the narrow water channel between Sicily and the mainland that held special significance for two of the cruisers. Lieutenant Robert Hughes aboard the *Scylla* later wrote how his skipper, Captain Macintyre, had explained this over the ship's tannoy: .

> Now, for a matter of interest. Later tonight we shall be passing through the Straits of Messina, and at the narrowest part lies the little village of Scylla. It was here, according to Greek legend, that the dreadful monster from whom we take our name lived. With wolves' or dogs' heads springing from her body she would reach out from her cave above the sea, and snatch sailors from passing ships. On a rock below the cave lived another monster, Charybdis, who three times a day swallowed the sea and spouted it out again to form a whirlpool from which no ship could escape. We will try to inform you when we pass the actual spot where these fearsome females lived.[1]

Macintyre's informed mythology contains just one inaccuracy: the monster Charybdis was said to dwell on the western side of the northern entrance to the Straits, opposite the cave which housed Scylla – the once beautiful virgin who had been turned into a six-headed fiend by the jealous sorceress Circe. To gain passage, ships would have to run the gauntlet between these two lethal viragos. Jason and the Argonauts, during their epic quest to obtain the Golden Fleece, managed the feat safely with the help of the sea-goddess Thetis. Odysseus was less fortunate. In steering well clear of Charybdis, six of his sailors were plucked from their oars by her terrible neighbour. Later, after his crew had angered the gods by feasting on some of Helius's immortal cattle, Odysseus's ship was wrecked and its remains driven back towards Charybdis by a storm. When the ship was sucked down, Odysseus managed to survive by clinging to a giant fig-tree which overhung the whirlpool. Later, Charybdis spewed up the mast and keel, and Odysseus used them to escape, using his hands as oars. Shortly after this episode, Scylla's days of terror were ended when she was turned into a rock.

Force V had remained at Salerno until 13 September, when heavy losses forced the carriers to return to Palermo to replenish with new fighters. Back at the beachhead the following evening, the three cruisers received the news to proceed to Tripoli without delay. Londoner Eric Wilmott was serving as a signalman aboard the *Charybdis*:

> There were three cruisers involved, including the *Euryalus* with Admiral Vian aboard. I remember him sending a signal to us saying that we were

going to take troops on a mission and asking how many we could fit in. The officers on the bridge began to debate this and eventually decided that we could probably squeeze in about 100. Before we could reply a second signal arrived saying we were to take 500 each!

It was not until well into the voyage to Salerno that some of the men were told of their true destination. Most of the veterans from the 50th and 51st Divisions were aboard the lead ship, *Euryalus*, when the tannoy crackled into life: 'Attention! Attention! You are not going back to your own units. You are to be landed as reinforcements at Salerno.'

Private Archie Newmarch, sitting huddled on deck with his mates Fred Jowett and Charlie Smith, could hardly believe his ears. Then, as the absurdity of the news dawned on him, he felt better. 'One of the boys must have got into the radio room and was playing a practical joke', he mused. The relief did not last. After a brief pause the message was repeated and this time he was forced to accept it was for real. As the shock wore off, the murmurings and discontent began: 'We've been shanghai-ed!' 'I'm not going there!' 'Where the hell is Salerno, anyway?' Amidst the general outrage, Newmarch's first reaction was one of disbelief that it could have happened:

> The army just didn't do things like that. If Green had not said in the first place, 'You're going back to your units,' then the whole situation would never have arisen. But it was that which caused it.

Corporal Hugh Fraser of the Camerons was also aboard the *Euryalus* – enjoying the thrill of riding in a big warship, as he enjoyed all journeys at sea – when the shocking news was announced. His determination to fight this perceived injustice was never in doubt.

> I didn't even know where Salerno was but my immediate reaction was, 'Oh dear no, I'm not going.' There was fury but it was a contained fury. There was no uproar, just an angry buzz all over the ship. I was dumbfounded; we had been told we were going back to our own units. I probably said to some of the other Camerons: 'I'm not going.' But there was no coercion, no conspiracy. Everyone was capable of making up their own minds. It was a matter of conscience, purely and simply. From the first moment I heard the news, I was determined not to join these strange divisions. I can't describe the feeling. Even now I have the same deep sense of being let down. During my time in the army I had never been, nor had I heard of anyone else, treated like this.

Private Edwin Scott, the man who had returned to 155 Camp on the advice of his adjutant and who now believed he was going home, was 'devastated' on hearing the news. A 21-year-old bricklayer from Ryton near Newcastle-upon-Tyne, he had joined the 8th Durhams in North Africa in the early summer of 1942. Like so many of the veterans on this draft, he first saw action at El Alamein, and from there he had gone right through the campaign without a break. While honoured to be a part of his local division – the 50th Tyne & Tees – he was particularly proud of his status as a 'Gallant Five-foot Guardsman', the honorary name accorded the Durham Light Infantry on account of their prowess in battle and their diminutive size. Most of his service in Sicily had been in a mortar-carrying half-track, although the carnage at Primo Sole had necessitated his fighting for a time as a rifleman. It was at the bridge that he fell victim to malaria. Now, with his hopes of returning to his unit dashed, he felt angry and frustrated.

Not yet over his malaria, Private Alec McMichael's heart sank when the announcement was confirmed. Although lying amongst a large group of men from the Black Watch – Scotland's oldest Highland regiment – his immediate emotion was one of sadness that he wouldn't be seeing his mates from the Pioneer Platoon of the 5th Battalion again.

At around the same time the message was broadcast on the *Euryalus*, men on the other two cruisers were told the truth. Signalman Joe Robinson of the *Scylla* remembers in particular a group of men from the Surrey Regiment and how 'although they weren't very pleased to hear they were being put into Salerno, they weren't comfortable aboard and were anxious to get off'.

Sergeant Wally Innes of the 8th Durhams – one of the few members of the 50th Division not on the *Euryalus* – was more than a little displeased. He was outraged. Born in Gateshead in June 1916 to an unmarried Scottish mother and an unknown Scottish father, Innes had never thought of himself as anything other than a Geordie. By the age of 20 he was working as a clay-digger at a brickyard near his home in Birtley, Newcastle-upon-Tyne. As holidays were unheard of then, he had joined the local Territorials as a way of getting two weeks off for summer camp without losing his job. When war broke out he was given his pay in one hand and his call-up papers in the other. An early indication of the inflexibility of the army – from which later he would suffer so dearly – was given to him shortly before embarkation for France with the 50th Division in 1940. While training at Castle Bromwich, he and a pal received word that both their wives had given birth, but when they asked for leave they were turned down. His pal never saw his baby daughter; he was killed by machine-gun fire during the May fighting. Innes survived the retreat to Dunkirk and reached safety by swimming to a small fishing boat.

Within two years he was again going backwards as the Eighth Army withdrew in the face of Rommel's onslaught to the final barrier at El Alamein. So costly was the fighting that the 50th Division only narrowly managed to escape encirclement at Gazala, losing a whole brigade in the process. At El Alamein the tables were turned and Innes faced death many times before the Axis forces were finally pushed out of North Africa. Sicily came next, and with it the horror of the bloodbath at Primo Sole, where so many of his friends and comrades were killed. Shortly after, relief from the fighting arrived in the shape of malaria.

At 155 Transit Camp, Innes had become suspicious about the real destination of the draft when he was issued with a rifle, because his was back with his unit. As the senior NCO on the draft he felt it his duty to check with one of the camp officers. 'Are you sure we're going back to our unit, sir?'

'Quite sure,' the officer replied.

A tough, handsome, square-jawed man of 27, he thought he had already seen every bad card that life could deal. On the cruiser to Salerno he realised he was wrong.

Royal Marine John Eskdale is unsure whether the troops on board his ship, *Charybdis*, were told of their destination over the tannoy or when they gathered at the mustering stations. Whichever method was used, the men were disgruntled at the news. Eskdale recalls:

> When we arrived at Salerno they weren't happy about being put ashore, they didn't want to go at all and one couldn't blame them. There was a big grievance. I remember it took about an hour to unload these men into LSTs at Salerno.

'When it sailed from Tripoli, the draft was in general contented at the turn in events and the men on it satisfied or glad at the prospect of rejoining their own divisions,' wrote Lieutenant Colonel Thomas Main, the army psychiatrist who submitted a report to the War Office in January 1945 after interviewing the scores of men convicted of mutiny at Salerno who were still in prison. Continuing, Main explained why this was so:

> Many had recently been discharged from hospital, and were eager to get back into the community to which they belonged; some were glad to exchange the disorder and inevitably difficult man-management of the transit camp for their own familiar officers and unit efficiency; some looked forward again to the freedom and friendliness of regimental life in the field; others, a proportion of whom were 'battle weary', had heard or suspected that the 50th and 51st Divisions were likely to go home . . .;

and a few were the nervous 'bomb-happy' men that any draft of experienced soldiers contains. The belief that there was a chance of going home was not however widespread at this stage, and it may be said that this draft consisted mainly of men willing or glad to face whatever the future might hold for them in these divisions.[2]

Given that almost all the men convicted of mutiny, and consequently those interviewed by Main, were veterans from the 50th and 51st Divisions, it is possible to excuse Main for implying that the whole draft was made up of such men. It was not. But seen in the context of the veterans, Main's report is highly relevant. The 'satisfaction' that these men had felt on boarding the cruisers vanished once the truth was known. The reaction, according to Main, was 'variously puzzlement, dismay, anger or incredulity'. On the other hand, 'other groups did not hear this news and remained in the belief that they were going to their own divisions.' A host of explanations were discussed within the many sub-groups – formed along regimental lines and stratified by age, rank and duration of past service – wrote Main:

> '50th Division was at Salerno'; '50th and 51st Divisions were in Italy moving up to Salerno'; 'the whole draft had been shanghai-ed'; 'all was well, for the camp orders at 155 Transit Camp prohibited transfer to other divisions'; 'the RSM had plainly stated that they were going back to their own division'. Moods now varied from uncertainty and anxiety to despair and anger. Some sub-groups remained in ignorance of any alteration of plan and others recalled that it was regarded as praiseworthy in their own divisions if they rejoined their units by illegal means. Among such men there arose a belief in the existence of such a crime as 'honourable desertion' for which they would get praise. A few individuals remained calm and determined in the decision that they would rejoin their own divisions with or without the co-operation of the transit officers.[3]

By the time the troops arrived at Salerno, Main wrote, three features of importance had appeared:

> A growing doubt in extra-divisional authority, an anxious need for news and direction, and the discussion of illegal methods should the need arise of rejoining their own division.

Recourse to this latter expedient became more attractive after 'certain officers appeared to have comforted the men by saying that if they stood firm it might be possible to get back to their division'.[4]

An ominous calm seemed to have fallen over the Gulf of Salerno as the two cruisers, *Charybdis* and *Scylla*, arrived four miles off X Corps' landing beaches during the afternoon of 16 September. The *Euryalus*, travelling at full speed, had arrived a few hours earlier and had already disembarked her quota of 500 reinforcements. Lieutenant Robert Hughes aboard the *Scylla*, greeted by the sight of the crew from a nearby landing craft swimming in the warm sea, might have been excused for thinking that the war was far away. He was brought back to reality by the deafening report of a salvo of 15-inch shells fired from the huge battleship HMS *Warspite* against the distant hills.

Both cruisers closed down their engines and lay with their bows facing the wind to enable landing craft to come alongside. The first to reach the *Scylla* was LCT 397. As the troops tumbled down the scrambling nets, an officer among them sought out the commander, Lieutenant Lew Hemming of the Royal Navy, on his bridge. 'We sailed at full speed right from Tripoli,' he told Hemming. 'We've been told the battle is bad, and there have been a lot of casualties.' Hemming replied that it had been touch and go but, in his opinion, the situation had eased considerably during the previous couple of days.[5]

Hemming's estimation was accurate. The knife-edge situation of 13 September was no longer applicable, the Germans had shot their bolt and the worst danger was over.

On 14 September the American VI Corps had defeated several attempts to pierce its defences along the Calore River, while the last regiment of the 45th Division had landed that day only to be put into reserve by Clark, an obvious sign that the emergency shoring-up of the front line was over. Clark's hand was further strengthened that night when 2,000 more paratroops from the 82nd Airborne Division were dropped near Paestum and added to his reserve. About the same time, German panzers and infantry launched a surprise attack against a brigade of 46th Division, but after initial gains they were held. Thanks to continual naval bombardments and largely unopposed air raids against their positions, particularly their communications, the Germans around Salerno were forced to pause for breath on 15 September. Such was the turnaround in circumstances that the War Cabinet's *Weekly Résumé* for the period 9–16 September stated: 'More Allied formations, including armour, arrived and by the 15th we had consolidated our positions and a very dangerous moment was past.'[6]

During the morning of 16 September the Germans made one last effort to crack the bridgehead. This time the British 56th Division faced the brunt of the assault, but by the time the last of the 1,500 reinforcements from Tripoli had been landed the Germans had once again been repulsed. That same day a reconnaissance party from General Montgomery's Eighth Army, advancing from the south, joined

up with elements of the American VI Corps from the beachhead. Clark
was now convinced that his position was sufficiently secure to allow him
to move on to the offensive. On 16 September he signalled to
Eisenhower:

> We are in good shape now. We are here to stay... I am prepared to attack
> Naples. We have made mistakes and we have learned the hard way, but we
> will improve every day and am sure we will not disappoint you.[7]

The official history of the battle, published in 1973, backs up Clark's
assertion that the danger was over:

> On the evening of the 16th September the Germans began to withdraw,
> partly because they had been out-fought and partly because of a change
> in their strategy. They now fell back through Naples to the Volturno river,
> but offered strong delaying action to the Allies who were hard on their
> heels.[8]

Referring to the situation 24 hours later, the official history is even
more conclusive:

> By 17th September the 5th US Army had won its beachhead at Salerno,
> and the 8th Army was advancing northwards.[9]

The fact that the existence of the beachhead was no longer in danger
by the time the reinforcements from Tripoli landed on 16 September
probably explains the lack of urgency in moving these men up the line.
From the minute they stepped ashore, they were confronted by
indifference and a lack of information. Eventually, after a delay of some
time, they were directed to a bare field a short way inland. From here,
just a few miles from the front line, they could hear sporadic gunfire and
see numerous Allied planes attacking enemy positions. Archie Newmarch was among the batch from the *Euryalus* landed at midday and
remembers the confusion:

> There was nobody there to meet us and we didn't know what was
> happening. Nobody came to tell us to join this division or that division,
> we were in a right muddle. While some men sat and stewed in the sun,
> others started wandering all over the bloody place, looking in the
> surrounding vineyards for grapes.

Suffering from the tell-tale symptoms of a malaria relapse – shivering
and sweating in turn – Newmarch went looking for a medical officer. He
found one in a field dressing station to the east of the field, but was told

that no quinine was available; aspirin was the best they could do. On returning from this largely fruitless quest he noticed a large group of men milling around. They turned out to be veterans trying to borrow bayonets off the better-equipped 'rookies' to open their tins of bully-beef, which had been issued without keys.

Around 4pm, by which time some of the troops from *Scylla* and *Charybdis* had arrived, a convoy of amphibious 'Ducks' (DUKWs) drove up and the reinforcements were ordered aboard. After a hot, slow, bumpy ride over rutted tracks, the men were dropped at a tented personnel transit area about a mile away. By dusk, the last of the draft had been dropped. Still no staff officers had come to speak to the men about what would happen next, and the many rumours that had begun on the ships were still rife. As they bedded down for the night, many on bare earth as the tented accommodation was inadequate, the men were disgruntled and apprehensive.

By the following morning, one man had a particular reason to feel aggrieved. While Private John Atterton of the Durham Light Infantry slept in the open, a small sand insect crawled into his ear. He awoke with a splitting earache, unaware of the cause. Later, in hospital, it needed an operation to remove the insect. Unfortunately it had pierced his ear-drum, and he never recovered his hearing in that ear.

During the morning of 17 September the majority of the men were moved again, this time a couple of miles further up the coast to the main X Corps' transit camp nearer to the town of Salerno. A group of the least fit men – including Captain Lee – stayed behind, but rejoined the main body a day later. The new camp was only a marginal improvement on the old. Bigger, with more tents, it covered a series of scrub fields fringed with tobacco and tomato plants. There were also a couple of makeshift huts which served as a camp office, and it was from staff working here that the first concrete information filtered out: the draft was due to join units of the 46th and 56th Divisions fighting on the beachhead perimeter. Also about this time, a rumour began to do the rounds of the various regimental groups among the draft, particularly the veterans, that the proper reinforcements for Salerno – X Corps' men – had been left behind in Tripoli. Not surprisingly, this heightened the anger already felt towards incompetent, or even worse, deceitful, transit authorities. Lieutenant Colonel Main, in his report, summed up the feeling of the men at this time:

> The absence of interest in them as individuals and the cavalier way their divisional loyalties seemed to be treated by transit camp officers produced a feeling of righteous indignation at being 'shanghai-ed', fears about

missing their chance of going home with their divisions, and discussions about how they could draw attention to their 'right' to join their divisions. A few men had already determined on a categorical refusal to join any division other than their own, but most remained uncertain and awaited a chance to make a formal protest.[10]

The fact that none of the draft were posted to units on 17 September is confirmation that the crisis at the beachhead was over. Instead they were left to stew in the heat. As they waited, the reinforcements inevitably split into two groups – Eighth Army veterans and others. It is not unusual in war for the former – instantly recognisable in this case by their bronzed limbs and faded, slightly dishevelled, desert khaki drill – to look down on the latter. The 500 or so veterans on this draft were further alienated by the knowledge that the 'rookies' were better equipped – most appeared to have rifles, ammo and bayonets.

As they marked time, some of the veterans spoke to officers on the draft and asked them about their chances of returning to their old divisions. According to Lieutenant Colonel Main, these officers 'appeared to have left the issue in doubt', and such sympathy 'encouraged the men' and confirmed 'the righteousness of their indignation'.[11]

Attitudes were now hardening. Private Robert Thompson remembers discussing the situation with other members of the draft. An apprentice bricklayer in Glasgow before the war, he had served with the 5th Seaforths in the 51st Division since El Alamein. Evacuated from his battalion with malaria and a temperature of 105°F after just five days in Sicily, he only found out he would not be going back when he arrived at Salerno:

> I only knew one man there, Charlie Keir, and we were just blithering away with other members of the 50th and 51st Division. They were saying things like, 'We won't be going back with our units now we've been landed in this.' We were all very, very angry and were determined not to join strange units at Salerno. We realised the seriousness of what we were doing, but we didn't care about the consequences. We felt very strongly about what had happened.

By 18 September, X Corps' staff officers at last woke up to the fact that 1,500 'emergency' reinforcements were languishing in the main transit camp. Instructions were issued that they should be detailed to join battalions with the heaviest casualties. Yet for some reason only a few hundred of the 'rookies' were ordered to move on this day. The staff officers must have known by now that they had been sent a large group of Eighth Army veterans who had thought they were on their way back to their units. Under the circumstances, they were probably attempting to sound out opinion before ordering them all up to the front line. One way of doing this was to detail them in batches. Despite this precaution, it was soon obvious that many of the veterans were not going to budge.

The matter came to a head on the morning of 19 September, when the transit camp officers tried to despatch the veterans to fighting units along with the remaining 'rookies'. Rather than meet these disgruntled soldiers head on, the staff officers spoke initially to the reinforcement NCOs. But already many of the NCOs had made up their minds not to go themselves, and their attitude only stiffened the resolve of the others. Finally, around midday, transit camp officers and, at their request, some reinforcement officers spoke personally to some of the men and asked them if, in Lieutenant Colonel Main's words, 'they were willing to go to 46th and 56th Divisions'.[12] The remainder of the 'rookies' complied, as did a sprinkling of veterans from each regiment of the 50th and 51st Divisions represented at the beachhead. Only one regimental group of veterans marched off *en bloc*: the Black Watch.

Major General Douglas Wimberley, the commander of the 51st in the desert and Sicily, later made strenuous efforts to find out the circumstances surrounding the Salerno mutiny in an attempt to force a review of the subsequent convictions. In his view, the men of the Black Watch were swayed because, luckily, they had one of 'their own regimental officers with them, whom they knew'. After this officer had spoken to them, 'all was well', wrote Wimberley in his unpublished memoirs. On the other hand, the 'Jocks of the other Highland regiments had ... none of their own known officers with them'.[13]

Wimberley was only partially right. The Black Watch reinforcement officer he mentions was Lieutenant J A Coulter of the 7th Battalion. Coulter had been wounded in Sicily during the fighting in the Sferro area, and had ended up in 155 Transit Camp after a period of hospitalisation. According to Private Alec McMichael of the 5th Black Watch, it was a speech by Coulter that persuaded the 100 or so men from the 1st, 5th and 7th Battalions to forget their grievances and join units at Salerno. McMichael recalls:

> Many of the men on the draft were refusing to go up to the front line in the mountains. I was one of about 100 Black Watch and we were taken aside by a Black Watch officer who told us that there were men at the front line who needed our help. It was put to us that if we did not go to their aid they would be pushed back to the beach and the boats waiting offshore would be used for their escape. We, therefore, would be left on the beach. The officer was very persuasive. Looking back I recall feelings

of hopelessness, dismay and anger. We had thought we were going back to our own units. Rightly or wrongly we followed orders.

Coulter, McMichael and the rest of the Black Watch reinforcements marched off to join the 6th Lincolns of 46th Division, fighting on the outskirts of the town of Salerno. But Coulter was not the only familiar regimental officer on the draft. There were at least two others. The war diary of the 5th Hampshires of 46th Division states that Lieutenant A R Tannahill of the 2nd Seaforths and Captain G L Paterson of the 5th Seaforths joined them on 19 September.[14] Both men had been wounded in the battle for the heights of Franco Fonte during the fourth day of the Sicilian campaign. Tannahill was a young officer who had only joined the 2nd Seaforths six weeks before his wounding, but Paterson was a company commander and his opinion should have carried some weight. Under the circumstances, it is possible that both officers were among those sympathetic to the plight of the men. Certainly, Private Robert Thompson of the 5th Seaforths cannot remember Paterson trying to persuade the men to obey orders:

> When they said we had to join 46th Division I didn't go because I had been told I was going back to join my own unit. Never before had we been lied to in this way. This type of thing could not have happened in the Eighth Army. My decision not to go was a personal one, not influenced by others.

Captain Albert Lee, the officer who had been ordered by the commandant at 155 Camp not to tell the draft of its true destination, recalls that he, like Coulter, tried to persuade the men to march off:

> All the men were in a huge field, with a hedge at the top and a metal road to the side. We reinforcement officers were congregated in slit trenches on the other side of the hedge. Besides me there were two other officers from my battalion – Captain Trevor Williams and Lieutenant Chris d'Iaga. On the 19th, Williams and I were instructed by an officer at the camp to encourage the men to join units fighting at Salerno. By now we were aware that the men were claiming they had been misled at Tripoli, that they had been told they were being sent back to their own units. Under the circumstances we decided that instead of confronting the men it would be better to let them know that we sympathised with them, which we did. We felt exactly as they did; we didn't want to be posted to unfamiliar units, but as officers we could not enjoy the luxury of saying: 'I'm not going.'
>
> At first we went to speak to the 15 or so York & Lancaster boys on the draft. Williams knew a sergeant among them, and he must have had some

influence because they all agreed to go. Then we went to speak to some blokes we didn't know, but most were adamant that they would not join any units other than their own. At no time did we actually order anyone to go.

Private Edwin Scott was one of the men that Lee failed to talk round. His memory of the incident is that Lee was 'very sympathetic'.

Ray Whitaker, then a private in the Argyll & Sutherland Highlanders, remembers an officer actually encouraging the recalcitrants to decide for themselves what to do. A Yorkshireman from Leeds, Whitaker had found his way into the Argylls by a roundabout route. In 1938, aged 16, he had joined the King's Own Yorkshire Light Infantry as a boy soldier. Following discharge a year later, and on the advice of a friend, he signed up with the Argylls as a Territorial. When war broke out he was called up to the 10th Battalion. If he had not been under 19 – the minimum age for overseas service – he would have gone abroad with the 7th Argylls and may well have shared the fate of most of its members, who were captured during the fall of France.

Short and stocky, with a strut like a bantam cock, Whitaker's love of a punch-up was to get him into hot water many times in his army career. In the summer of 1940 he volunteered for the Commandos, Churchill's fledgling shock force that was being specially trained to harry the coast of German-held Europe, but within nine months had been returned to the reformed 7th Argylls after a drunken brawl with MPs. Unrepentant, he continued to wield his fists with gay abandon until, tired of a spell in the guardroom, he escaped and went absent without leave. Court martialled on recapture, he was sentenced to nine months imprisonment and discharge from the army. This was reduced by three months with continued service on the recommendation of his brigadier, who sensed that he would make a good fighting soldier. Even before this reduced sentence was up, the battalion was sent to North Africa and he was released to go with it.

Whitaker's first chance to redeem himself came at El Alamein, yet, the terrific opening barrage apart, his most enduring memory of the battle is the capture of an Italian army mobile brothel! Injured by shrapnel at Wadi Akarit – the battle in which his CO, Lieutenant Colonel Lorne Campbell, won a VC – he finally rejoined the battalion after an eight-week spell in hospital, convalescent depot and transit camp. As the desert campaign neared an end, he heard many rumours that the Highland Division would be going home to prepare for an invasion of France – but then, he recalls, 'you hear a lot of rumours in the army, that you're going here or there, and you often end up somewhere else'.

That 'somewhere else' was Sicily. It was an unlucky five weeks for the 7th Argylls, who had already been through so much. In savage fighting during the two-day battle for Gerbini aerodrome the battalion suffered over 180 casualties – more than a third of its fighting strength – including the death of the new CO, Lieutenant Colonel Mathieson, who was awarded a posthumous DSO and OBE. Whitaker was one of just seven members of A Company to come through the ordeal unscathed. As the campaign drew to a close, he fell victim to jaundice and was evacuated to Tripoli.

Now at Salerno, Whitaker was surprised when an officer from the Durham Light Infantry spoke in confidence first to the NCOs and then to some privates:

> He said to us: 'I've been told that if I don't go, I'll be shot. So I've got to go. You decide amongst yourselves what you want to do. All I will say is that it's a liberty what they've done.'

By the afternoon of 19 September some 350 veterans were still unwilling to join units at Salerno. Realising that the situation was getting out of hand, staff officers at X Corps' command post in the village of Pontecagnano decided to give the bad news to the corps commander, Lieutenant General Sir Richard McCreery.

Despite his Celtic-sounding name, McCreery was a true Englishman, born in Leicestershire and educated at Eton. His military career had begun in 1915 when he was commissioned at Sandhurst at the age of 17. Distinguished war service in the 12th Lancers followed, capped by a fine reconnaissance action in 1918 which, ironically, enabled troops of the 50th Division to continue their advance and which won him a Military Cross. Like many cavalry officers he was a fine horseman, and in the inter-war years had twice won the Grand Military Gold Cup at Sandown as well as leading the 12th Lancers' polo team to victory in the inter-regimental competition of 1936.

While less spectacular than that of Alexander, his army career had prospered in the 1930s. Command of his regiment for three years was followed by a posting as Alexander's chief of staff in the 1st Division in 1939. By May 1940, he had been promoted to brigadier and was awarded the DSO for the gallant extrication of the remnants of his armoured brigade in the June battles, long after the majority of the BEF had escaped at Dunkirk. Back in Britain, he spent two years commanding an armoured division before being sent to North Africa as armoured adviser to GHQ Cairo. When his mentor, Alexander, was appointed commander-in-chief he resumed his old role as his chief of staff. McCreery was anxious to be involved in the fighting, though, and

Alexander rewarded his hard work by promoting him to lieutenant general and giving him X Corps in 1943. Salerno was his first front-line command of a formation bigger than a brigade. It was this inexperience that caused Montgomery – who was always scathing about staff officers and cavalrymen – to write to the Chief of Imperial General Staff, General Sir Alan Brooke, some weeks after the battle for Salerno was over, voicing his 'doubt' that McCreery 'understands the infantry division'.[15]

On hearing that battle-hardened reinforcements from Tripoli were refusing to join his divisions, McCreery decided to speak to the men personally. He was filled in on the details of the men's grievances by staff officers during the bumpy ride in his jeep to the transit camp. After a brief consultation with the camp officers, he directed the driver across the field to where the defiant troops were gathered. Hardly waiting for the jeep to come to a halt, McCreery vaulted out, climbed on to the bonnet and unfolded his thin, tall frame to its full height. Speaking as loudly as he could, he told the men to gather round. At first they listened in silence.

'I'm shocked to find you men here,' he began. 'I had expected all of you to be with your new divisions by now. They have been having a hard time, which is why it was necessary to ask for urgent reinforcements.'

'We were told we were going back to our units!' a lone voice cried out.

'Obviously there's been a cock-up,' McCreery replied, glancing in the direction of the speaker. 'As soon as the military situation allows I promise you I will do everything in my power to return you to your units.'

Amid the response of boos and catcalls, one man shouted: 'Promises, promises. That's what they said at Tripoli!'

Unperturbed, McCreery continued: 'If you go now, we'll forget this whole little incident. If you don't, the consequences could be very serious indeed. You know the penalty for mass disobedience.' He was careful not to mention the word 'mutiny' for fear of inciting the men further.

But they were angry now, and the booing resumed. McCreery seemed to be appealing to their better judgment, implying they had a choice. 'Send us back to our units,' said one. 'We won't fight at Salerno,' shouted another. Then, an anonymous voice of compromise: 'We'll only fight as a unit, together.'

McCreery was losing patience. 'I'm afraid that's not possible. I'm asking you, for the last time, to change your minds before it's too late!' More boos. Defeated, McCreery jumped down and drove off to the edge of the field, where the camp officers were waiting. He told them to give the men a chance to think it over, then to get tough. Before nightfall, another 50 men had agreed to join units at Salerno and had been marched off. A hard core of 300 remained.[16]

Months later, when General Wimberley, the former commander of the 51st, learnt about the incident he was convinced that a golden opportunity to defuse the situation had been missed. In his memoirs he wrote that the 'tragic side' of the whole affair was that the commander of the 56th Division at Salerno, Major General Douglas Graham, a former brigadier in the Highland Division, 'heard nothing about the incident at the time'. He continued:

> Had only someone thought of getting him to talk to our Jocks for fifteen minutes, I feel certain the whole affair would never have occurred. To my mind it was quite obvious, to anyone who understood our Jocks, what should have been done. Indeed, it was what we ourselves had done in the 51st after Akarit. Then we suddenly got large drafts from other English regiments, as there were, at that time, no more Scots reinforcements immediately available in Africa. We at once arranged to send these men by whole platoons, still wearing their own regimental cap badges and Divisional flashes . . . to be attached to certain of our regiments. Moreover, they were . . . told as they arrived that as soon as the fighting was over . . . any who wished would be returned to the Corps reinforcement camps . . .
>
> I remain convinced, that if the Jocks had really believed, from an officer they knew and trusted, that they would be kept together, and merely attached to the English regiments, still wearing their HD flashes and tartans, there would have been few, if any, Courts Martial.[17]

In his report for the War Office, Lieutenant Colonel Main wrote that the hard core of 300 left by the evening of 19 September contained men of different calibre with varying motives. In his opinion, it included:

> . . . the man of high divisional morale who hoped that his action would be subsequently approved; the angry affronted patriot of high personal morals, who believed he was right whatever the consequences; the man whose sense of justice was outraged and who had been encouraged in this by the attitude of the draft officers and NCOs, and by the number of his companions who were taking the same course; a few men whose anxiety about future battle in strange company led them to follow the firm lead given them; and a few useless men who preferred idleness to discipline and service in any formation.[18]

Tellingly, Main went on to state that, in his professional opinion, the more scurrilous members of the group making up the last two categories 'were few enough to have no directing influence on the others'. On the contrary, it was those 'with the highest divisional morale and a combative family spirit' that 'grouped themselves together in the decision to refuse all divisions but their own'.[19]

So what was this 'combative family spirit' that was powerful enough to cause veterans with mostly spotless disciplinary records to disobey orders? Undoubtedly, its most general form was a pride in belonging to Montgomery's by now world-famous Eighth Army. Addressing members of the Highland Division in Sicily in September 1943, Montgomery put his finger on the major factor that he believed had contributed to his army's success: teamwork.

> I wonder whether you have had time to think why it is this great Army of ours is what it is; wherein lies its great strength . . . I believe our great strength lies in the fact that in this Army we are one great family. Everybody knows everybody else, and, as in a good family, we are a great team. Team work in this Army; I don't think there is anything like it in any other part of the world. When you get that spirit in an Army there is nothing you cannot do, and I would like to say that in what has been done your Division has played a very great part.[20]

Enhancing this teamwork was Monty's unique practice of keeping the troops informed. Not only would he regularly speak to them himself, but he also instructed his officers to explain to them their role in a battle, and how it fitted into the larger picture. In an address to his officers before the battle of El Alamein, he explained the effect this would have:

> Once every soldier knows and understands what is wanted of him, and why, he will always do his stuff and will never let down his side. And so you see, we've got a hard fight in front of us. But tell the men all about it, work them up to a state of great enthusiasm and send them into the battle determined to fight, and to kill, and to conquer.[21]

Andy Scott, for one, recalls being as attached to Monty's army as he was to the Highland Division and the Gordon Highlanders. Others, like Hugh Fraser, saw their division as more important:

> It may seem strange, but we felt in the 51st Division – and they probably felt the same in the 50th – that there was nobody like us, and no matter what we always had to get back to our units. This was drummed into us. We were the 'HD', we were the ones that were winning the war.

According to Lieutenant Colonel Main, the prime loyalty felt by

Highlanders was towards their division, whereas members of the 50th worked on a 'different system of loyalties':

> Pride in the division was there, but it was overridden by battalion loyalties, and in the men of the DLI [Durham Light Infantry] by a peculiar family affection for the DLI brigade.[22]

Certainly Wally Innes and Joe Pettit felt this 'affection', as did Edwin Scott and Percy Aveyard. In the past it had been guaranteed by, in Aveyard's words, the 'accepted practice to always return the wounded and sick to their own units'. Andy Scott remembers that it was Montgomery who instituted the practice as a way of promoting the *esprit de corps* of his troops:

> Before that, if you landed back at one of the base camps you would be sent to whichever units was short. Monty sent out orders to these base camps that if you were still A1, you were to be sent back to your own unit. The first time I caught jaundice in the desert, the one thing that worried me was that I might not get sent back to my own unit. I needn't have worried, because they kept each regiment separate until there was a vacancy in the battalions.

Wimberley, also, was instrumental in ensuring that casualties returned. As well as instructing the staff at 155 Camp to this effect, he also gave specific instructions to the men of his division. In his memoirs he admitted that during the North African campaign he had:

> ... often told the officers and men of the 51st ... that if wounded etc. and sent to the base, they should not allow themselves to get drafted to other Divisions, but should see that they came back to us.[23]

The combination of expecting always to be sent back to their own units and the familiarity of being kept informed to a much greater extent than private soldiers were used to meant that members of the Eighth Army, more than any other, were likely to react unfavourably when neither of these practices was upheld. Such 'rebellious' behaviour could be justified by the fact that their officers – and in the case of the 51st, their general – had expressly told them 'not' to 'allow themselves to get drafted to other divisions'.

At the subsequent trial of those accused of mutiny at Salerno, the chief prosecution officer stated in his opening speech that he knew 'of no circumstances' which placed those men who agreed to join divisions at Salerno on 18 and 19 September 'in any different category' from those who refused.[24] He was trying to convince the court that the men who made up the Tripoli draft were essentially the same – all Eighth Army veterans – so implying that, however unwillingly, the majority did their duty while a minority of 'bad hats' refused. In fact, the vast majority of those who agreed to go on 18 and 19 September were almost certainly inexperienced troops, many recently arrived from Britain. With no firm attachment to a particular battalion or fighting unit, and therefore no reason to be lied to, they had nothing to complain about when they learnt they were being sent to reinforce the 46th and 56th Divisions. Only the veterans, bonded to their battalions by the crucible of combat, had cause to object to the way they had been deceived. Apart from the Black Watch – cleverly persuaded to march off by an officer whom many knew and trusted – the majority of men from battalions of the 50th and 51st Divisions were united by the evening of 19 September in their determination not to fight at Salerno with strange units.

Chapter 4

Mutiny

A hot sun had already burned off the thin sea mist by the time a group of officers arrived to speak to the 300 or so veterans lying in the field that served as X Corps' transit camp during the morning of 20 September. They did not order the men to move, they simply advised them to, warning them of the dire consequences of refusing. Nevertheless, the majority remained determined not to join any divisions but their own.

One officer who had some limited success was Captain Rankin, a 46th Division medical officer. Tipped off by his sergeant about trouble at the transit camp involving men from the Durham Light Infantry, Rankin, a former member of the 6th Durhams of 50th Division, decided to see what he could do. A mile down a dusty track he came upon a crowd of men milling in a field, and soon sought out a group of Durhams. 'What's the problem?' he asked.

'It's a conspiracy, sir,' replied a man with a white bandage round his forehead. 'They want us to join divisions here but we were told we were being sent back to our own units.' It seemed to Rankin that some of the men were obviously unfit for combat, while others appeared bewildered as to what to do next. Suspecting that there were ringleaders encouraging the rest, Rankin tried to persuade the Durhams to change their minds and agree to go. Only about a dozen were swayed; the rest stood fast.[1]

The showdown came at 3.30pm. Under the directions of Major G G Ellison, the deputy assistant adjutant general of X Corps, a parade of the men who were unwilling to be posted was held. It was also attended by officers of the camp commandant's staff and 12 reinforcements officers, including Captain Lee. Lee had been given the job of formally ordering the men to join the 46th Division, but only after another officer had wriggled out of this unenviable task. Lee recalls:

> Captain Williams and I were in our slit trench when an officer ordered us to attend a parade of the men still refusing to join units. On the way the officer asked Williams if he would give an order for the men to join 46th Division. As Williams was older than me, a big man with a bull-like voice,

it seemed a logical choice. But he got out of it by replying in a hoarse whisper which I hadn't heard before: 'Ask Lee, he's got a stronger voice than mine.' That was how I got the job!

With the men paraded in three ranks, Lee's first task was to take a roll-call to establish exactly who was present. The comprehensive roll he held contained the names of all 1,500 men who had disembarked at Salerno, with a tick next to those who had already joined units. First, Lee called out the unticked names of the Durham Light Infantry and those present were directed a short way off. Then the names of men from all the other regiments involved were called, and they were sent to a separate area. A handful of unticked names went unanswered. The end result was two roughly even groups, about 50 yards apart.

Major Ellison, Captain Lee and a handful of other officers then approached the body of Durhams. At Ellison's request, Lee produced a copy of the *Manual of Military Law* and began by reading out Section 7 of the Army Act, relating to mutiny and sedition:

> Every person subject to military law who commits any of the following offences; that is to say causes or conspires with any other persons to cause any mutiny or sedition in any of His Majesty's military, naval, or air forces; or endeavours to seduce any person in any such force as aforesaid from allegiance to His Majesty, or to persuade any person in any such force as aforesaid to join in any mutiny or sedition; or joins in, or being present does not use his utmost endeavours to suppress, any mutiny or sedition in any such force as aforesaid; or coming to the knowledge of any actual or intended mutiny or sedition in any such force as aforesaid, does not without delay inform his commanding officer of the same, shall, on conviction by court martial, be liable to suffer death.[2]

Ignoring the loud gasp that followed the mention of the word 'death', and pausing only to flip over a few pages, Lee then read out the relevant passage defining mutiny:

> The term 'mutiny' implies collective insubordination or a combination of two or more persons to resist or to induce others to resist lawful military authority.[3]

Most Durhams reacted with horror to this first actual mention of the crime of 'mutiny' and its chilling penalty. It also produced indignation and, for some, indecision about what to do next. They did not have long to make up their minds. Lee bawled out an order made up on the spur of the moment: 'Pick up your kits, fall in on the road and march off to 46th Division area!'

Many were in a quandary. For some, this was the first specific order to join units at Salerno they had received. All were aware that their actions up to this point were illegal, but they had hoped that, once the circumstances behind the incident were fully known, the authorities would decide not to punish them and would return them to their units. Never, in their wildest imagination, had they supposed that their stand could lead to their being court martialled on a capital charge. About 20 men cracked and obeyed the order. This still left over 120, including Lance Corporal Percy Aveyard. Despite the threats he was more indignant than worried:

> They hadn't honoured what was said and we weren't pleased, but there was no conspiracy. We had talked with our mates about what we would do as individuals, not what we would do as a group. We were all individuals, we had our own ideas. I wasn't worried at this point because I didn't think that what we had done was mutiny. We didn't take up arms, or anything like that. All we did was stand still. I was convinced that, if it came to a trial, we would be let off.

At this point Major Ellison, certain that many more were wavering, stepped forward and addressed the men:

> You must realise the seriousness of mutiny. Any man who continues to disobey the order will answer separately for his crime and will be individually court martialled. I appreciate that a mistake was made in sending you here, and I repeat once again the promise made to you yesterday by General McCreery. When circumstances permit, all efforts will be made to return you to your own units.[4]

Captain Lee, for one, was unconvinced that this promise would ever be fulfilled. He could not imagine a situation in which reinforcements posted to the 1st York & Lancasters would be allowed to return to their original units at a later date. Lost in such thoughts, Lee was brought back to reality by a signal from Ellison to repeat his original order. This time a sullen group of around 45 broke ranks and moved off. Seventy-five were left. As a last resort, Ellison took the remaining three sergeants – Wally Innes, Joe Pettit and George Middleton – to one side so he could speak with them in private.

'I'll put a crown above your stripes if you go up that road, because if you go others will follow,' Ellison told them.

To be asked to betray their principles for the reward of promotion to sergeant major only made the three more determined to stand fast. Innes, the most senior, replied for all three: 'You can keep your crown and you can have these three stripes and let me get back to my unit.'

'What about you two,' said Ellison, nodding towards Pettit and Middleton.

'I'm with Sergeant Innes,' Pettit replied. Middleton nodded his agreement.

'You're making a big mistake. You've got two minutes to persuade the men to move. After that you'll face the consequences,' Ellison concluded.

As the sergeants returned to the men, the assembled officers withdrew. Once again, it was Innes who spoke. He began by telling them what Ellison had said, how he had offered to promote them if they went and how they had refused. Edwin Scott remembers that Innes concluded by telling them to make up their own minds:

> Innes said to us: 'Don't take any notice of what we do. It's up to yourselves what you're gonna do. I'm not going to influence you in any way. Whatever you do, you do it off your own bat; it's your neck.' It made no difference. I wasn't going.

When the two minutes were up, the officers returned. Lee's voice rang out: 'I order you for the third and final time to pick up your kit, fall in on the road and march off to 46th Division area.'

Not a soul among the three depleted ranks of Durhams stirred. None stared ahead more defiantly than 27-year-old Private John McFarlane, proudly wearing the ribbon of the Military Medal on his chest. A short, wiry Scotsman from Holytown in Lanarkshire, McFarlane had worked with pit ponies at the local colliery before the war. Originally enlisted into the Argyll & Sutherland Highlanders, he was disappointed to be transferred soon after to the Durham Light Infantry. But service with the Durhams had changed all that, and he was now as proud a member of the 6th Battalion as any Tynesider. 'They're a grand crowd of chaps,' he wrote to his wife from North Africa. 'We're all as thick as thieves.'

McFarlane's finest moment came during the desert fighting. During the long retreat from Gazala to the El Alamein line, he worked tirelessly as a stretcher-bearer. He was almost captured at Tobruk, but narrowly escaped through the encircling German net in a truck full of wounded. About a week later, as the remaining two brigades of the 50th Division tried in vain to stem Rommel's advance at Mersa-Metruh, McFarlane was with a portion of the 6th Durhams pinned down beneath an escarpment by a storm of enemy fire. When the agonised screams of a badly injured gunner rang out, McFarlane was the first to volunteer to rescue him from the exposed ridge.

Reaching the gunner, McFarlane saw to his horror that his arm was pinned under the overturned carriage of his two-pounder anti-tank gun. To relieve his agony, McFarlane tried to administer a morphine tablet, but the gunner, deranged with pain, spat it out. Out of morphine and without the strength to release the gunner, McFarlane made his way back down the ridge. Once there he made up his mind. Armed with a borrowed jack-knife and more morphine he once again braved the storm of steel on the ridge. This time he forced the gunner to swallow the painkiller by holding his jaws shut. Once it had begun to take effect he nervelessly cut through the fragments of bone and flesh still connecting the gunner's trapped arm to his shoulder, quickly clamping two field dressings over the gaping wound. Then, holding the wounded man by the heels, he dragged him down the ridge to safety. Sadly, the gunner died a few days later, but McFarlane's courage was recognised with the award of an MM.

Now, with a different type of danger facing him, he was just as unflinching. Years later McFarlane explained why:

> I had no intention of moving ... because I knew that if I left ... I was going to get pushed into another unit ... I was either going back to the 6th Battalion of the Durhams or nobody. At the third time they put the order to us, I just stood tight. I said: 'I'm not moving ...' They could have shot me if they had wanted, I wasn't caring.[5]

Faced with a complete lack of response to the final order, Ellison's patience snapped. 'Arrest these men,' he told Captain Dallenger of the Royal Artillery, the commander of the guard surrounding the men. In all, three sergeants, four corporals, seven lance corporals and 61 privates of the 6th, 8th and 9th Battalions, the Durham Light Infantry and their brigade support group were disarmed and placed under close arrest,

Ellison, Lee and the other officers then moved across to the second group. The procedure was exactly the same as for the first. As before, a number of men obeyed the first order. About 140 did not. One of them was Corporal Hugh Fraser, the senior NCO among the Cameron Highlanders present:

> They explained to us the offence we were alleged to be committing, that it was rather serious, and that we were liable to be sentenced to death. My feeling then was, 'if you're going to sentence us to death, just put us against the wall and shoot us now'. It's difficult to describe how I felt. A deep, deep feeling of having been deceived and let down. Of having been lied to. And I'm sure other lads felt the same.

Once again Ellison addressed the men, in almost identical terms as before. Then Lee repeated the order for a second time. For many, Ellison's reference to a 'mistake' being made only confirmed their sense of grievance and strengthened their resolution not to go. But 20 took heed of the warning and left. Among them was Private Andy Scott of the Gordon Highlanders:

> I didn't want to go. I felt like the rest of the men standing there: we had been told we were going back to our units and instead we had landed at Salerno. But I realised this was my last chance; I either agreed to join 46th Division or I would be court martialled for mutiny.

Scott broke ranks, collected his kit and fell in on the road. Not once did he look back at the men he had left standing to attention in the field. He could not bear to. He was destined for the 5th Hampshires of 46th Division, fighting in the hills to the east of Salerno.

In an attempt to break the deadlock, a Cameron Highlander officer stepped forward. His identity has never been documented, but it is likely that he was Lieutenant D W Milne, a member of the draft from Tripoli.

'Now come along, Scotsmen,' he began. 'Obey the order that has been given or you will be in serious trouble. There was no mistake made in sending you here. It was deliberate. So you had better make the best of it.'

Seeing he was getting no response, he walked up to Corporal Fraser and, out of earshot of the other officers, told him that he 'understood' his anger at having been misled but he 'strongly advised' him to obey the order. Fraser was unmoved, partly because he had never seen the man before; he may have been a Cameron Highlander but he was not from the 5th Battalion.

As with the Durhams, Major Ellison then took the NCOs aside. Corporal Fraser does not recall being offered promotion, but he was told he would be given a few minutes to try to persuade the men to obey orders before it was too late. His reaction was much the same as that of Sergeant Innes:

> I recollect saying to the private soldiers: 'You make up your own minds. I know what I'm doing, but you can do what you want to do. If you want to go, go.' Each man in that lot was capable of making up his own mind. They were all good men, they had all seen some action, and they knew what they wanted to do. To be honest, there might have been one or two shirkers who wanted to avoid fighting, but the great majority were refusing to obey orders for the same reasons I was.

With the couple of minutes up, the officers returned and Lee gave the same order for the third and final time. Not one of the 117 men still on parade obeyed. One 'old sweat' among them was 30-year-old Private Andrew 'Cushy' Mills of the 2nd Seaforths. A powerfully-built Glaswegian with a penchant for slicking back his dark hair from a middle parting, he had started work as a pit boy before joining the Seaforth Highlanders as a regular aged 17. When the 2nd Battalion went to France with the original 51st Division in 1940, Mills went too and was captured with them after a heroic last stand outside the village of St Valéry in Normandy. He escaped twice during the march to POW camps in Germany, the second time successfully with three RAF men, using a rope to scale the prison wall. It took him a full 14 months to get back to Scotland, via Marseilles, Spain and Gibraltar. Serving in a front-line unit after escaping was always a risk, in case you were captured again, but Mills was happy to take it. He rejoined the reformed 51st Division in North Africa, and was only forced to leave his beloved 2nd Battalion when he was bitten in the rear by a venomous spider during the fighting in Sicily. Now, if he could not go back to his mates, he was not going anywhere else.

Nor was Private Robert Thompson of the 5th Seaforths. He did not believe Ellison's assurance that they would be returned to their own units when the situation allowed. The draft had already been let down once and there was no guarantee it would not happen again. For him, it all boiled down to a matter of principle:

> We all realised that we could be killed if we joined units at Salerno. But then we had all been in action before and had faced those dangers. I stayed put on a matter of principle; the fear of dying came second. After all, I had fought right the way through the desert. If Salerno had been a quiet battlefield, like Sicily when we first arrived, I think I would still have refused to join 46th Division. We had never been treated in this way before and we weren't going to put up with it.

Private Ray Whitaker, the fiery Yorkshireman serving in the Argylls, was not worried by the threats. To him, mutiny meant armed rebellion. This had not been anything like that and he did not believe such a charge would stick.

Like the Durhams before them, the remaining men in the second group were disarmed and placed under arrest. They included 29 members of the 50th Division: 23 privates from the 5th East Yorkshires, one lance corporal and four privates from the 1st Devons, and one private from the 1st Dorsets. Both latter battalions were part of 231 Brigade which, only the day before, had become part of the 50th. Of the other 88 men, 83 were members of the 51st Division: 23 privates of the

Seaforth Highlanders, one lance corporal and 19 privates of the Argyll & Sutherland Highlanders, one corporal and 21 privates of the Queen's Own Cameron Highlanders, two lance corporals and 14 privates of the Gordon Highlanders, and just two privates from the Black Watch. Only five men, all privates from Scottish units in the Eighth Army – three from the 1st Argylls and two from the Cameronians – had no connection with either the 50th or 51st Divisions.

The arrested men remained in the field for a further two hours while their weapons were confiscated and their kit searched. It was early evening before the Royal Artillery guard led them down to the prisoner-of-war cage on the beach that was to serve as their temporary jail. As the head of the column neared the entrance to the cage, an 88mm shell landed towards the rear, seriously injuring a member of the guard and lightly injuring four prisoners. Trained to react in such circumstances, the prisoners and guards alike broke ranks and took cover in the orchards flanking the road. It would have been easy for many to have escaped in the mêlée, but none made the attempt; they still saw their actions as honourable, and unlikely to result in a conviction by a court martial.

It was probably during the 15 minutes that it took to round everyone up that a Royal Engineer, Sapper W DeLong, accidentally joined the column of prisoners. The true story may never be known, but it seems likely that DeLong, separated from his unit, heard an explosion and then saw a large body of British infantry being herded into a cage. Possibly he assumed that this was being done for their own safety and, conscious of his own, he joined them. Yet when he discovered the men had been arrested for mutiny he made no attempt to proclaim his innocence to members of the guard. Whatever his motive, he remained with the prisoners and was subsequently put on trial with them.

As the Eighth Army veterans entered the large barbed-wire enclosure, about 40 yards square, one more humiliation awaited them. Next door to the cage was another of similar size filled with Germans. Spotting the horde of shamed British infantry, they let out a chorus of catcalls, the better English-speakers shouting 'cowards!' and 'deserters!' This was too much for Sergeant Wally Innes:

> When they were catcalling and shouting, and when they said 'British cowards', I went immediately over to the wire and asked if someone could speak English. I got an English speaking German and told him: 'We're the same cowards that drove you 3,000 miles from El Alamein, halfway through Sicily, and them's the cowards that you've got facing you now.' And I just walked away, back into the middle of the compound.[6]

Hugh Fraser had never known such humiliation, and remembers feeling 'utterly degraded and shamed'. In that moment his thoughts went back to all he had been through the previous year just to end up as a prisoner of his own side, next to a crowd of jeering Germans. It was a 'bitter pill' to have to swallow.

For many, though, considerations of safety were uppermost in their minds. Packed into such a small area, the prisoners were sitting ducks for enemy artillery. Apart from two small slit trenches with a total capacity of eight men there was no protection, and a stray shell would have wreaked terrible havoc. So when some rounds did explode nearby, they were enough to unnerve a handful of men. One in particular was Private Charlie Smith, formerly hospitalised with 'shell-shock'. As the men fell to the ground, some on top of each other, Smith went berserk, screaming and crying. He had been sent from 155 Camp without even a helmet, and it was not until his mate Fred Jowett gave him his that Smith calmed down a little.

With the onset of darkness men struggled to find a space to sleep in the crowded cage. Some remarked bitterly that their one comfort, their cigarette ration, had been withdrawn, while the Germans prisoners still had theirs. Their world had been turned upside-down.

The following morning, as the prisoners awoke from an uncomfortable slumber, one man was preparing to desert them. Private Kemp of the 7th Argylls had spent a sleepless night agonising over whether to continue in his stand. By the morning he had decided not to. He approached Wally Innes, the senior NCO, and Innes in turn spoke to one of the escort officers, Lieutenant Creed.

'Sir, one of the men has changed his mind and is willing to join the party going to 46th Division. Would that be possible?' asked Innes, handing over a scrap of paper with Kemp's name, rank and number on it.

'I'll make enquiries, sergeant,' Creed replied. But when he brought the matter up with the commander of the escort, Captain Dallenger, he received the curt reply that it was too late. He had refused a specific order three times and would have to suffer the consequences.[7]

Shortly after, the four men with light wounds from the shell explosion the previous evening were reunited with their fellows. A little later still, at around 9.30am, Captain Dallenger supervised a ramshackle parade inside the cage. Lieutenant Creed, assisted by Lieutenant Rees, the third officer on the escort, conducted a roll-call from a list compiled the previous evening by X Corps' transit camp staff from the original comprehensive roll of all 1,500 men who had arrived from Tripoli. It was surprising, then, when a number of errors were discovered.

The first problem was one of numbers. A rough count by Captain Dallenger of those left on parade on 20 September had come to 191; now the figure was 193. The escort officers simply assumed that the two extra men were the result of a mistake in the counting. When the roll-call was over, two names had been called without reply, while the names of four men present in the cage had not been. These men then approached the escort officers and had their names added in pencil. They were Sapper DeLong, Private W Malloy of the Durham Light Infantry, and Privates J Mulligan and J Rae of the Black Watch. The names that received no answer – Privates Davison and Davies of the Durham Light Infantry – were subsequently deleted from the list. In addition a number of names were wrongly spelt and these were amended. One man, Private T Milne of the Gordons, was listed with the right regimental number but the wrong name – he was down as Long. This, too, was changed by hand.

What is the explanation for this error-filled roll? The original comprehensive roll of the 1,500 reinforcements who had arrived from Tripoli was used by Captain Lee during the roll-call at the beginning of the parade on 20 September. All those who had already left were marked in pencil, so Lee then put a blue tick to distinguish those remaining. At the end of the parade a X Corps' transit camp staff officer put a second blue tick against all those still refusing to go. The names with two blue ticks against them were then transferred to a second nominal roll written in purple ink and known as the 'purple roll'. But when Captains Lee and Williams were asked to check the purple roll against the comprehensive roll they found one mistake. The name of Private W Malloy of the Durham Light Infantry had two blue ticks against it, but it was not present on the second roll. Lee rectified this by hand by adding it in pencil in the top right corner of the first page, giving a total of 192 names. When Lieutenant Creed called the roll on 21 September, he must have missed this amendment and failed to call Malloy's name.

This accounts for Malloy, and DeLong's presence in the cage has already been explained. Apart from typographical errors, this leaves just Privates Mulligan and Rae. Given that two men, Privates Davison and Davies, were on the roll but were not present in the cage on 21 September, it is tempting to conclude that Mulligan and Rae had impersonated these two men the day before. On the other hand, the two missing men were from the Durham Light Infantry, and would have been separated from the rest during the parade. This would have made it almost impossible for two members of the Black Watch, with their regimental insignia prominent, to have impersonated them. However unlikely, it is just possible that Davison and Davies absconded between the time of their arrest and the incarceration of the prisoners in the POW cage, while Mulligan and Rae joined during this period, as DeLong undoubtedly did.[8]

With the roll-call over, the men were fed. Bully-beef, hard-tack biscuits and water in discarded petrol cans were passed through the wire. Captain Dallenger later testified at the trial that Lieutenant General McCreery had ordered that, as a punishment, the prisoners were to have their 'compo' rations removed and replaced with these 'iron' rations.[9] 'We were already being treated like we were guilty,' Fred Jowett recalls.

After a long, hot day in the cage, praying that a stray shell would not land amongst them, the 193 prisoners were moved under cover of darkness to another holding area closer to the port of Salerno. At 5.30am on 22 September they were embarked on an infantry landing craft, LCI 350, and soon after were transferred to a bigger tank transport, the LST 305. Accompanying the prisoners were three reinforcement officers who were needed as witnesses for the prosecution (Captains Lee and Williams, and Lieutenant R D Busson), and an escort of three officers (Captain Dallenger and Lieutenants Creed and Rees), three sergeants and 20 men.

One of the crew of LST 305, Able Seaman James West, recalled years later in a letter to the *Blackpool Evening Gazette* the harsh treatment meted out to the prisoners during the voyage. 'They were all herded on to the upper decks, although there were plenty of bunks down below, and were kept under constant armed guard,' he wrote. Whereas before they had been allowed bully-beef with their rations, now, according to West, 'they were treated like animals and kept alive on a diet of thick hard-tack biscuits and water'. West also noted that 'many were wounded and covered in bandages and plaster'. During the slow 48-hour crossing to Bizerte, West spoke to many of the men and was amazed by what he heard: 'It has been a story that I have thought about nearly every day of my life since.' In his letter, written 39 years after the event, he noted down what the men had told him as if it had happened the day before:

> The men said they felt betrayed and cheated. They all said they would have been glad to fight along with their own units, even though many were wounded and clearly sick.
>
> But they refused to fight with novices fresh from home after serving with Montgomery and having already been involved with some of the heaviest fighting of the war. They were the cream of the British Army's fighting force and they wanted to fight with their own colleagues.
>
> They said they had been promised that they would be taken from

North Africa to join their units in Sicily for a period of recuperation. So when they were asked to join the fighting at Salerno they simply refused and had the courage of their convictions.

All the men looked shattered but they never showed any fear, though many knew they faced the death sentence.[10]

Not every member of the crew, though, was as sympathetic to the plight of the prisoners. From the guards, some heard a one-sided version – that the men had been arrested for refusing to fight – and they shunned them accordingly. A few went even further. Hugh Fraser recalls that 'some of the crew insulted us quite a bit, saying we were cowards and had refused to fight'. And yet, despite his despondency, he was not without hope:

> I always believed that something would happen, someone would realise the mistake that had been made, and I would get back to my unit. I didn't even know what a court martial was at that time, and I certainly didn't expect to be tried. I had never been in any kind of trouble before. I had only ever been on two charges: the first was for being in bed during reveille; I think I got seven days confined to barracks. The second was for gambling with private soldiers when I was a corporal. I went up before the CO who reduced me to the ranks, but I was made up to a corporal again soon after this.

Despite the apparent seriousness of the prisoners' predicament, Fraser was not alone in his optimism. Percy Aveyard remembers not being worried 'at this point because we didn't take up arms and I didn't think they could prove it was mutiny'. Even if it came to a trial, he was 'certain the men would be let off'. Ray Whitaker had similar thoughts, and expected the outcome to be that they would all be returned to their own units. In general, the prisoners were convinced that they would never be convicted of mutiny once the full story was known. If a trial was needed to bring all the facts to light, then so be it, but no one was in any doubt as to its outcome. Such naïve faith in the 'fairness' of the system they had served so well was to be rudely disappointed.

While the men steamed towards their judgment day in Algeria, arrangements for their trial were already under way. No sooner had the men been arrested than the normally cumbersome wheels of military justice were put into motion – for the prosecution team at least. During the evening of 20 September, McCreery's staff sent a signal to Clark at Salerno, Alexander at Bizerte, and Lieutenant General Gale – the senior British officer – at AFHQ in Algiers:

> Of 1,500 reinforcements from Tripoli, 191 men battle casualties from

Sicily have refused to join formations to which posted. These men now under close arrest and being returned to Bizerte ... Officers with escort are necessary witnesses.

Require AFHQ arrange reception Bizerte and subsequent disciplinary action which impossible here.[11]

Four days later, Gale received a follow-up signal, referring to the first, from Alexander's headquarters. It was sent by Major General Miller – ironic, given his role in sending the reinforcements to Salerno in the first place – and contained a list of recommendations made by Alexander: all the men involved 'should be court martialled'; in the event of sentences of imprisonment and penal servitude being awarded, the 'maximum of such sentences should be served in the North African theatre'; men given lesser sentences 'should thereafter be employed in the North African theatre'.[12]

Such harsh suggestions indicate that Alexander had assumed, incorrectly, that the men's main motive in refusing to join units at Salerno was a desire to return with their divisions to the UK. As a punishment, he wanted to keep them in North Africa for as long as possible. In fact, the definite decision to send the 50th and 51st Divisions home was not made until 18 September.[13] By then the reinforcements were already at the beachhead, and could not have known. Indeed, most members of the 51st Division – scheduled to leave in early November – were not told of the move until well into October. Of course there were rumours that the divisions were going home, and some of those who were arrested on 20 September undoubtedly believed them. Even so, this can only have been a contributory factor in their desire to rejoin their units; only a fool would be prepared to risk his life for the sake of rumours, which, true and false, fly round an army at war like bees round a honeypot.

Alexander's final recommendation to Gale was that 'in future, officers and other ranks of 50th and 51st Divisions are not drafted as reinforcements out of North Africa provided they have had six months' service overseas or there is no other special reason for not returning them to UK with their divisions.' Obviously, it was intended to prevent further 'incidents' of a similar nature. Subsequently put into force, it was too late for the men arrested at Salerno. In conclusion, Alexander stated: 'Essential that trials should be dealt with utmost despatch.'[14] He need not have worried. Arrangements were already well in hand.

On receipt of the first telegram, Gale had instructed Lord Russell of Liverpool, deputy judge advocate general and the senior army legal officer in the Mediterranean, to initiate proceedings. Born Edward Frederick Langley Russell in 1895, his father had died when he was just four and he had been raised by his grandfather, Sir Edward Russell (later first Baron Russell of Liverpool), editor of the *Liverpool Daily Post* and a noted liberal. The younger Russell had joined the army at 18, serving until 1930 when ill health forced him to resign his commission. Instead he entered law, and within three years was back in the army as a military prosecutor in the office of the Judge Advocate General (JAG). His views on the necessity for iron army discipline had been formed during his experience of the trenches in the First World War, where he was wounded three times and won three Military Crosses. At a time when young men were being sent to their death like cattle, it was felt by many officers that only draconian penalties could prevent wholesale desertion, strikes and even mutiny.

The man Russell chose to start putting together the case for the prosecution was Captain Lionel Daiches. Short, with a sensitive, handsome if slightly cherubic face, Daiches was the descendant of Dutch-Jewish ancestors who had arrived in Britain in the 18th century. Born in the north-east of England and educated in Edinburgh, Daiches had qualified as a solicitor in Scottish law before the war. His appointment in North Africa in the autumn of 1942 as a First Army staff officer had lasted just six months, when a chance meeting with Russell led to his transfer to the JAG Branch. By September 1943 he was one of three legal officers on the headquarters staff of North Africa district, the recently-formed military-controlled area that included most of Algeria and Tunisia.

Two days after the arrest of the men, Daiches was informed that Russell wanted to see him in Algiers on a matter of urgency. Hitching a lift on the next available plane, he reached AFHQ the same day. Daiches recalls his meeting with Russell:

> Russell told me: 'We're hearing of some extraordinary stories of mutiny. I've got a general pass for you signed by Eisenhower. Find yourself whatever transport you can and see if you can get to X Corps, which at the moment is somewhere south of Naples.'

Making full use of his *carte blanche*, Daiches immediately left for Italy without delay, catching one plane to Sicily and another across to the mainland. After losing his way a number of times, he borrowed a jeep and finally located X Corps' headquarters in the vicinity of the ancient Roman city of Pompeii. On 23 September, the Fifth Army had gone on to the offensive and had managed to break out of the Salerno beachhead. Eight days later its troops would enter Naples. Now, it was about halfway between the two.

Daiches spent a day discussing the events of 19 and 20 September with staff officers, notably Major Ellison, the DAAG. A busy man, Ellison made a brief statement recounting General McCreery's address of 19 September and the parade the following day. When the prosecution presented its case at the trial, however, there was no reference to the role played by the corps commander. Why? In December 1943, in a letter to a senior British staff officer at AFHQ, Lord Russell of Liverpool explained:

> It was impossible to give evidence of this [McCreery's address] at the trial ... as it could not be strictly proved that they were present on the corps commander's parade.[15]

In other words, as there was no roll-call preceding the address it would have been impossible to prove that all those on trial were present. While technically true, this explanation fails to mention that any reference to McCreery's address at the trial might have done the prosecution more harm than good. After all, McCreery's admission to the veterans that their arrival in Salerno was due to a 'cock-up' could have been used by the defence as evidence of a genuine grievance. In addition, the general tone of the address could have been seen as just another example of the inability of the authorities at Salerno to act decisively and order, rather than encourage, the men to join divisions there. Arguably, this indecision bolstered the veterans' belief that they had a choice. During an interview with me in 1993, Lionel Daiches confirmed much of this with a startling admission:

> If it had been established as a fact that the corps commander had admitted that a mistake had been made, and had assured the men that they would be returned to their units if they obeyed the command to join units in X Corps temporarily, then this might have undercut, a little, the case for the prosecution, could have resulted in further enquiries, and might have led to a rewriting of the charge in a less serious form [than mutiny].

Chapter 5

Six days to prepare a defence

The white, flat-roofed houses of Bizerte shimmered like a mirage in the morning sun as the prisoners' cumbersome transport approached the harbour during the morning of 24 September. In ancient times a Phoenician outpost, Bizerte had become an important military base with the imposition of the French protectorate over Tunisia in 1881. Now the Allies were in control, General Alexander had his command post there, and the bay was thick with shipping.

After the usual interminable delay, the hungry men were dis-embarked in the afternoon and taken to a nearby transit camp to be given their first proper meal for 10 days. All, that is, except Private R Middleton of the 5th East Yorkshires. He had suffered a severe relapse of malaria during the voyage, and on reaching land was taken to the local military hospital. Their hasty repast over, the rest of the prisoners were driven to the railway station and loaded aboard a waiting train. The officers and guards occupied two passenger carriages at the front, the prisoners were herded into cattle trucks behind. At 7.30pm, amid the usual hustle of an Arab station, the engine whistle blew and the train began its tortuous progress south-west towards the Algerian border. The prisoners now numbered 192.

At an average speed of little more than seven miles per hour, the old locomotive toiled for more than two-and-a-half days to cover the 400 miles of railway between Bizerte and the small village of Ouled Rahmoun in the north-east highlands of Algeria. It hauled its cargo of captives through the hilly region of northern Tunisia, over the Algerian border and across the Medjerdan Mountains, before finally arriving at its destination in the early afternoon of 27 September.

One incident that occurred during the journey demonstrates the prisoners' faith in their innocence and their unshakeable belief that justice would be done. The hell of sitting in the filthy, strawless cattle trucks for up to six hours at a time was only relieved by occasional stops at small stations where the men were fed and watered and allowed to stretch their legs. During one of these breaks, Archie Newmarch and his two mates, Fred Jowett and Charlie Smith, eager to supplement their meagre rations, wandered off to buy some fruit. They returned to discover the train had left without them.

Here, then, was a golden opportunity to escape that most guilty men due to go on trial for their lives would have taken. Instead, without hesitation, the three men set out to catch the train up. Exploring a small hamlet near the tiny station, they came across an old, ramshackle solid-tyred lorry with half its tail missing. Its owner, an old farmer, appeared, and after much gesticulation, mimicking and pointing they managed to make him understand their dilemma. Signalling the three to get into the frail rear of the truck, the farmer leapt into the front, started up the ancient engine and set off. After a hair-raising trip of some distance, during which the solid tyres bounced clean off every pot-hole and threatened to catapult the three men through a gaping hole at the back, they were relieved to spot the slow train approaching the next station. After a minor scare when it looked as if it was not going to stop, the train halted in the station yard and the three men, pausing only to thank their elderly deliverer profusely, jumped aboard. They had not been missed by their lax Royal Artillery guards.

Talking of the escapade years later, Jowett told me: 'If we'd been guilty we wouldn't have done nothing like that. You could say we thumbed a lift to our own court martial.' For Newmarch, the important thing was not his own welfare but the 'unity and integrity of all the men under arrest'.

Arriving at the broken-down settlement of Ouled Rahmoun, the men were detrained and marched a short distance to a huge tented compound, surrounded by barbed wire. From their earlier experience, it did not surprise them to learn that this was 209 Prisoner-of-War Camp. As recently as August it had housed more than 10,000 German and Italian inmates, but had been evacuated on 31 August and had remained empty ever since. At the gateway to the camp Captain Dallenger formally handed over responsibility for guarding the men to Lieutenant Ted Everett of the 30th Battalion, the Bedfordshire & Hertfordshire Regiment.

By now a second prisoner – Private Harry Merrikin of the 5th East Yorkshires – had become dangerously ill and Everett instructed that he be taken directly to the military hospital at Oued Athmenia, a town about 35 miles to the east. Merrikin may have been the only prisoner who required urgent medical attention at this time, but many others were still far from fit. Archie Newmarch, soon to succumb to another malaria relapse, recalls:

Many of the prisoners, owing to cramped conditions and rough treatment during the trek from Italy to Algeria, were showing signs of sickness, weeping and inflamed wounds, infections, malarial relapses and other illnesses.[1]

In the remaining five weeks before the trial, a further ten prisoners were hospitalised and one man died of his illness. Many more were confined to beds in the compound.[2]

Once inside the camp, Lieutenant Everett ordered the prisoners to form up on parade in three ranks. From his first words, it was clear he was a reasonable man. He told them that if they gave their word they would not escape, he would give them as much freedom as possible. It was his job to guard them, and he would do it to the best of his ability. They could make it much easier on themselves by co-operating. The men all gave their word.

The prisoners were fortunate that the fates had decided on Everett as their new keeper. A short, pleasant-looking, moustachioed officer in his thirties, Everett was the type of sensitive, humane man often found in second-line battalions like the 30th Beds & Herts. Consisting of men not in their physical prime, such units were used to ensure security in the rear areas. The fact that the 30th Beds & Herts had seen no front-line service, and had been in North Africa for barely a month, meant that its members held veterans in high regard. And they did not come with any bigger reputations than those from the 50th and 51st Divisions. While Everett was not in awe of his charges, he did respect what they had done and, as he gradually heard their story, he came to sympathise with their plight.

The three sergeants – Innes, Pettit and Middleton – realised that if the prisoners were to convince a court martial that they were essentially good soldiers who had come to such a pass through no fault of their own, it was important that they created a good impression while they waited for their trial. So they immediately set about running the camp themselves on strict military lines. Archie Newmarch recalls that the NCOs 'organised those men who were reasonably fit to carry out fatigue duty'. The result was that the compound was thoroughly cleaned: the open, box-type latrines were washed and disinfected, and all rubbish was bagged and removed. Periodically there were camp inspections by Everett, and Newmarch remembers that 'on more than one occasion' the prisoners were 'complimented on their self-discipline and combined efforts to maintain high standards'.

Everett even arranged for cooking facilities to be installed inside the compound, allowing the men to enjoy better-quality food than they were used to. In addition, there were sick parades held each morning by a medical officer who was housed, along with Everett and the guards, in a marquee outside the compound perimeter. In a written account of his time at the camp, Newmarch describes the relaxed atmosphere:

> With the provision of regular substantial meals, an atmosphere of joviality and a sense of relief gradually spread over the prisoners. The environment and the knowledge of being under the care of an officer with principles and fair-mindedness, and the close bonds of friendship that sprang up between the Scottish, Tyne Tees and Humber regiments no doubt attributed to this easy relaxed air.[3]

The strong competitiveness between members of the two divisions was most evident in their sporting activities. Those men fit enough battled it out in running races and football games. Such antics were loudly applauded by the guards, who eventually put up a football team of their own that was soundly beaten by the best the prisoners could muster. The three sergeants were all members of the talented team, as was Robert Thompson of the Seaforths, a fine amateur footballer in pre-war days. He recalls they were jovially known as the 'Mutineers XI'.

The mutual respect between the prisoners and their gaolers steadily grew. Everett was impressed by the veterans' strength of character and enjoyed chatting to them. It soon became routine for Everett and his senior NCO, Sergeant Terry Corbett, to enter the compound each morning to drink cocoa with the prisoners in the cookhouse area. Years later, Corbett recalled one such humorous incident:

> On this particular morning our commanding officer arrived for a snap inspection and held us in conversation outside the compound. The conversation went on for a few moments when behind us was a voice which said, 'Your cocoa, sir.' When we turned, there was one of the prisoners with three mugs of cocoa on a tray. The commanding officer immediately said: 'Who let you out?' 'No one, sir, I got through the wire.' 'What, with the cocoa?' 'Yes sir, we're trained to get through wire.'[4]

Like Everett, the more Corbett got to know the prisoners, the more he was convinced that they were the victims of an injustice. In 1959 Corbett wrote to the now-defunct *Reynold's News*, which was running a series of articles on the mutiny. 'I came to know most of these men intimately,' he stated. 'These were no "mutineers", but men with a conviction and the courage to stand fast for that conviction.' Corbett went on to describe the men as 'heroes of the then élite divisions of the British Army' who had 'played their part in driving the Afrika Korps from North Africa and lifting Britain's waning prestige once more on high'. In his opinion they should never have been tried for mutiny.[5]

On 29 September, after just two days at Camp 209, the men were visited by Captain Lionel Daiches. No sooner had Daiches arrived back in Algiers from Italy to report to Lord Russell of Liverpool, than he was despatched to Ouled Rahmoun with a sergeant from the JAG Branch to take down the summary of evidence. Before any court martial, it is correct procedure to disclose the case for the prosecution to the accused. Witnesses are sworn and examined, as they would be in court, and the accused are given the opportunity to cross-examine. A copy of the summary is then given to each of the accused.

Although it was Daiches' duty to do his utmost to gain convictions for men who had allegedly refused to join front-line units in action, he found it difficult to equate the impressive soldiers he met at Camp 209 with such a crime:

> When I arrived I was correctly received with a guard provided by the men using proper military procedure. The three sergeants, who had to maintain their own discipline, arranged for all the men to be present on parade. It is true that other officers had arranged a notional guard outside the perimeter of the camp, but within that area their discipline was superb. Given that these were men who were due to be court martialled for mutiny, I was not only surprised, I was impressed.

The taking of the summary of evidence lasted two days. In the morning of both 29 and 30 September, before he began, Daiches conducted a roll-call using a list of names compiled during the voyage from Salerno by Captain Dallenger with the assistance of Sergeant Joe Pettit. Six men missed either one or both days through illness: Privates Middleton and Merrikin were still in hospital; Archie Newmarch was suffering from a malaria relapse; Charlie Smith was bed-ridden with exhaustion and fatigue; Privates A Johnson and W Clark of the Gordons had bad infections.

Before opening proceedings on 29 September, Daiches addressed the men:

> This is not a trial. I am here to take a summary of evidence with regard to certain incidents alleged to have taken place at Salerno. You have all been charged under Section 9(2) of the Army Act with having disobeyed a lawful command given by a superior officer. Other and more serious charges may later be preferred against you. Witnesses will now be called and I shall write down what these witnesses will say on oath in your presence and hearing. Every one of you may cross-examine each witness and call witnesses on your own behalf if you wish.[6]

Two points of interest arise out of this address. Firstly, the charge at this stage was 'disobeying the lawful command of a superior officer' rather than 'mutiny'. The difference between the two is slight – if two or more men combine together to disobey a lawful order then they are committing mutiny – but in terms of sentencing it represents a gulf. The maximum penalty for the former is a term of penal servitude, the maximum for the latter is death. Ominously, Daiches mentioned that 'more serious charges' might later be made, and this is exactly what happened. Secondly, Daiches correctly pointed out to the men their right to cross-examine the prosecution witnesses, and many subsequently exercised this right. But a soldier has no defending officer at a summary of evidence and none of the accused had any legal experience. Consequently, few of them raised points that might have aided their cause.

In all, seven prosecution witnesses were examined: Captains Dallenger, Lee and Williams; Lieutenants Creed, Rees and Everett; and Sergeant L Learmouth, one of the guards at Camp 209. By far the most important evidence was provided by Captains Lee and Williams, because both were reinforcement officers who had been with the draft since Tripoli. As already mentioned, it was during the taking of the summary of evidence that Lee inadvertently admitted details that were of some help to the defence of the accused. He knew at 155 Camp that the destination of the draft 'was Salerno', while the men were only informed 'after sailing'. He 'had received an order from the Officer Commanding 155 Transit Camp... that the troops were not to be informed [that their destination was Salerno]'. He 'did not know' that 'members of certain Regiments at 155 Transit Camp had previously been informed that they were definitely going to return to their units in Sicily', but he 'heard about it at X Corps' Transit Camp at Salerno'.[7] This evidence is important. Even if Lee did not know that the men had been misled as to their destination at Tripoli, he did hear about it later and this tends to support the prisoners' claims that it actually happened. Unfortunately, partly due to time constraints imposed on them, the defending officers failed to pick up on these important points at the actual trial.

By the afternoon of the second day, the taking of the summary of evidence was complete. The accused had all been asked by Daiches if they wished to give evidence on their own behalf, and all had declined. Daiches then typed up his handwritten notes and a copy was given to all the men at Camp 209. It is surprising, then, that the team of defending officers who were allotted to the prisoners some weeks later did not make better use of the testimony that supported the claims of the accused. By coincidence, the code-name for the secret trial was now 'Case 191'. This had come about as a result of Dallenger's mistake in counting the men on 20 September, and it had been confirmed by McCreery's signal referring to the arrest of 191 men on the same day.

On 1 October, the day the motorised vanguard of Clark's Fifth Army entered Naples, some of the veterans who had agreed to join units at Salerno were setting out on the first leg of a journey that would take them back to their own battalions in Sicily. True to his word, General McCreery had taken advantage of a lull in the fighting to give the reinforcements from Tripoli the chance to return to their divisions.

One of the first to take up the offer was Lieutenant A R Tannahill of the 2nd Seaforths, the officer who with Captain G L Paterson of the 5th Seaforths had joined the 5th Hampshires of 46th Division on 19 September. Now, just 12 days later, Tannahill was posted to X Corps' transit camp. After a few delays, he and 39 men finally reached the 2nd Seaforths training at Catania, Sicily, on 10 October.[8] Paterson was unable to accompany them because he had been wounded in action on 26 September and evacuated to hospital.[9]

Private Andy Scott, also serving with the 5th Hampshires, was sent back at the same time. Scott recalls:

> The battalion was badly in need of a rest and was taken out of the line. The next morning the sergeant major came round and said: 'All 50th and 51st Division men are to report to the company office.' We thought we were in trouble but the officer only wanted to ask whether we still wanted to go back to our own units. If you said 'yes', he put a tick against your name and the next morning we were told to get our kit and report to the beach. I didn't hear of anyone who turned down the offer.
>
> I joined up with about 20 other men from the 5/7th Gordons and when we got back to the battalion the CO and all the officers were out to welcome us. Nobody said 'Well done', or anything like that, but we knew they were pleased to see us by the way they treated us. The officers were very angry about the other men who had been arrested.

Another officer returning to Sicily was Lieutenant J A Coulter, the man who had single-handedly persuaded a large body of the Black Watch to join units at Salerno. Like Tannahill, he left his surrogate unit, the 6th Lincolns, on 1 October and joined up with the 7th Black Watch at Catania eight days later. With him were 24 other ranks who had also joined the 6th Lincolns.[10] Strangely enough, Private Alec McMichael was not one of them. Lucky enough to have been given the cushy task of looking after the battalion store, he had settled in well by this time and did not see the point in returning to the 7th Black Watch, which was rumoured to be returning to Britain to prepare for the invasion of France. 'They were going back for a lot worse than we were getting,' he recalls, 'for the invasion, and I couldn't see me tackling that!' A number of other Black Watch men must have felt the same, because they also stayed.

Other veterans of the 50th and 51st Divisions on the draft to Salerno who returned to their units from Italy were 29 members of the 5th Camerons who arrived on 10 October, 10 members of the 1st Gordons who arrived on 11 October, and 32 members of the 9th Durhams who arrived on 12 October.[11] Undoubtedly there were more, but their unit war diaries make no mention of their return.

The two prime movers in the return of the reinforcements to their units were Generals Alexander and Montgomery. During a morning conference at Montgomery's headquarters near Bari on 7 October, the two generals discussed the Tripoli draft. Montgomery told Alexander that although it may have been 'necessary' to send recently-recovered casualties from the 50th and 51st Divisions to units in the Fifth Army as 'an emergency measure', he did not agree with the move in principle and advised that it was 'vital that these men be sent back to their Divisions at once'. Furthermore, he suggested that his own head-quarters should make the arrangements.[12] As X Corps was due to transfer to the Eighth Army anyway, Alexander agreed. He also told Montgomery that he had already instructed General McCreery 'to collect the reinforcements from 50th and 51st Divisions' at the earliest possible moment and to 'return them'.[13]

Clearly, it was Alexander who had initiated the return of the men, while McCreery was carrying out his orders. Given that, according to Montgomery, Alexander would not have given his permission if he had known his staff were planning to send Eighth Army veterans as reinforcements to Salerno, it is safe to assume that he was trying to rectify the mess General Miller, his administrative chief, had landed him in. It was too late, of course, to save the 192 men who had refused to be treated like livestock.

If Alexander had doubts about General Miller following the balls-up over the draft to Salerno, they were reinforced at the conference when Montgomery told him that the Eighth Army's administrative supply lines were in such a muddle that he would need 'a pause of from two to three weeks' before he could even think about continuing his advance. Once again, Montgomery blamed Miller. The inadequacy of supply to the Eighth Army had been getting steadily worse for some weeks. On 27 September, Montgomery had noted in his diary that the 'problem is not made any easier by the fact that Miller . . . is quite out of his depth, and merely tries to wave the problems aside'. In Montgomery's opinion, Miller was 'useless in his present job' and a 'menace'.[14]

Embarrassed by the administrative failings of his staff, Alexander assured Montgomery that he would do everything in his power to turn the situation around. The sticking point was Miller. Montgomery wanted him sacked. Alexander gave in, effectively stalling Miller's career by arranging for him to take up a staff appointment in Britain. At the same time, all administrative responsibility for armies in the field was transferred from Alexander's headquarters to AFHQ.

A week after the conference, Montgomery twisted the knife in a letter to General Sir Alan Brooke, the CIGS. Miller 'is not fit to be a Major General in charge of Administration in the field, and I doubt very much if he has the ability to hold down the job in England', he wrote. 'He has risen beyond his ceiling.'[15] Montgomery's attempt to stymie the career of the staff officer he blamed for sending the 'wrong' reinforcements to Salerno was successful. Miller remained in Britain for the duration of the war, was repeatedly passed over for promotion, and retired from the army in 1946 aged just 52.

* * *

The decision to try the men as a body in one mass court martial was taken by Lord Russell of Liverpool. In his memoirs he explained why:

> There were over a hundred of them and there were no ringleaders. The [NCOs] had apparently taken no active part in suborning the others, and I could see no alternative but to try them all together. To have tried them by separate courts in small batches would have been most unsatisfactory, and I considered that the whole story and all the facts should be put before one General Court Martial.[16]

Russell's words are important. If the authorities accepted that there were no ringleaders, that the NCOs had made no effort to persuade the others, then it is arguable that there was no conspiracy and that each man made up his own mind not to join units in 46th Division. If that was so then, at worst, they can only have been guilty of the lesser charge of disobeying a lawful command, and then with extenuating circumstances. Sadly, it would prove almost impossible to convince the court martial of this.

The city of Constantine was chosen as the venue for the secret trial because it offered seclusion and security. Perched more than 2,000 feet above sea level on a rocky, diamond-shaped plateau surrounded on three sides by a precipitous gorge, the ancient settlement was a natural fortress. Known as Cirta, the Phoenician word for city, it had been one of the most important towns in the Roman colony of Numidia until it was razed during the war against Alexander, the Numidian usurper.

Restored at the beginning of the fourth century AD, it was renamed after its patron Constantine the Great, the first Emperor of Rome to embrace Christianity. A provincial capital of the Ottoman empire from the 16th century, Constantine declared its independence in 1826, only to be reconquered by the French 13 years later. By 1943, although still nominally under the French, the city, and indeed the whole of the coastal region of North Africa, was controlled by the Allies.

While the prisoners did their best to keep their spirits up at Camp 209, a new compound was being built at Constantine to hold them during the trial. To ensure secrecy the spot chosen was a shaded clearing in the Legion of Honour Wood on a hillside overlooking the city. It was an ironic choice. Each tall pine tree in the wood represented a fallen French hero of the First World War. Now it would be home to a group of soldiers due to be tried for allegedly failing their country in wartime.

At midday on 17 October, 186 prisoners arrived at the newly-completed compound. With them came Lieutenant Everett, two of his NCOs and seven men. A second Beds & Herts officer, Lieutenant L S Newman, and his platoon of 35 men had also been detailed to act as guards, but Everett remained in overall command. Six of the seven missing prisoners were in hospital: Privates Middleton and Merrikin (no change), Private John Atterton (recovering in the American 61st General Hospital from an operation to remove the tiny sand insect from his inner ear), Private Johnson of the Gordons, and Privates Neasham and Greally of the Durhams.

The seventh man, Private John Dobson of the Argylls, was dead. He had fallen victim to the most virulent form of malaria – cerebral, which attacks the brain. When the medical officer at Camp 209 had realised that Dobson was seriously ill, he arranged for him to be taken to the 61st General Hospital. During the evening of 10 October, as his condition deteriorated, four of his mates were allowed to visit him. He died the next day and was buried at Medjez-el-Bab war cemetery in Tunisia with six of his fellow Argyll prisoners as pall-bearers. He had paid the ultimate price for his principles.

As the men marched through the sturdy gates of their new prison they were amused to notice that it was much more secure than Camp 209. Covering a smaller area, it was enclosed by a high barbed-wire fence and overlooked by watch-towers in each corner. Clearly, the authorities were more anxious to ensure their captivity than if they had been prisoners of war. In other respects little had changed. The men were still housed in eight-man, high-ridge canvas tents, and cooking facilities had once again been provided inside the compound.

With the date for their trial approaching, the NCOs were even more determined than before to put on a good 'show' and the men responded enthusiastically. A duty roster was set up for orderly sergeant and sick and sanitary corporal. The grounds of the compound were kept immaculately clean, fixtures were whitewashed, and the men displayed their devotion to their units by reproducing their regimental badges in shells and coloured sand outside their tents. When one man put the integrity of the group in danger by breaking out of the camp to look for wine, Sergeant Innes spoke firmly to him and there was no repetition.

By now the men had been forced to accept that they were to be tried, yet still they were convinced that the members of the court, or some higher authority, would understand their motives as honourable and let them off. Already, though, their chances of acquittal had received a severe, arguably a fatal, blow. While Captain Daiches had been working on the prosecution case since the end of September, priming his witnesses and streamlining their stories, the 14 officers detailed to defend the accused did not all meet until 23 October, just six days before the trial was due to begin.

Captain Bill Murgatroyd, 29, of the Royal Army Ordnance Corps, was stationed at a vehicle park near the Algerian port of Bône when he received orders on 22 October to report at once to the town major at Constantine for two weeks' special duties. A tall Yorkshireman with a military regulation moustache, Murgatroyd was possessed of a down-to-earth, unflappable nature that was ideal for the cut and thrust of courtroom battles. In 1938, a couple of years after qualifying as a solicitor in his home town of Halifax, he had gone to work in the rival county of Lancashire as a prosecutor. This legal experience had caught the eye of the JAG Branch soon after his arrival in North Africa in May 1943, and he had already been detailed to defend at a couple of minor courts martial. Suspecting that this latest call might mean more of the same, he set off the same day in a jeep originally earmarked for General Alexander. After an exhausting drive of more than 150 miles, most of it through hilly country, he arrived at Constantine in the early evening and went straight to see the town major:

He handed me a copy of the *Manual of Military Law* and a copy of *King's Regulations*. 'What's this for?' I asked. 'What am I doing?' 'I can't tell you, it's secret,' he replied. I was to spend the night billeted with a French family and to report the following morning at 9 o'clock to the Cirta Hotel. It was then that I met the 13 other defending officers and discovered that we were all defending a large body of men charged with mutiny at the Salerno beachhead.

The 14 officers making up the defence team were a mixed bag: nine were legally qualified (eight solicitors and one barrister); seven were the traditional 'soldier's friend' – representatives from the men's own units – although three of these were also lawyers; just one was neither qualified nor knew any of the accused.

During the defending officers' first meeting, one man was thrust irresistibly to the fore: Captain Hugh Quennell of the Welsh Guards. Not only was Quennell the senior officer in terms of age, he was also, in Murgatroyd's words, 'the most impressive and imaginative lawyer present', having worked as a solicitor with the highly-respected London firm of Slaughter & May before the war. By force of personality, Quennell quickly took control, and the rest were happy to let him do so. Murgatroyd was made secretary, and took care of all the paperwork relating to the trial. The happy coincidence of this appointment was brought home to me when I endeavoured to track down the defending officers and discovered only one, Murgatroyd, still living. If it had been any of the others, the crucial defence papers which he generously made available to me might have been lost to history for ever.

At this stage, the defending officers did not have a lot to go on. Their only knowledge of the incident at Salerno came from their reading of the summary of evidence. Tacked on to their copies of this was a new charge sheet. It read:

> When on active service joining in a mutiny in His Majesty's military forces in that they in the field on 20 September 1943 when ordered by Captain A G Lee, 1st Battalion, the York and Lancaster Regiment, to pick up their kits, fall in on the road and march off to 46 Division Area, joined in a mutiny by combining among themselves to resist lawful authority and disobey the said order.[17]

Daiches' earlier warning to the prisoners that a more serious charge might be preferred had come about. The defending officers would be literally fighting for their clients' lives.

With time of the essence, Quennell advised his fellow officers that their first step should be to talk to the accused. To facilitate this, they agreed to divide responsibility as far as possible along battalion lines. Quennell took charge of 16 men from the 6th Durhams and six from the 151 (Durham) Brigade Support Group, among them John McFarlane and Edwin Scott. Captain Jimmy Kailofer, a company commander in the 8th Durhams who had been a solicitor before the war, was happy to represent all 21 members of his battalion, including the three sergeants. Captain John Wheatley, like Kailofer an 8th Durhams' company commander, had originally been asked for by 10 men from his company. Generously, he volunteered to defend 15 members of the 9th Durhams – including the ailing and absent John Atterton – as none of their battalion officers were available. The remaining 17 men from the 9th Durhams were given to the sole barrister, Captain G L Taylor of the Pioneer Corps. Ironically, Murgatroyd remembers Taylor as 'worse at advocacy than most of the solicitors'.

Captain Goldsmith of the Royal Artillery, a lawyer serving as a staff officer, took charge of the 21 fit members of the 5th East Yorkshires, and Corporal Hugh Fraser and the 21 privates from the 5th Camerons were taken by Captain John Mitchell, a solicitor and former member of the battalion who was serving as staff captain of 152 (Seaforth & Cameron) Brigade of the 51st Division.

The surviving 22 Argyll & Sutherland Highlanders were divided between three officers from the regiment: Captain H P Samwell, MC, a company commander in the 7th Argylls, had been requested by his 10 charges – including Private Ray Whitaker – all of whom had served in his company. Lieutenant F M H Edie, also from the same battalion, was asked to represent the three men from the 1st Argylls – an Eighth Army unit but not part of the 51st Division. Like Wheatley, Edie had been chosen because their own battalion officers were not available and he, as an officer from the same regiment, was the next best thing. Lieutenant W J Howat, a solicitor and former private in the 7th Argylls who was serving as camp commandant at 154 Brigade headquarters, 51st Division, was given the remaining nine, most of whom he knew.

The 16 members of the Gordon Highlanders were split down the middle: eight from the 1st Battalion were taken by Captain Murgatroyd, eight from the 5/7th Battalion by Lieutenant D R H Gardiner, a young solicitor serving with the Royal Armoured Corps.

All 21 Seaforth Highlanders, from both the 2nd and 5th Battalions, were given to Captain Evers of the Duke of Wellington's Regiment, the one officer who appears to have had neither legal experience nor a regimental connection with any of the accused. Murgatroyd recalls that he might have been a staff officer at GHQ Middle East, the Cairo-based headquarters with authority over 155 Camp. If correct, it was probably for this reason that he had been chosen.

The 13th defending officer was Lieutenant H Hammonds of the Royal Engineers. He was almost certainly asked for by Sapper DeLong, the lone Royal Engineer among the accused. Instead, bizarrely, he was asked by Quennell to defend Private H Swadkins of the Devonshire Regiment. It is possible that he was given Swadkins as a sop after Quennell had decided that DeLong should be grouped with the other two men – Privates Mulligan and Rae of the Black Watch – whose presence at the parade was also in doubt, and the intricacy of whose case demanded a lawyer's skill. The officer chosen for these three men was Lieutenant Tom Magnay, a canny young solicitor from Tyneside. Aptly, the remaining men – the two Cameronians and the private from the 1st Dorsets – were also given to Magnay.[18]

With their responsibilities divided, the defending officers went straight from their preliminary meeting to the compound in Legion of Honour Wood. The problems encountered there by Captain Murgatroyd were typical. Lack of time meant he had to speak to seven of his men (the eighth, Private Johnson, was back from hospital but was still not well enough to be interviewed) as a group. Although impressed with their smart, soldierly appearance and cheerful demeanour – especially laudable given their predicament and the fact that by this time many prisoners were weak with dysentery – the more Murgatroyd heard, the more pessimistic he became about their chances of acquittal. They admitted that they had disobeyed orders, but only because they were angry that they had been misled and were anxious to return to their own units. Being returned to your own battalion was standard procedure, they told Murgatroyd, and many times they had been instructed by officers to ensure they came back.

This was not much to go on. Murgatroyd realised that if the prosecution could convince the court that they had conspired to disobey orders, they would be found guilty of mutiny however genuine their grievance. Unfortunately for the prisoners, there was no time for Murgatroyd or the other defending officers to go into their stories in detail. Murgatroyd recalls: 'We were not able to take individual statements from each of the 192 men – there simply wasn't time. A number of lines of enquiry probably passed us by because of this.'

When I interviewed Murgatroyd in 1993, I discovered just how many lines of enquiry the defence team had missed. He admitted that he was 'unaware that there were some "rookies" among the draft, men with no allegiance to any particular units and so different to the 192 arrested'. As far as he could recall, the defence team 'never discussed the fact that none of the draft was instructed to join units of X Corps until 18 September at the earliest', a point that would have undermined the prosecution argument that the reinforcements were desperately needed. At no time were he or the other defending officers aware that General McCreery had addressed the accused at Salerno, admitting that their presence was the result of a 'cock-up'.

So, at least in part because of the constraint of time, the defending officers missed many of the facts that would have put the case for the defence in a better light. Instead, they concentrated on more fundamental statistics. Murgatroyd, for example, made a list of his defend-ant's battle honours. All seven had fought in at least three major battles during the North African campaign: six had fought at both El Agheila and Wadi Zem Zem, five at Wadi Akarit and the Mareth Line, four at El Alamein, and three at Enfidaville. But while emphasising that the men had done their bit was all very well, it could offer no defence as such to a charge of mutiny; at best, it could be put forward as mitigation and might encourage a lighter sentence if the men were found guilty.

During this first visit to the compound, Quennell was already beginning to envisage the type of defence strategy he would adopt. The accused were top-notch soldiers, experienced in battle, who had been messed around by insensitive staff officers and had each taken an individual decision to disobey orders because they were desperate to return to the family atmosphere of their own units. To convince the court of this, it was vital that the prisoners' conduct was impeccable during their period of incarceration. It had been so far, but Quennell was determined that it should remain so. For this reason he arranged with Captain Samwell to speak privately to the one man whose record suggested he might fracture the unity of the group: Private Ray Whitaker. The fiery Yorkshireman recalls:

> When the defending officers came to speak to us, Captain Samwell came with Captain Quennell to speak to me alone. They realised I had a bad disciplinary record and wanted to make sure I wouldn't escape. Samwell said: 'Look, I know you could escape if you wanted to, but my advice to you is to stay put. If you go it will jeopardise the case for the rest of the men. It will look better if you all stay together.' I said: 'I'm not going to escape.' I suppose he spoke to me in this way because I had been in and out of that many guardrooms.

On 23 October, the day the defending officers took their first faltering steps towards putting together a case, some of the units that the accused had risked their lives to return to were setting off on the long boat journey back to Britain. The whole of the 50th Division and part of 152 Brigade of the 51st Division set sail from Augusta in Sicily. It also happened to be the first anniversary of the battle that had blooded so many of the accused, the battle that had changed the course of the war – El Alamein. While many of the battalions of the Highland Division in Sicily enjoyed a holiday to mark the occasion, and the officers who been with the 51st at El Alamein attended a dinner at 153 Brigade HQ, their erstwhile comrades nervously paced the confines of their barbed-wire enclosure, awaiting their fate.

After breakfast on Sunday 24 October, the defending officers assembled for the second time at the Cirta Hotel to discuss the summary of evidence and the various group statements they had taken from the accused. Certain conclusions were reached. The draft had been misled as to its true destination; it had been sent to reinforce units in a different army in contravention of current orders and normal procedure; many of the draft had been unfit for combat; many had been despatched without the proper kit; the identity at the parade of at least three men (Mulligan, Rae, and DeLong), and possibly four (Malloy), was in doubt. If the defence could prove these facts, then it could argue that the men had a genuine grievance and consequently a reason to decide *individually* to refuse orders to join the 46th Division. Without proof, it might appear that the men were shirkers who were using the insistence on returning to their own units as an excuse to avoid combat at Salerno. Everything depended on getting the necessary evidence.

A list of likely witnesses and documents was drawn up. Most of the witnesses were members of the permanent staff at 155 Reinforcement and Transit Camp, including Lieutenant Colonel Richards, Sergeant Majors Green and Thompson, Sergeants Richardson and Brown, Corporal Floodgate, and the medical officer, Major Morton. Clearly, it was hoped that some or all of these men would confirm that the veterans had been told they were returning to their own units, and that some were sent away unfit and underequipped for battle.

From the events at Salerno they required three witnesses: the DAAG of X Corps (they did not know his name), in the hope he would testify that at the parade on 20 September he had told the men that a mistake had been made in sending them to Salerno; Lieutenant Busson, a reinforcement officer present at the parade who had been brought to Algeria as a prosecution witness and then discarded (Quennell inferred from this that he might be of some use); and any witness from 77 Field Ambulance, a medical unit at Salerno, who could confirm the claim made by Privates Mulligan and Rae that they had arrived at Salerno unfit for service and had spent four days, from 16 September to some time on 20 September, receiving medical attention.

The documents required were standing orders regarding both transfers and the medical fitness of drafts; medical inspection reports on reception to 155 Camp and routine medical inspection reports at 155 Camp between 1 and 15 September; the ship's roll of troops embarked on 15 September; the comprehensive roll at X Corps' transit area; all the service records (1157s) of the accused; the GHQ (Cairo) orders regarding kit deficiencies and hardening of casualties prior to posting; Corporal Floodgate's marking-out book; and Sapper DeLong's sick report from No 1 Infantry Reinforcement Depot.

The request for the last document tends to imply that DeLong had told his defending officer, Lieutenant Magnay, that he had not been properly fit for action when he was posted from the reinforcement depot at Philippeville to Salerno. What his ailment was we can only speculate. In the light of his strange behaviour on the beach at Salerno, and his tardiness in denying his participation at the parade on 20 September, it is just possible that he was suffering from 'shell-shock'.[19]

The list of evidence required is notable chiefly for its omissions. There was no mention of Lieutenant General McCreery, who could have confirmed that he had indeed spoken to the men on 19 September, admitting that a 'cock-up' had been made in sending them to Salerno. As the prosecution had decided to leave the corps commander out of the case, and there was no mention of him in the summary of evidence, this is hardly surprising. If the defending officers were ever informed about McCreery's speech by the accused, they must have considered it of insufficient importance to warrant further investigation. In any case, calling as a witness such a senior army commander, embroiled in important operations, would have been next to impossible.

The defence team also failed to request a staff officer from the headquarters of either the Eighth Army or the 51st Division (part of which was still in Sicily), who might have confirmed that men were habitually told to ensure that they always returned to their units. General Wimberley, the erstwhile commander of the 51st, could also have confirmed this, but he was back in Britain. When I mentioned the omission of the staff officer to Bill Murgatroyd in an interview in 1993, he said: 'We'd have liked a staff officer from the Eighth Army, but I suppose we thought it would not be possible given the campaign in Italy.'

With the list of evidence completed, it was only left to decide which officers would take responsibility for collecting the various witnesses and documents. Captain Evers volunteered to deal with 155 Transit Camp and left the same day by plane for Tripoli. Captain Mitchell took charge of trying to track down the GHQ orders regarding kit deficiencies and the hardening of casualties. Lieutenant Magnay offered to make enquiries at X Corps' headquarters about calling the DAAG and a witness from 77 Field Ambulance.

Within 24 hours of this meeting, the defence team got an important break. Lord Russell of Liverpool had instructed the assistant prosecutor, Captain Daiches, to meet the defending officers and, as Daiches recalls, 'ask them if there was any assistance the authorities could give them for obtaining evidence, or helping them in any other way'. Daiches duly arrived on 25 October. At first Quennell was hostile, but when he realised the possibilities of such an offer he took full advantage. After much discussion, Daiches agreed to sign on behalf of the prosecution a document entitled 'Statement of Agreement between the Prosecution and the Defence'. It contained six points:

1.   The Defence will state and the Prosecution will admit that each of the 192 accused is a first-class fighting soldier, and, subject to any entry in his 122, is a man of good character.

2.   The evidence in support of the charge which the accused have to meet, is as set out in the Summary of Evidence, and they will not be confronted with any new evidence, or new witnesses.

3.   The Defence made, on Sunday 24th October, a request for the following witnesses and documents:-
       [a full list was included]

4.   The Prosecution admits any Hospital Discharge Certificates.

5.   The Prosecution, subject to being given an opportunity to verify the same, will accept a scheduled statement of their operational services etc.

6.   The Trial opening on Friday – if any witness required for the defence does not become available, the Prosecution will support any application to adjourn at any time, to give the Defence time on the arrival of the witness to take his statement.[20]

Only the third point, listing the witnesses and documents the defence were trying to procure, could be said to be a concession to the prosecution. The other five points were clearly advantageous to the defence, particularly the last one. Fully aware that there were just five days to the trial, Quennell was obviously anxious not to begin the cross-examination of any of the prosecution witnesses, nor indeed the examination of his own witnesses, until he had all the relevant evidence. Unfortunately for the accused, the chief prosecutor, Major Robert Money, was later to weaken the case for the defence by reneging on this agreement.

With the agreement signed, Daiches departed. Moving on to other business, Quennell issued each defending officer with a single sheet of paper containing a thumbnail sketch of each of the five officers who had been assigned as members of the court. In 1943, a field general court martial – the special tribunal designed to try serious offences committed on active service – was made up of a minimum of three members, headed by a president, who were in effect judges and jurors. Advised on matters of law by a deputy judge advocate – a legally qualified representative of the JAG Branch – they alone had the final say regarding verdict and sentence. The only curb to their authority was that all sentences were subject to confirmation or otherwise by a senior officer, while sentences of detention and death also had to be scrutinised by the local commander-in-chief. Consequently, the members of the court – none of whom needed to have legal experience – had extraordinary power. Quennell realised that if they were to be swayed in favour of the accused, it was important to play on their emotions, and to do this the defending officers would need to know the type of men they were dealing with.

Given the time constraint, the knowledge gleaned about the members of the court was limited. The senior officer and president was listed as 'Major General Alexander Galloway, CBE, DSO, MC', a regular soldier and former member of the Camerons who had passed through staff college. The comments about Galloway included the fact that he was a probably a Scotsman, and so might sympathise with his fellow countrymen among the accused. They also noted that he was the 'commander of the 1st Armoured Division', and that the division had fought with the Eighth Army for most of the desert campaign, including the battle of El Alamein (it was eventually transferred to the First Army in Tunisia in April 1943). This point was important because it might mean that Galloway would understand the close 'family' allegiance within the Eighth Army, and the determination of its men always to return to their own units.

The defending officers were correct in their guess that Galloway was a Scotsman. Born in 1895, the son of a Lowland minister, he had made the army his career and had served with some distinction in the First World War. But unbeknown to the defending officers, he had fought at Gallipoli in 1915 and so may have had little sympathy for troops who had appeared to refuse to fight in a similar situation. Furthermore, he had not taken command of the 1st Armoured Division until July 1943, long after it had left the Eighth Army. As such, he was a First Army man and may well have held the belief – prevalent in that under-acknowledged formation at the time – that Montgomery's men were a law unto themselves and deserved to be taken down a peg.

Next on the list was another regular officer, 'Lieutenant Colonel M G Kerr of the Rifle Brigade', noted as 'commanding a regiment of the Yorkshire Hussars in the 1st Armoured Division since El Alamein'. As with Galloway, the assumption was that as he had served a lengthy period in the Eighth Army he might sympathise with its displaced members. Once again the assumption was wrong. Not only had the

Yorkshire Hussars not fought at El Alamein, they had not fought with
the Eighth Army anywhere else during the desert campaign. In
addition, there is no record that a Lieutenant Colonel M G Kerr was
ever with the Yorkshire Hussars during its tour of duty in the Middle
East. If once a Hussar, Kerr must have been posted to another job long
before, possibly as a First Army staff officer.

Little was known of the third member, 'Major A C Smart' of the
'1/6th East Surreys', other than that he had obtained an 'emergency
commission', was 'probably second-in-command of his battalion' and
'probably reasonably young'. The inference Quennell drew from this
was that such an inexperienced, wartime-only officer would defer to the
older, regular soldiers who would be more likely to understand the
fierce regimental and divisional pride that had caused veteran soldiers
to disobey orders. Quennell was not aware, however, that Smart's
battalion had, as a unit of the 4th Division, provided 23 officers and 504
men as emergency reinforcements for the Fifth Army since late August,
leaving it understrength by roughly two-thirds.[21] However bitter Smart
must personally have felt at seeing his battalion reduced to the role of
a replacement unit, his men had obeyed orders and done their duty. He
was unlikely to be too sympathetic to others in a roughly similar
situation who had not.

The fourth member was 'Major William Harris', listed as a company
commander of the 2nd Coldstream Guards, part of the 1st Guards'
Brigade of the 6th Armoured Division. Like Smart, Harris was noted as
having an emergency commission, and being 'probably young, but may
be older than other members'. What the defence team did not know was
that Harris, at 31, was the youngest member of the court. They were also
unaware that he had trodden the well-worn establishment path through
Harrow and Cambridge before becoming a barrister in 1937. Despite
his comparative youth, this legal expertise was likely to accord him a
disproportionate influence with the other members. Posted to the 2nd
Coldstream shortly before it left Britain in 1942, Harris had served with
it as part of the First Army from the TORCH landings in November of
that year to the Axis surrender in Tunisia in May 1943.

The last officer on the list was 'Captain J A C Gribble' of the
'Lancashire Fusiliers'. As with Kerr, there is no record of Gribble as
being a member of the only Lancashire Fusiliers unit in the theatre – the
2nd Battalion. Although initially with this regiment, he had probably
been transferred to a staff job. Unable to decide whether Gribble was
fish or fowl, Quennell had him down as a regular soldier who seemed
to have 're-enlisted in January 1941' on an 'emergency commission',
and who was 'probably very young'. In fact, he was a major and older

than Harris, the junior member, who was higher in rank than the most senior defending officer. The inherent weakness in this arrangement is obvious.[22]

At midday on Tuesday 26 September, with just three days to the trial, a telegram arrived for Quennell from Captain Evers at 155 Transit Camp. It was bad news:

> Most Secret. For Quennell from Evers. Nothing in Part 1 Orders. Richards could be hostile. Kit deficiency story will not repeat not hold water. Impossible return by Friday air service cancelled. Will bring witnesses requested if you insist. Suggest revised list signal instructions.[23]

The likely scenario is this. Evers, a relatively junior officer without even the clout of legal experience, had turned up at 155 Transit Camp seeking witnesses and evidence to support claims that recuperated veterans had been sent to Salerno in contravention of common practice and standing orders, that they had been deceived as to their destination, and that many were sent underequipped and still unfit for battle. Evers had drawn a blank with the first claim: either there were no existing orders in writing, or they could not be found, or they had been concealed. As regards the second claim, if Lieutenant Colonel Richards, the camp commandant, was the man who took the decision to mislead the men, as he almost certainly was, he was hardly going to admit it. This would explain Evers's comment that 'Richards could be hostile' if called as a witness. The fact that the 'kit deficiency story' would 'not hold water' was presumably for the same reason: if admitted it would reflect badly on the camp staff. Richards had denied everything.

Desperately disappointed with the news, but anxious for any scrap of evidence, Quennell sent a brief reply. 'AFHQ Algiers are cracking on your air passage', he wrote. 'Please bring all witnesses and documents. Will explain reason on return.'[24]

The following morning the defending officers met again. After dealing with a number of administrative details, such as entry permits to the prisoners' compound, transport arrangements, and cigarettes for the accused, Quennell turned to the matter of evidence.

'Things aren't looking good. So far Mitchell has drawn a blank with Middle East orders, Magnay is waiting to hear from X Corps, and Evers' cable does not hold out much hope of any worthwhile evidence from Tripoli. In my opinion, if we cannot get our hands on any useful witnesses or documents, as looks the case, we may be forced to offer no evidence and rely on the prosecution failing to prove that the men combined together to refuse to join 46th Division. On the other hand, if we can convince the court that each man acted individually and on his own conscience then we just might be able to get the charge of mutiny dropped to the lesser crime of disobeying the orders of a superior officer, which is what they were originally charged with.'

Such words struck a chord with Bill Murgatroyd. While he was convinced that the men had committed an offence by refusing orders, he did not feel it amounted to mutiny in the true sense of the word. The problem was how to defend them. If they offered unconvincing and uncorroborated arguments that the men had been shabbily treated, this might only serve to alienate the court.

Shortly after the end of the meeting, Quennell received word that Sergeant Major Green, the warrant officer who had organised the draft from 155 Camp and one of the witnesses Evers had been sent to collect, was already in Constantine. The fact that he had originally been called as a witness for the prosecution, and then discarded, indicated to Quennell that his testimony might be of some use to the defence. Bill Murgatroyd was sent to question him. As luck would have it, Green confirmed much of what the accused had told their defending officers: it was contrary to all previous practice for men to be sent from 155 Camp to units other than their own; there was a specific order that all casualties from the Sicily campaign should be returned to their units; Green himself had been under the impression that the men were returning to their own units, and he may have passed on this information; the detailing of the draft was chaotic, and there were no medical or kit inspections before it left.[25]

Murgatroyd was delighted. While at this stage Green would not go so far as to admit that the draft had been deliberately misled (although he would come close to doing so during the trial), his other admissions were extremely revealing. Without further ado, Murgatroyd took down four statements – or 'proof of evidence' – from Green which would serve as the basis for any examination during the trial. A further two statements were taken the following day. Here, at last, the defence had evidence of irregularities that went some way to explain the subsequent actions of some of the draft.

Not surprisingly, Green's 'proof of evidence' was one of the first items discussed at the meeting of the defending officers during the morning of Thursday 28 October. With Evers still in Tripoli, no news from X Corps in Italy, and just one day to go to the trial, Quennell had been forced to base his case on the assumption that Green might be the only favourable witness available.

'It is extremely unlikely that Green's evidence alone will be enough to get us a mass acquittal,' Quennell argued. 'If Evers or Magnay can pull something out of the hat, that might be different. But as things stand, we might have a better chance if we decline to present evidence and instead put forward a submission that the prosecution has no case. This would also give us the advantage of speaking last, as the prosecution are denied their summing-up speech when the defence offer no evidence. Then, if things go badly, we can use Green's evidence in mitigation of sentence.'

Most of the lawyers in the defence team agreed. Aware that even genuine grievances offered no defence to a charge of mutiny, they were not sanguine about the chances of getting the men off with emotional arguments about deception, accepted practice and regimental loyalty. Like Quennell, they felt that the best chance of acquittal lay with convincing the court that there was no proof that the men had agreed among themselves to disobey orders to join units at Salerno. A charge of mutiny could not be sustained without proof of such a conspiracy.

Those defending officers who had fought alongside the accused, particularly those with no legal experience, felt differently. To them, the emotional argument was relevant. Alongside them, the accused had repeatedly put their lives on the line for the sake of their country. They had suffered unspeakable privations in the long desert campaign without complaint, and during this time they had forged powerful ties to their units that only men who have shared common danger can understand. In return, these men expected nothing more than to be treated fairly as individuals, not cattle. Clearly this had not happened.

Undoubtedly the most charismatic of the 'regimental' officer clique was Captain Samwell. With his clipped moustache, fair hair, aquiline nose and regular features, Samwell cut a dashing figure. A pre-war Territorial officer with the Argyll & Sutherland Highlanders, Samwell had first seen action at El Alamein with the 7th Battalion, receiving a bullet wound in the leg for his troubles. In action again on the Mareth Line, he was wounded a second time when an exploding mine blew shrapnel into both his legs. During his recuperation in a Tripoli hospital, he was told he would have to vacate his bed to make way for more serious casualties. Declining an offer to be sent back to Egypt to continue his convalescence, he elected to go instead to 155 Transit Camp, as this would hasten his return to his unit. Clearly it was no less unusual for unfit officers like Captain Samwell to be convalescing at 155 Camp in March than it had been for Captain Lee later in the year.

Samwell's determination to secure acquittals for the accused was in some way driven by his first-hand knowledge of 155 Camp. In a book about his wartime experiences, published in 1945, Samwell noted that nobody 'bothered' about him at the camp, and that if he had wanted he could have 'stayed on indefinitely', like a young artillery officer he met who had already been there three months.[26] This account fits well with Archie Newmarch's own recollection that the camp was poorly run. After just six days there, Samwell learnt of the attack on the Mareth Line and used his influence as an officer to commandeer a truck for the journey back to his unit. He was still far from fit on arrival, though, and was ordered by his CO to remain with the rear party until he had recovered. Although he spent much of the Sicilian campaign away from his battalion, as a brigade transport officer, he returned to it six days before the end as casualties among its officers had been so high.

As the only defending officer to have been decorated for gallantry (he had won a Military Cross at El Alamein; one other, Captain John Mitchell, would later receive the MBE for service in Sicily), Samwell commanded the respect of his colleagues, particularly the behind-the-lines lawyers. Yet he was content to defer to the 'experts' on matters of trial tactics, not least because he held a naïve faith in British fair play and deep down was certain that such 'first-class soldiers' would never be convicted of mutiny by their own side. Most of the other regimental officers felt the same. Bill Murgatroyd recalls how the lawyers were less optimistic:

> The 'regimental' blokes like Samwell didn't believe for a minute that these men could be convicted of mutiny. Those of us who were ordinary lawyers were not so certain. In a sense we were divided into two halves between those who thought these men were in grave danger of their lives and those who thought that there wasn't anything to worry about and the men were bound to be acquitted.

It was tragically inevitable that Quennell and the other lawyers would get their way on the question of offering no evidence if Evers was unable to pull a rabbit out of the hat. They found it easy to convince the 'regimental' officers that the 'grievance' argument would not in itself be enough, particularly given the paucity of evidence. Yet any decision to offer no case would mean that even the accused would not be able to testify. Murgatroyd recalls:

> Of course we were we were horrified at the thought of the death penalty for 192 men and we felt that they had a very good chance of being acquitted for mutiny without testifying. On the other hand we reckoned that if we put them in the witness box, they might incriminate themselves. If Major Money, the chief prosecutor, had been able to cross-examine 10 or 15 of these men, he would have been able to niggle them to such an extent that they might have made a few admissions which would tend to prove the very thing that we were trying to deny – namely that they had

discussed not joining units other than their own and so had not acted independently.

Even so, this tactic had potentially dire consequences for the four men whose identity was in doubt, as Quennell and the other lawyers appreciated. Murgatroyd recalls:

> It was a particularly tough decision because four men – Sapper DeLong and Privates Rae, Mulligan and Malloy – were missing off certain rolls and there was no evidence that they had been on parade on 20 September. By not allowing them to testify we were taking a chance that they would be convicted along with the rest. The defending officers assigned to these men explained to them exactly what they were giving up if they agreed not to testify. They were taking a hell of a risk, but they were happy to do so for the good of the whole group. We knew DeLong had not been on the parade as he was an engineer and only infantrymen were present. The other two could have been there, and might have answered to false names. All we could show was that they were missing from the nominal roll.

In an attempt to reduce the risk that they were asking these four men to take, the lawyers devised for them a special defence – discussed at the Thursday meeting – that would come into play during the cross-examination of prosecution witnesses, particularly Captain Dallenger. The plan was to play on the confusion of Dallenger's original count of 191 men entrusted to his care at Salerno, and to argue that the four extra men joined after the parade.

The final major item discussed at the meeting was the amended charge. Since the summary of evidence, the charge had already been changed from 'disobedience' to 'mutiny'. Now, the defence team were informed, the wording of the mutiny charge had been altered. The amended version read as follows:

> When on active service joining in a mutiny in His Majesty's military forces in that they in the field on or about 20 September 1943 joined in a mutiny by combining together and with other persons unknown to resist lawful authority and to disobey the orders of their superior officers.[27]

Gone was the exact date on which the offence was alleged to have been committed ('the 20th'), and gone was the specific order that was alleged to have been disobeyed ('pick up your kits, fall in on the road and march off to 46 Division Area'). In the opinion of the lawyers, the defendants were prejudiced by the lack of 'particularity' or exactness, and they agreed to put forward an application to amend the charge at the beginning of the trial.[28]

Cunningly, the prosecution had made the charge deliberately vague so as to encompass their claim that a mutiny was in existence before 20 September. The fact that there had not been a roll-call before that date, and consequently no evidence that any of the accused had been involved, was not going to deter the prosecution from implying that the offence was more serious than just one order being disobeyed three times.

Chapter 6

Court martial

Roused at dawn on Friday 29 October, the opening day of the trial, the prisoners stumbled from their beds pale and bleary-eyed. A cold night and the lingering effects of dysentery had denied many a temporary release from their predicament in sleep. Some had lain awake agonising over the unfairness of it all. Others had endured a fitful slumber, punctuated by nightmares of 'guilty' verdicts and firing squads. Only a handful had been able to doze undisturbed, naïvely confident that justice would be done.

It was a beautiful autumn morning, crisp and clear. After washing and shaving, the men returned to their tents to dress. Determined to show the court they were 'good' soldiers, each man had carefully washed and pressed his uniform as best he could. Their shorts and shirts were immaculately creased; boots, buckles and cap badges gleamed. After breakfast, a medical parade was held. Only one man in the compound, Private Alec Johnson of the Gordons, was considered sick enough to warrant his absence from court, although many others were far from well. Including Johnson and the deceased Private Dobson, a total of seven men would miss the opening of the trial. Privates Middleton, Merrikin and Atterton were still in hospital; since the move from Ouled Rahmoun, they had been joined by Privates J Ball and V J Little of the Durhams.

Shortly after 8.30am the men were called on parade and a roll was taken. At its conclusion, Sergeant Wally Innes, on behalf of all the accused, presented Lieutenant Ted Everett, the camp commandant, with a leather belt bearing the cap badges of all their regiments. Occupying pride of place in the centre, on account of its size, was the badge of the Argylls. The gift was a big thank you to Everett for all the kindness he had shown, for treating them like soldiers rather than criminals. In Fred Jowett's words, Everett was simply 'a real gent, a toff'. Archie Newmarch is convinced that there never would have been an 'incident' if officers of the calibre of Everett had been involved from the start.

The presentation over, each man was handed a numbered card with a string attached. These were to be worn round the neck in court, so enabling the accused to be easily identified. Whatever the practical justification, the cards were a humiliating confirmation that the men were to be herded to their trial like cattle. His job done, Everett handed over to an officer from the the the 3rd Battalion, the Welsh Guards, who had come with a platoon to escort the prisoners to court. As they were being lined up in numerical order, Fred Jowett, number 141, overheard the Guards' sergeant major bark at his men: 'These prisoners are smarter than you, but you'll be smarter tomorrow morning!'

With number 1, Lance Corporal Blake of the Durham Light Infantry, at their head and number 192, Private Ede of the Dorset Regiment, bringing up the rear, the prisoners marched out of the camp and down the hill into the town. The gymnasium of the *École Normale* – the secondary school – had been chosen as the venue because of its discreet and secure location. Passing between two MPs guarding the doorway of this slightly shabby, nondescript stone building, the prisoners were directed to a large group of chairs in the main body of the room. Sitting at a trestle table directly ahead was Major General Alexander Galloway, the president of the court, with his four fellow members on either side. On a separate table just to the left of the court sat Major Geoffrey Raphael, the deputy judge advocate and adviser to the court in matters of law. Ranged down a number of tables to the left of the accused was the defence team, while the two prosecuting officers sat at a single table away to the right. It was now shortly before 10am.

Any observant Seaforth Highlanders among the accused would have noticed with surprise that their defending officer, Captain Evers, was absent. Unable to arrange a flight, he was still in Tripoli. Equally worrying for the now 13-strong defence team was the lack of success with their other efforts to procure witnesses and documents. By the opening of the trial, the only significant witness they had was Sergeant Major Green. To allow them time to gather more evidence they would need an adjournment, but first there was another matter to address.

As soon as the prisoners were seated, Captain Goldsmith, the officer defending the East Yorkshires and most of the Devons, rose and informed the court that he had a legal objection to make on behalf of all the accused. A tall man in battle dress, with a hawk nose that jutted over his clipped moustache, Goldsmith said that in his opinion the charge did not comply with Rule of Procedure 13(D) which stated that the 'particulars should state the circumstances respecting the alleged offence as will enable the accused to know every act, neglect or omission which it is intended to be proved against him as constituting the offence'. Instead, the charge merely alleged 'a general disobedience to the orders of their superior officers' and consequently it was 'bad in law'. The 'original mutiny charge', on the other hand, did comply with 13(D) because it 'specified a distinct order which it was alleged they did not obey'. The new charge was prejudicial 'first as to date – "on or about 20 September" – and secondly as to disobedience, that they did not know which orders they are alleged to have disobeyed', Goldsmith concluded.[1]

Bound to adjudicate on such matters, Major Raphael was unimpressed. Aged 49, he had a wealth of legal experience behind him. A barrister for almost 20 years, and a junior counsel in the Court of Criminal Appeal since 1934, he had been drafted straight into the JAG Branch after his call-up in 1940. As resident DJA at North Africa district headquarters, it was his duty to attend all major trials. But this was no ordinary court martial. It had been set up with the intention of punishing almost 200 men accused of the worst crime that a soldier can commit – mutiny. While it was important that the men were seen to be getting a fair trial, convictions were crucial. For men in a combat zone to disobey repeated orders, for whatever reason, and get away with it would be unthinkable. As such, Raphael was not going to allow minor legal quibbles to obstruct the course of the trial. In any case, he was well aware that – in the event of a field general court martial – Rule of Procedure 13(D) could be overridden by Rule 108, which stated that a charge 'may be made briefly in any language sufficient to describe or disclose an offence under the Army Act'.[2]

His reply, therefore, was predictable: 'What you are charged with here is a combination or an agreement amongst you to disobey orders, whatever those particular orders might be. If you were charged with a substantive act of disobedience I agree that the particular acts would have to be specified.'

Despite Goldsmith's interjection that 'there might have been a number of orders which they combined to disobey', leading him to affirm again that the original charge was the 'proper charge', Raphael was adamant: 'In my view this is a perfectly good charge. It sufficiently states the allegation against the accused and it complies, as I understand it, with the Rules of Procedure. In my view the objection is not a good one.'[3]

Although Raphael's role was to advise rather than decide, the court were well aware that under Rule of Procedure 103(F) they had an obligation on points of law to be 'guided by his opinion, and not disregard it, except for very weighty reasons'.[4] Such an imperative was doubly necessary as only Major Harris among the members of the court had legal experience. After a brief conference, Raphael stated that the court had overruled the objection. With this obstacle out of the way, the accused were formally arraigned. The charge was read, and each man was asked in turn how he pleaded. Without exception the answer was 'Not guilty'.

Normally, the prosecutor would now begin his case with an opening speech. Lieutenant Tom Magnay postponed this by rising and asking for an adjournment on the grounds that there had not been 'sufficient opportunity for the defence to prepare their case'. When asked by the court's president, Major General Galloway, when the defending officers had first met, he replied: 'A week ago. On that occasion we were asked to supply by Sunday a list of our requirements as to documents and the witnesses we would like to see in order to consider whether or not to call them. That list was submitted at the time suggested. Facilities were given for Captain Evers – the defending officer who is not present this morning – to fly to Tripoli to ascertain what documents and witnesses were available to assist the defence there. He has not yet returned, so we have not had an opportunity of considering what the evidence is which he will bring back. In addition, certain witnesses and documents were asked for from the Middle East and Italy and they are not yet forthcoming.'

As a result of this, he explained, the defence did not have a complete picture, and until they did they would not be able to formulate their cross-examination. He suggested, therefore, that prosecution witnesses could be called but all cross-examination would have to wait 'until such time as the witnesses we require have turned up and we have had an opportunity of taking their statements'. If that was unacceptable to the prosecution, it would be necessary to 'apply for a complete adjournment' until statements had been taken from all the witnesses requested.[5]

Turning to the chief prosecutor, Major Robert Money, Major Raphael asked him his opinion. From the West Country, a handsome man with a quick mind, Money had originally joined his local regiment, the Duke of Cornwall's Light Infantry. But, like Daiches, his legal training was soon noted and he was invited to transfer to the JAG Branch. At the time of his appointment he was serving on the legal staff of the Algiers sub-district headquarters. Although aware of the 'Agreement' that his deputy, Daiches, had made with the defence to support any application for an adjournment they might make to allow them time to obtain witnesses, Money was determined in his opposition.

'I do not want to do anything in this trial which is in any way going to hamper the defence or make it more difficult for them,' he began obsequiously. 'I am well aware that certain witnesses have been asked for as well as certain documents, which have not yet come to hand. I cannot agree to the suggestion which has been made by the defence that each of the prosecution's witnesses should be called and the cross-examination of each such witness postponed until after these witnesses for the defence have been obtained. I do not feel that I could properly conduct the prosecution on these lines.

'Formally I must oppose this application on the grounds that the defence have had ample opportunity of considering the evidence for the prosecution, which is contained in the summary, and that the prosecution is ready to proceed with that evidence. I do not know whether the cross-examination referred to by Lieutenant Magnay applies to all the prosecution's witnesses. As I understand it, it does. At any rate, I oppose this application insofar as it prevents me calling my first witness. If at the end of his examination-in-chief the defence asks for an adjournment I would offer no objection.'[6]

Unwilling to accept in entirety either of Magnay's suggestions – to examine all the prosecution witnesses first and postpone their cross-examination until the defence had all its evidence, or simply to adjourn – Money had made one of his own which effectively gave the defence the breathing space before cross-examination they had been looking for in the first place. Naturally, Magnay agreed to it, explaining to Major Raphael that Captain Evers and the witnesses had been held up by a suspension of the air service from Tripoli, and that had the defence anticipated this they would never have assured the authorities that they would be ready by 29 October. He went on to say that as far as he knew all efforts were being made to get the witnesses to Constantine 'as quickly as possible'.[7]

What Magnay had not counted on, though, was the opposition of members of the court to Money's concession. The manner of Money's rejection of the original request, with fatuous words like 'the defence have had ample opportunity of considering the evidence for the prosecution', had obviously had an effect. After a brief conference to consider the request, the court insisted that the trial went ahead as planned. Their only concession was to allow the defence 'every latitude to recall any witnesses' after they had had an opportunity to speak to Captain Evers.[8] Unsatisfied, Magnay repeated his earlier point that the defence would not have agreed to start on 29 October unless they had assumed all their witnesses would have arrived by then.

General Galloway's response was ambivalent. While he wished to give 'every attention to any request for an adjournment which may be made', too many might cause the case 'to go on for weeks or months', and it was his 'duty to see that this did not happen'. Although Rule of Procedure 15(A) stated that the accused had to be 'afforded proper opportunity of preparing his defence', Galloway was clearly guided by

Rule 104 which allowed Rule 15 to be dispensed with if 'military exigencies, or the necessity of discipline, render it impossible or inexpedient to observe'.[9]

Understanding only too clearly that Galloway was not going to agree to a lengthy adjournment, Magnay tried to placate him by saying that he did not 'anticipate' the adjournment extending beyond Monday morning, which would give the defence ample time as it expected the witnesses to arrive 'today'.[10]

Anxious to keep the trial going, Major Raphael unfairly argued that the accused should have been able to give the defending officers enough material on which to base their cross-examinations, while General Galloway rather lamely backed him up by citing the summary of evidence as a document they had had a chance to examine. Realising that these comments were having little effect, Major Raphael lost his patience: 'Mr Magnay, do you press this application? You realise, do you not, it would be disastrous in the public interest to adjourn a trial of this size unless it was absolutely necessary?'[11]

After a brief conference with his colleagues, Magnay insisted that he would press for an adjournment until Monday, particularly in view of the 'seriousness of the charge'. Once again the court conferred, and once again their decision disappointed the defence. An adjournment was granted, but only until 9.30 the following morning. The original application could then be renewed if necessary.[12] At this point, Captain Samwell, the Argylls' officer who had won a Military Cross serving with many of the accused in the desert, stood up, resplendent in his regimental kilt. Begging the court's indulgence, he asked if it would be possible for the court to give the necessary permission for the men to be able to buy their NAAFI ration of cigarettes, which had been denied them up to this point.

'It is nothing to do with the court,' General Galloway curtly replied.

'I submit it is to do with the court,' insisted Samwell.

'It is not. You can take it up with the proper authority, but the proper authority is not this court.'[13]

Defeated, Samwell slumped into his seat and the court was adjourned.

* * *

When the trial resumed at 9.30am the following morning, three more of the accused were absent. Privates Pratt and Devaney of the East Yorkshires and Private Baudains of the Seaforths had all fallen sick and been taken to hospital. This brought the number attending the trial down to 183. In addition, Captain Evers had still not returned from Tripoli with the witnesses and documents that the defence had requested.

Once again, Lieutenant Magnay rose to explain the situation. The defence had been led to believe, he told the court, that Captain Evers would arrive by air that evening. A separate witness – unnamed – who was due to arrive the following day would be delayed indefinitely because of illness. Despite this, Magnay said, the defence were prepared to go ahead with the case, but only up to the cross-examination of Captain Lee because they were expecting witnesses who were material to that cross-examination.[14]

Major Money's response was to inform Magnay that, contrary to the order of witnesses called at the summary of evidence – Captain Dallenger, followed by Lieutenants Rees, Creed and Everett, Sergeant Learmouth, Captain Lee and finally Captain Williams – he intended to call Captain Lee first. As a result, the court ordered the case to proceed in the order the prosecution had chosen, with the proviso that it would consider an application to defer some of Lee's cross-examination until the arrival of any relevant witnesses. At the same time, General Galloway made it clear that the court would 'definitely... have to proceed without' the mystery witness who was ill. Oddly, Magnay agreed by telling Galloway that the defence were writing off this particular witness.[15]

The roll of the accused was then taken, followed by Money agreeing to Raphael's suggestion that the trial of all those absent should be adjourned to a future date. Money then opened the case for the prosecution. 'If you please, sir, and members of the court,' he began. 'The accused are all men who have served with the Eighth Army. They come from 10 well-known regiments [he listed them], and one man comes from the Corps of Royal Engineers.'

Next he read out section 7(3) of the Army Act describing the offence of mutiny and its penalty. 'In my submission,' he explained, 'the term "mutiny" as applied to persons subject to military law implies collective insubordination or disobedience or a combination of two or more persons to resist or induce others to resist lawful authority.

'The accused are charged under sub-section 3 of the section I have just read, with joining in a mutiny in His Majesty's forces on active service. The prosecution allege that on or about 20 September the accused committed this offence by combining together and with other persons unknown to resist lawful authority and to disobey the orders of their superior officers.

'As far as the number of the accused is concerned, this trial must rank among the most stupendous trials ever heard in the British Army, and possibly in the British Empire.

'The charge is a grave one; the punishment can be death or such less punishment as is provided for by the Army Act. But in spite of this, the facts are short and the issue is, in my submission, a simple one.'

Pointing out that the offence was alleged to have taken place near Salerno, Money emphasised that the prosecution were not proposing to call any evidence outlining the military situation at Salerno around 20 September. This was just as well, or the court might have been made aware of the fact that the crisis was long since over by this time, thus enabling the authorities, if they had felt so inclined, to have arranged for the men to be sent back to their own units.

Money then launched into the chronology of events. On 14 September the accused were in 155 Reinforcement and Transit Camp at Tripoli. On 15 September they, with other men making up a total of 1,500, sailed for Salerno. They disembarked on 16 September and were moved to a transit area a mile inland. The following day, with the exception of a baggage party, they moved to X Corps' transit area. On 18 September the baggage party rejoined the main group, and on that day and the following day around 1,200 men of the draft joined units in either the 46th or 56th Divisions. Up to this point, Money's account was relatively straightforward. His next comment was not. 'The prosecution knows of no circumstances which places those 1,200 men who obeyed orders and went to those two divisions in any category different from the category in which the accused were at that time.'[16]

In fact, as already noted, those who were left by 20 September were almost all veterans from the 50th and 51st Divisions, casualties from the Sicilian campaign who had departed from Tripoli under the impression that they were returning to their own units. Some of those who agreed to join units at Salerno on 18 and 19 September were also in this category, but many others were not. A significant number were 'rookies' from Britain who were yet to forge strong ties with particular units. Others were almost certainly X Corps' troops who would have had little objection to being posted to Salerno. In addition, many of the 300 had not fully recovered from wounds and illness.

Furthermore, Money mentioned in his address a 'baggage party' which stayed behind for a day at the first transit area. Yet, as Captain Lee told me in an interview in 1993, there was no 'baggage party' because the draft was so poorly equipped it did not have any baggage. Instead, this 'party' was a group of the worst cases of the walking wounded and ill, which explains the delay in its movement. However, during both the taking of the summary of evidence and the trial, Lee failed to correct the prosecution's erroneous description of the group left behind at the first transit area as a 'baggage party'.

Continuing his address, Money described how Captains Lee and Williams had interviewed members of the draft on 19 September, stating that the prosecution believed the mutiny was in existence as early as 18 September. The remainder of his speech dealt with the events of 20 September up to the arrest of the men, followed by their movements since that date. He concluded: 'Gentlemen, it will be for you to decide in this case whether this mass disobedience on the part of these accused and any others amounted to mutiny. I suppose there could be no tribunal better qualified to answer that question than you. If you determine that the answer to the question is yes, then the other question to be decided is: are you satisfied that the accused before you joined in the mutiny?'[17]

As a parting comment, Money rightly pointed out that it was for the prosecution to establish beyond reasonable doubt that the accused were guilty of the offence they had been charged with, not for the accused to establish their innocence. Warming to this generous theme, General Galloway then told the accused that if at any time they wished to consult with their defending officer they only had to indicate and they would be allowed to do so. With that, the prosecution's first witness, Captain Lee, was called to the stand, a chair facing the court.

As was planned, Captain Lee's testimony backed up Money's opening address. He had sailed from Tripoli with 1,500 reinforcements. At Salerno he remained behind with the 'baggage party', rejoining the main group on 18 September. The next day he was ordered by the officer commanding the infantry wing of X Corps' transit camp to 'advise various bodies to leave'. The attitude of the men was that they 'obeyed any other order' but 'they did not wish to join' units other than 'their own'.

On 20 September, Lee told the court, he had attended a formal parade in the afternoon which, as he understood then, was made up of approximately 300 men who 'had disobeyed the order' to join units. After a roll-call the men were separated into two groups, Durham Light Infantry and others. First the DLI group were approached, and after extracts were read from the *Manual of Military Law* he gave an order for them to move off. Some obeyed.

Then the DAAG of X Corps spoke to those who remained. Lee's memory of this speech unwittingly indicated a chink in the prosecution's armour. The DAAG warned the men of the 'seriousness of their crime of mutiny' and threatened that 'each man would have to answer separately for his crime'. The defence would later pounce on this as evidence that the men were acting individually and not in combination. Lee then went on to recount how he gave the order a second time, at which a larger number of men obeyed. This caused the DAAG to beckon and speak in private to the three DLI sergeants remaining. Following this, the officers withdrew for about two minutes 'to allow these three sergeants to speak to the men'. When this time was up, a third and final order was given. The names of those remaining were called from the roll, then they were 'disarmed and placed in close arrest'.

Lee then explained, step by step, how the second group were dealt with in almost exactly the same way. The main difference was that, after the order was given for a second time, one of the reinforcement officers, a Cameron Highlander, addressed the men, saying, 'Now come along, Scotsmen', and appealing for them 'to obey the order'.

Finishing off his testimony, Lee described how he and Captain Williams, on being ordered to check the rolls after the arrest of the men, had noticed that Private Malloy was missing off the second, or 'purple', roll and had added it in pencil. He admitted that four names – DeLong, Mulligan, Rae and Milne – were added to the purple roll after it left his keeping, but Milne's number had been present on the roll next to a different name, Private Long, and he did recognise the man now answering to the name of Private Milne as having been at Salerno.[18]

Money's examination over, Captain Quennell stood up and applied for an adjournment. Despite an attempt by Major Raphael to stall him by incredulously asking that surely he had some material upon which he could cross-examine Lee, Quennell insisted. Raphael tried a second time to keep the trial moving by suggesting that the prosecution call other witnesses, but this time Money was the stumbling block, as he maintained that he would only be able to decide how much evidence his subsequent witnesses would need to give when he had seen how much of Lee's evidence was challenged by the defence. All out of ruses to prevent an interruption in the proceedings, Raphael was silent and General Galloway had no option but to grant another adjournment until the following morning. The second day's session had lasted a little over three hours.[19]

As the men trooped back up to their compound, they were at a loss to decide whether the trial was going well or not. Most of them were young, with little formal education, and the complex legal arguments of the first couple of days had passed straight over their heads. With Lee's testimony, though, they had perked up, noting with amusement his description of the 'baggage' party, and with unhappy resignation his omission of McCreery's speech. Despite this, most were optimistic that when the true facts about their maltreatment were known they would be acquitted.

That evening, Captain Evers arrived from Tripoli. He brought with him just one document, the ship's roll of men despatched from 155 Camp on 15 September, and one witness, the camp medical officer, Major R S Morton. His failure to return with any of the other witnesses or evidence listed in the 'Statement of Agreement' can only be explained by the camp staff's unwillingness to make admissions that would have put them in a bad light.

Surprisingly, given that Evers had seen fit to fly him to Constantine, Morton was to prove equally unhelpful. After a preliminary interview, Quennell decided that Morton's testimony would do more harm than good and he was discounted as a witness. In 1961 Morton wrote a letter to the *Daily Telegraph* challenging a recent book – Hugh Pond's *Salerno* – which argued that the blame for the mutiny lay largely with 'bad or inexperienced officers at base reinforcement centres in North Africa'. The draft to Salerno 'were marshalled and fully equipped with the multifarious paraphernalia deemed necessary by the authorities' and sent off in warships at 'some eight hours' notice', Morton wrote. This was 'hardly a task likely to be so rapidly executed by ill-prepared or inefficient officers'.[20]

Given that there is overwhelming evidence to refute Morton's claim that the men were sent off 'fully equipped', it is tempting to conclude that his recollection of events to the defending officers at Constantine was less than comprehensive. After all, he was responsible for the medical parade that was never held, and it might not have been in his interest to have been entirely open about the night of 14 September.

This rejection of Major Morton meant that of the 11 witnesses originally listed by the defence, only one – Sergeant Major Green – was both available and suitable. Magnay's enquiries had failed to procure a witness from 77 Field Ambulance, Lieutenant Busson had been questioned and then discarded, and Major Ellison, the DAAG of X Corps, was unavailable. Magnay was almost certainly referring to Ellison when, at the beginning of the second day, he mentioned a 'separate witness' who would be 'delayed indefinitely because of illness'. As the most important witness not from 155 Camp, Ellison would have been scheduled to arrive separately from Evers. Even if he was not genuinely ill, his absence from X Corps, fighting its way up Italy, would not have been welcomed by his superiors, while he may not have relished the prospect of being cross-examined about his actions of 20 September.

Evers' failure to procure more than one written piece of evidence from Tripoli – the ship's roll of the 15 September draft – meant that, along with the service records of the accused which had been acquired separately, the defence had just two of the 11 sets of documents listed in the 'Statement of Agreement'. Why it should have been so difficult to obtain a copy of the standing orders relating to transfers and the medical fitness of drafts, or a copy of the GHQ (Cairo) order concerning kit deficiencies, is hard to explain beyond the twin factors of unco-operative staff officers and the lack of time.

Whatever the reason, the consequences for the defence were dire. With just one main witness, Sergeant Major Green, and no solid documentary evidence, the lawyers among the defending officers were forced into a corner. They did not feel that Green's evidence alone would be enough to get the men an acquittal, not least because even genuine grievances are no defence to a charge of mutiny. They also did not feel that it was worth putting any of the defendants on to the witness stand because of the danger that they might implicate themselves. As Bill Murgatroyd recalls, there was only one alternative:

> We were driven into offering a case based on no evidence, on letting the prosecution prove that these men had combined to mutiny because we did not have time to obtain evidence that would support any other form of defence.

* * *

With the return of Captain Evers, the defence team was back to its full complement by the morning of Sunday 31 October, the third day of the trial. No more of the accused had been stricken with illness, so the number of clients they were defending was the same as the day before. Prior to commencing his cross-examination of Captain Lee, Captain Quennell opened by asking if he could make a statement with regard to the character of the accused. 'For reasons which I think will appear obvious,' he told the court, 'the prosecution and the defence have agreed that each one of the men now accused is a first-class fighting soldier and, subject to anything in his 122, is a man of good character.'[21]

To Quennell's surprise, Major Raphael ruled that the agreement between the defence and the prosecution that had established this premise was not permissible because it did not 'comply with the rules of evidence'. If Quennell wanted to 'establish good character', Raphael told him, he could do it 'out of the mouth of any witness for the prosecution' but not by an '*ex parte* statement'.[22]

Chastened, Quennell let the matter drop and asked for Captain Lee to be called. His first aim was to establish that the names of four of the accused were missing from certain rolls. On Quennell producing the original embarkation (or ship's) roll of the 1,500 reinforcements, Lee accepted that it consisted only of infantrymen and that it did not contain Sapper DeLong's name. He also admitted that the comprehensive roll, from which he called out the names of the men on the afternoon of 20 September, did not include the names of Mulligan, Rae or DeLong; though it did, he insisted, include Malloy's name. Quennell then moved on to the purple roll, compiled by X Corps' transit camp staff after the arrests, and Lee confirmed that when it was handed to him it contained just 191 names, none of which were Mulligan, Rae, DeLong or Malloy. But while acknowledging the logic of Quennell's arithmetic – that two men on the purple roll, Privates Davies and Davison, had later disappeared, leaving a total of 189 which was made up to the 193 shipped to North Africa by the four whose identity was in doubt – Lee would not accept that this proved that Mulligan, Rae and DeLong were not present on the parade. They could have been there but no one answered to their names, he suggested, implying that they had answered to someone else's. The most that Lee would concede was that there was a difference between DeLong on the one hand and Mulligan and Rae on the other, because the former did not even appear on the ship's roll.

Quennell then turned to 155 Camp in an attempt to establish that, as many of the accused believed, the wrong reinforcements had been taken. Surprisingly, Lee's answers did not rule out this possibility. When asked if he knew whether X Corps' reinforcements had been left behind at the camp after the draft had left, he replied: 'I should imagine so. I do not know.' Moving on to the events of 20 September, Lee stated that it was 'an orderly parade' and that the 'order to fall in was complied with'. He also confirmed that when the parade was split into two groups, DLI and others, they were placed between 50 and 100 yards apart and could not have heard each other. While he could not remember whether the DAAG had said in his address to the men that 'a mistake had been made', he did confirm that the DAAG had told the men 'to act individually' and it 'looked as though they did so'. At all times during the parade the men were 'perfectly quiet and absolutely obedient'.

When pressed by Quennell on the question of motivation, Lee backed up his earlier comment by stating that he imagined the men were 'thinking individually'. The defence team were delighted. Here was the prosecution's star witness actually providing evidence that the men had been acting on their own individual consciences to disobey one particular order. If the court were to interpret what Lee had said in this way, the accused could not be found guilty of mutiny. Flushed with success, Quennell concluded by asking Lee if he could identify the man he had added to the purple list, Private Malloy. Unable to, Lee did settle the issue of Malloy's identity once and for all by telling the court that Malloy had personally told him on 21 September that he was 'present on the parade'.[23]

Quennell's job done, Lieutenant Magnay briefly took over. Was Lee aware that while DeLong was an engineer, the 1,500 reinforcements were all infantrymen? 'I was under the impression until yesterday that DeLong was an infantryman,' Lee lamely replied. Pressed on the unlikelihood of DeLong, Rae and Mulligan being present at the parade, Lee conceded that the only possible explanation 'was that they were impersonating other soldiers'.[24] There were no more questions. Lee's ordeal was over and he gratefully rose from his seat and left the gymnasium. The following day he was on his way back to Italy to rejoin his unit. If it had not been for the 'incident' at Salerno, he would have been fighting with unfamiliar troops in X Corps.

Next, the prosecution called Captain Williams. His testimony was little more than a confirmation of what Lee had stated. He also had been left behind with the 'baggage' party but rejoined the main group on 18 September. During that day and the next, 'approximately 1,200' men 'were allocated to and despatched to the 46th and 56th Divisional areas'. He could not say whether the men remaining on 19 September had received any order to join units, but he did speak to some of them and advise them to go. As he was about to give details about what he said to them, Quennell objected on the grounds that the identity of those he had spoken to was unproved. Money countered with the argument that he was trying to show that the mutiny was in existence by 19 September at the latest, but, for one of the few times in the trial, Major Raphael ruled for the defence.

Money then moved on to 20 September and once again Williams backed up what Lee had said. There were only two exceptions: firstly, he remembered that the DAAG, in his speech, had told the men that a promise had been made that they 'would be returned to their own divisions when the circumstances permitted'; secondly, he did not see any of the NCOs from the second group speaking to their men after they had been privately spoken to by the DAAG.[25]

The cross-examination of Williams offered the defence another chance to hammer home the points they had scored off Lee. First Quennell asked how many names there were on the 'purple' roll, and Williams immediately confused everyone by stating that there were 193, including Malloy's. Quickly realising that he was getting nowhere, Quennell switched to the parade. Referring back to Williams' testimony in the summary of evidence, Quennell managed to get the witness to admit that some of the Durhams 'obeyed' Lee's order after being spoken to by the three sergeants and before the final order was given. This was a major *coup* for the defence. If men who had disobeyed the second order went after words from the NCOs, the implication was that, far from pressuring them to stay, the latter had encouraged them to make up their own minds what to do.

After further questions, Williams admitted that the DAAG had told the men 'that any man who continued in his disobedience would have to answer personally for his crime'. He did not recall that the DAAG had also said that they would all be 'subject to individual court martial', but he would not disagree if Captain Lee had stated that was so. He also said that the two groups on parade were about 50 to 100 yards apart and could not have heard each other.[26] When Magnay asked him about DeLong, Mulligan and Rae, he replied that he knew nothing about them.[27] All too soon he was allowed to stand down.

Unlike Lee, Williams did not return to his battalion. Unsuited to the pressures of front-line combat, he had applied for and received a new posting to a non-combat job on account of a physical deformity of his foot. Only Lee was aware that he had had this particular 'ailment' since birth.

Following Williams on to the stand was Captain Dallenger. He had been ordered to take command of a guard surrounding two large groups of prisoners, he told the court. His rough count of both groups came to 191. They were left standing for about one-and-a-half hours before he took them away. During the march to the POW cage on the beach, a shell landed at the rear of the column, causing the men to scatter. It was 15 minutes before they were collected together. Dallenger did not see any men join the column, nor did he see any leave due to enemy action. The following day, when a roll was called in the cage, three men were found who were not on the roll – Mulligan, Rae and Malloy. In addition, two who were on the roll were absent – Davison and Davies. No one, Dallenger assured the court, had suggested to him that he had been 'wrongly included' in the cage. While he did not remember a man called Milne, he admitted there was a query regarding his name and number and that it was added in his own handwriting.[28]

As Dallenger's evidence only had a bearing on the men with 'special' defences, Magnay was chosen to cross-examine him. In response to Magnay's questions about numbers, he replied that when he 'first received the purple roll' there were '193 names on it', although his 'count of the prisoners' was only '191'. While he was satisfied that the three – Mulligan, Rae and Malloy – were in the party when he took over, he could not swear to this. Next, Magnay concentrated on the possibility that some men might have departed and others joined the prisoners

after their arrest, and Dallenger did not rule this out by admitting that
he had 'released' the men from the parade in 'small batches to get their
kit', while he had only 'kept the pickets under observation for part of
the time'. Up to this point, Dallenger had not mentioned DeLong, and
Magnay, seeing this as an advantage, did not refer to him either.[29]

Dallenger's brief testimony over, Lieutenant Creed was called by
Major Money. An officer of the guard under Dallenger, Creed's version
of events was very similar. A picket was placed round the prisoners in the
field and he did not see 'any man join the party'. Similarly, he 'did not
see any man join or leave the column before the men dispersed' at the
sound of the shell exploding during the march to the beach. The
following day he was 'approached' by Sergeant Innes who 'wanted to
know whether Private Kemp could join the party going to 46th Division'.
He passed the request on to Captain Dallenger and heard no more
about it.[30]

Again, Magnay spoke first for the defence, asking Creed if there were
any air raids on 20 September. He was trying to prove that there had
been opportunities for men to have both left and joined the group of
prisoners. Creed remembered two, one in the morning, one in the
afternoon at about 4.30pm, but he could not remember if it took place
while the prisoners were waiting in the field.[31]

Pressed by Major Raphael on why Sergeant Innes had spoken to him on
behalf of Kemp, Creed answered that 'apparently Kemp had approached
him and wanted to go back to 46th Division'. On hearing this, Raphael
quite naturally asked Kemp's defending officer, Lieutenant Howat, if he
wished to cross-examine Creed. Presumably feeling that Kemp's change
of heart had been adequately explained, Howat declined.

Lieutenant Rees, another of the escort officers, came in next. During
the two hours that he was with the prisoners in the field, he told the
court, he did not see 'any man enter or leave the area, but it could have
happened' as he was 'busy with the kits'. Likewise, prior to the shell-
burst he 'did not see any man leave or join the column'.[32] His brief
examination by Major Money over, Magnay asked him if there were any
air raids on 20 September. 'I don't think so', he replied.[33]

The last prosecution witness to be called was Sergeant Learmouth, a
guard at 209 POW Camp. He told the court that not one of the accused
had approached him during their time in his camp. This was the
prosecution's attempt to argue that if any of the accused had not been
present at the parade on 20 September, as the defence were alleging,
then surely they would have proclaimed their innocence during this
period. Their silence, the prosecution were implying, proved their
guilt.[34]

Stuck for anything to ask Learmouth that would have reversed this impression, the defence declined to cross-examine and the witness was allowed to stand down. With the opportunity now to recall any witness the defence chose Lieutenant Rees. After his denial that there were any air raids on 20 September, two of the accused – Lance Corporals Wade and Brannaghan, both of the Durham Light Infantry – had conferred with their defending officer, Captain Wheatley. They could both remember incidents that might help to jog Rees's memory. After an air raid while the prisoners were still in the field, Brannaghan had found a wallet that someone had dropped and had handed it over to Rees. When this was put to Rees by Quennell, he admitted the episode with the wallet but denied it was 'immediately after an air raid'. Finally, Rees remembered there being an air raid, but denied going up to Lance Corporal Wade after it and saying: 'Where has the guard gone?'[35]

With this line of questioning exhausted, Rees was released a second time and the case for the prosecution was over. Money did call one more witness, Lieutenant Ted Everett, but this was simply to allow the defence to establish the premise that Major Raphael had denied them at the beginning of the day. Money did not bother to examine Everett, but turned him immediately over to Captain Quennell. As administrative officer for the accused since 27 September, Everett described them as 'first-class fighting soldiers and, subject to 122s, of good character'. The NCOs had run the inside of the camp for him, while the men's morale had been consistently high, 'particularly their divisional morale', he told the court. To illustrate this he explained how they had carved their divisional badges and battle honours outside their tents.[36]

With Everett's departure, it was the turn of the defence to present its case. Quennell surprised the court, the prosecution and the deputy judge advocate by rising to his feet and stating that the defence wished to make two submissions that there was 'no case to answer'. He would make one in 'general terms' that referred to 'all the accused'; Lieutenant Magnay would make the other 'on behalf of Mulligan, Rae and DeLong'.

With the permission of Major Raphael to deal with the 'special case' first, Magnay took the floor. With a frame too small for his baggy battle-dress, a gap-toothed grin and slicked-down, carefully parted dark hair, Magnay could have been mistaken for a boy if it had not been for his bushy, black moustache. Yet his talents as a lawyer belied this youthful impression, and he certainly needed them now. He began: 'May it please the court. May I refer you to page 644 of the *Manual of Military Law*, which, so far as it relates to my submission, reads as follows: "It is open to the defending officer at this stage to submit that the evidence given for the prosecution has not established a *prima facie* case against the accused and that he should not therefore be called upon for his defence." I now make that submission on behalf of Privates Mulligan and Rae and Sapper DeLong.

'The prosecution must prove first of all that Mulligan, Rae and DeLong joined in a mutiny by combining together and with other persons unknown to resist lawful authority and to disobey the orders of their superior officers . . .

'I would like to review what evidence, if any, there is before the court that Mulligan, Rae or DeLong were present at the time of the alleged offence. There is no evidence at all as to the three of them as to where they were or what they were doing in the days immediately preceding their being discovered in the prisoner of war pen on 21 September. With DeLong it is even more clear than that, because he was not on the original ship's nominal roll. No one has proved that they were with this body of men up to Captain Lee's parade and no one has proved that they were on Captain Lee's parade. The fact that they were in the prisoner-of-war pen the next morning cannot, in my submission, count against them, because the offence, if any, had then concluded and they were merely with a body of men who were alleged to have committed this offence.'

At this point Major Raphael interrupted: 'But apart from the escort, nobody was put into the prisoner-of-war pen except those men believed to be those who had refused to obey orders.'

'There are three opportunities for these men to have got into the pen,' Magnay explained. 'First, on the parade in the two-and-a-half hours standing about. That is confirmed by the fact of the air raid; they could have got in among them then. Then there was the incident going down the road towards the beach when the shell or bomb exploded.

'It is for the prosecution to establish beyond all doubt that these men were there all the time and that, in my submission, can only be proved by more evidence than is before the court today.

'The only thing which I consider may be influencing the court's mind is the suggestion put forward by Captain Lee that these three men were in fact on that parade but that they impersonated three other men. With respect, the prosecution cannot have it both ways. If that was the case and subsequently there was no opportunity for anybody to join or leave the parade, it necessarily follows that when these men's names were accurately checked up there must be three less than there are before the court today.'

Again Major Raphael interjected: 'There were two less, were not there?'

'Yes,' Magnay replied, 'but no explanation has been given with regard to those two as to how they disappeared. If the check was as strict as Captain Lee and Captain Williams make it out to be they could have given clear evidence as to what happened to Davies or Davison, but they have given no such evidence. In my submission, it is quite possible that the simple explanation is the true explanation in this case, which is that the three of them somehow or other got on to that parade after the final order had been given by Captain Lee. What they did after that order is not evidence against them and therefore is no case against these three.'

Admitting that the evidence was not entirely satisfactory, Raphael then gave it as his opinion that the fact Mulligan and Rae were present when the roll was checked in the prisoner-of-war cage was 'some evidence that they were on parade'. Magnay's response was to point out that, as DeLong did not even appear on the ship's roll, there was 'no evidence at all'.

'DeLong is on a special footing, I understand that,' Raphael conceded. 'I was dealing for the moment with Mulligan and Rae.'

Turning to these two, Magnay calmly went through the facts: 'The purple list was compiled by double check in the afternoon, after the parade in question, from a comprehensive list. There is no evidence before the court that Mulligan and Rae were on that comprehensive list; they were not ticked; also, as I have said before, they were not put on my purple list until the next morning. It necessarily follows, in my submission, that here is therefore *prima facie* evidence, which the prosecution have not rebutted, that they were not on that parade.'

Raphael was not to be persuaded: 'I agree that so far as Mulligan and Rae are concerned the evidence of identity is by no means altogether satisfactory; but that does not establish the proposition, does it, that there is no evidence against them that they were present on the parade?'

Magnay disagreed, pointing out the additional discrepancy of numbers: 'Then of course there is the question of the count which is mixed up with the compiling of the purple list, the 191 and the 193. Altogether it is so contradictory, even in the slight manner in which it has been brought before the court by the prosecution today, that there is an additional ground for deciding that there is no case to answer.'[37]

Weary with trying to rebut Magnay's clever arguments, Raphael turned to the chief prosecutor for help: 'Major Money, what do you say about this?'

Money's response was predictable: 'Firstly, how did these three men come to be in the cage if they were not on the parade? I would remind you of the evidence of Captain Dallenger, Lieutenant Creed and

Lieutenant Rees. They gave evidence that none of them saw anybody join the men in the field or join the column while it was on its way to the cage. The second point is that if these three men were not on that parade, how is it that although they had ample opportunity of saying so afterwards not one of them has opened his mouth to this day about it? You will remember that I particularly put the question to several witnesses: "Were you approached at any time by any of the accused?" That may not be a very strong point but I would say that on those two points there is some evidence that these men were on the parade when the three orders were given.'[38]

With that, Major Raphael gave his final opinion. Admitting that on the one hand the evidence of identification was 'not altogether satisfactory', on the other he pointed out that if a mistake as to identity had been made, 'nothing would be easier than for that mistake to be explained'. If the court decided that the circumstances in which the men were found in the POW cage was 'evidence that they were part of the parade', they were 'entitled to call for an answer' by the defence, he said. On the other hand, if they thought that the evidence was 'so unsatisfactory that it would be unsafe to call on them to put forward their defence', then they were entitled to rule that there was no case to answer. For his part, he felt there was a 'scintilla of evidence'. Whether the court thought this was sufficient was 'entirely a matter for them'.[39] At this point the court adjourned to consider their finding.

A quarter of an hour later, Major Raphael read out their response: 'I am directed by the court to say that solely so far as the question of identity is concerned in relation to Mulligan, Rae and DeLong there is some evidence which calls for an answer.'[40]

So that was that. It was now Quennell's turn to achieve the impossible. 'May it please the court,' he began, 'it now falls on me to submit on behalf of all the accused that they have no case to answer. I admit at once that if a charge had been brought against each one of these 192 men under section 9(2) I should not have been in a position to make such a submission. If I may remind the court, section 9(2) reads as follows: "Every person subject to military law who commits the following offence, that is to say, disobeys any lawful command given by his superior officer, shall on conviction by court martial, if he commits such an offence while on active service, be liable to suffer penal servitude or such less punishment as is in this Act mentioned."'

Continuing, Quennell read out the relevant footnote: '"The disobedience must be immediate or proximate to the command, and actual non-compliance must be proved." Obviously there is evidence of an order having been given. There is evidence that disobedience was

Sergeant Wally Innes, Durham Light Infantry, one of the three NCOs sentenced to death.

Private Archie Newmarch, East Yorkshire Regiment, seven years' penal servitude. Had not fully recovered from malaria when he was sent to Salerno.

Private John McFarlane MM, Durham Light Infantry, seven years' penal servitude.
Was forced by the War Office to return his gallantry medal after going absent without leave
while under suspended sentence (seen here as an Argyll & Sutherland Highlander in 1940
before his posting to the DLI).

Corporal Hugh Fraser, Queen's Own Cameron Highlanders, 10 years' penal servitude and reduced to the ranks. Joined the Aberdeen police after the war and retired as an inspector. (Seen here as a private in 1939.)

Lance Corporal Percy Aveyard, Durham Light Infantry, seven years' penal servitude and reduced to the ranks. Tried to re-enlist in 1952 but the army would not have him.

Private Fred Jowett, East Yorkshire Regiment, seven years' penal servitude. Still suffers from a nervous condition brought on by his time in prison.

Private Edwin Scott, Durham Light Infantry, seven years' penal servitude. Discharged himself from a convalescent home in Tripoli two days before being sent to Salerno.

Private Robert Thompson, Seaforth Highlanders, seven years' penal servitude. Lucky to be posted to a Seaforth battalion with which he saw out the war.

Private Charlie Smith, East Yorkshire Regiment, seven years' penal servitude. Sent to Salerno still suffering from 'shell shock'. (Seen here in India in 1946.)

Private Herbert Crawford, East Yorkshire Regiment, seven years' penal servitude. Victimised in his new unit, he lost both legs at Anzio.

Captain Bill Murgatroyd, defending officer, as a second lieutenant in the Royal Army Ordnance Corps.

Private Ray Whitaker, Argyll & Sutherland Highlanders, seven years' penal servitude. Blames his mutiny conviction for turning him to a life of crime (seen here during a recent visit to Naples, his old stamping ground).

Private Alexander McMichael, Black Watch, was taken from a convalescent camp at Tripoli and added to the draft of reinforcements (at Salerno he and most of the other Black Watch were persuaded to join the 46th Division by an officer from his regiment).

Private Andy Scott, Gordon Highlanders, narrowly avoided being arrested for mutiny by reluctantly agreeing to join the 46th Division at Salerno only after Captain Lee had given the order for a second time. (Seen here in Palestine in 1946.)

This photo of the 14 defending officers, standing outside the Constantine school gymnasium that served as a courtroom, was taken at the end of the trial by an Algerian bystander using Captain Murgatroyd's camera. From left: Captain Goldsmith, RA; Captain Bill Murgatroyd, RAOC; Lieutenant DRH Gardiner, RAC; Captain John Mitchell, Queen's Own Cameron Highlanders; Captain HP Samwell MC, Argyll & Sutherland Highlanders; Lieutenant FMH Edie, Argyll & Sutherland Highlanders; Captain Evers, Duke of Wellington's Regiment; Lieutenant WJ Howatt, Argyll & Sutherland Highlanders; Captain Hugh Quennell, Welsh Guards; Captain John Wheatley, Durham Light Infantry; Lieutenant Tom Magnay, RA; Captain Jimmy Kailofer, Durham Light Infantry; Lieutenant H Hammonds, RE; Captain GL Taylor, Pioneer Corps.

Lionel Daiches QC in 1993.

*Captain Albert Lee, York &
Lancaster Regiment, the chief
prosecution witness at the trial.
He was sent on the draft of
reinforcements without proper
equipment and still recovering
from a serious wound (he later
rejoined his unit and won a
DSO during the fighting in
Italy).*

Major William Harris, Coldsteam Guards, one of five members of the court. Described the trial, in a letter to his wife, as 'absolute HELL' and 'an awful cold blooded responsibility' (seen here in England, late 1944).

Lieutenant Lionel Munby, Royal Artillery, got to know the convicted mutineers on the voyage back to Italy and strongly sympathised with their plight.

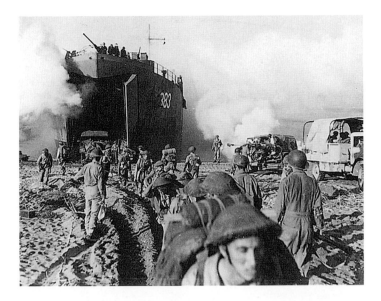

Troops and vehicles being unloaded from landing craft at the Salerno beachhead, 9th September 1943.

General Sir Harold Alexander (left front), with Lieutenant Generals Mark Clark (middle) and Sir Richard McCreery (right), during Alexander's visit to the Salerno beachhead on 15th September 1943.

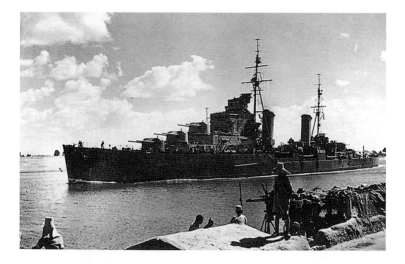

HMS Euralus, one of the three cruisers used to transport the 1,500 emergency reinforcements from Tripoli to Salerno (seen here in the Suez Canal).

General Sir Ronald Adam, the enlightened Adjutant General who described the treatment of the mutineers as 'one of the worst things that we have ever done' and who ordered the suspension of their sentences. (Seen here as GOC Southern Command.)

General Sir Bernard Montgomery, commander of the Eighth Army, later wrote: 'If I had known what was to be done I would have said "No". Alexander would also have said "No".' (Seen here as Field Marshal Viscount Montgomery of Alamein in London in 1947; photo courtesy of Bill Murgatroyd.)

Major General Douglas Wimberley (second from left), former commander of the 51st Division, who did much to secure the early release of the mutineers who had their sentences reimposed for going absent without leave.

immediate and proximate to the order. It is also interesting to observe that all the 192 were originally charged under section 9(2).'

In contrast, Quennell then recited the section of the Army Act relating to mutiny, 7(3), in full. 'The *Manual* also contains a note,' he told the court, 'that a charge under section 9(2) should be considered adequate even in doubtful cases and that unless the clearest possible case of mutiny arises no charge should be made under section 7.'

When asked by Major Raphael which note he was reading from, Quennell replied: 'Page 16, paragraph six: "In framing a charge under section 7 the specific act or acts which constitute the offence must always be alleged; and the offence is so grave that a charge for it should only be brought on very clear evidence. Cases of insubordination, even on the part of two or more, should, unless there appears to be a combined design on their part to resist authority, be charged under section 8 or section 9, or, if these sections are inapplicable, under section 40 ..." Then it goes on: "Provocation by a superior or the existence of grievances is no justification for mutiny or insubordination though such circumstances should be allowed due weight in considering the question of punishment." That, of course, is inapplicable in the submission which I make.

'I pause again to point out that the *Manual* is appearing to say that unless, before any question of defence, even before any question of cross-examination, there appears to be a combined design on their part to resist lawful authority, a charge of mutiny should not be brought. Of course I have only to point out this. It is not a question now of appearing; it is a question of the prosecution proving. It is for the prosecution to prove the charge which they allege before I can be called upon to answer on behalf of the defence.'

Continuing, Quennell began to outline the sequence of events relating to the three different charges made against the men, but he was interrupted by Raphael who pointed out that the court were not aware of any previous charges and were only interested in the charge as it stood. Confined to discussing that charge, Quennell ploughed on: 'I am going to quote from the words of the learned judge advocate on the first day: "What you are charged with here is a combination or agreement amongst you to disobey orders, whatever those particular orders might be. If you were charged with a substantive act of disobedience I agree that the particular acts would have to be specified in the charge."

'In my submission, therefore, accepting what the learned judge advocate has said, the prosecution must prove three things before any verdict of guilty can be brought in. They must prove the orders, disobedience and agreement or combination.'

While conceding that the evidence thus far proved that three orders were given by Captain Lee on 20 September, Quennell went on to argue that the circumstances in which the prosecution had alleged they were given did not support a charge of mutiny. The second order was given 'after the men in the two separate groups had been addressed by the DAAG', Quennell reminded the court. 'The substance of the DAAG's remarks was this: the order in each case had been given in all seriousness; if disobeyed each man would be individually responsible; each man, if he disobeyed it, would be the subject of an individual court martial; and in the case of the DLI at least he said: "Later you will go back to your own divisions."'

While Quennell did not dispute that the three orders were disobeyed, he emphasised that there was 'no other evidence before the court of any single order given to these men which was not immediately obeyed'. This brought him, he told the court, to the 'third element which must exist in the case presented to you by the prosecution'. Namely, an 'agreement' between the men to 'resist lawful authority or to disobey the orders of their superior officers'.

'It may well be that the term "to disobey the orders of their superior officers" is synonymous with "resisting lawful authority",' Quennell mused. 'If that is so, you are again faced with only three facts, namely, the disobedience of three individual orders by Captain Lee. If it is suggested by the prosecution that the two terms are not synonymous and that "resisting lawful authority" means something other than disobeying, in this case, the orders of their superior officers, then there is no evidence at all before the court, in my respectful submission, on which you could find that these men have resisted lawful authority.'

'One may be a consequence of the other,' Raphael interjected. 'If you disobey orders, the consequence may be that you resist lawful authority.'

'Then in my submission the two terms are synonymous; one merges into the other. It is like a leasehold merging into a freehold,' retorted Quennell.

'They may merge into each other, but they are not necessarily synonymous,' Raphael persisted.

Clearly running out of patience with the deputy judge advocate's petty objections, Quennell had to force himself to stay calm: 'May I put it this way? The only facts before the court are that three orders were given and three orders were disobeyed. The point which I was making to the court was that there was no evidence at all that these men did anything in disobedience to authority, in contravention of authority, except to disobey three individual orders given at one parade by the same officer.

'The evidence is this: The men were told to parade. There is no question but that they did parade. Captain Lee and Captain Williams have both told the court that the parade was an orderly parade. It was a parade at which there was no talking. There is no evidence that the men were warned what the parade was for. When they got on parade they were told: "Pick up your kits, fall in on the road and march off to 46th Division area." On that order being given a number of men obeyed it and some were left. Upon the second order, given after the remarks made by the DAAG, other people obeyed the order.'

After a brief pause, Quennell continued. The DAAG, he reminded the court, had told the men that if they disobeyed the order they would be 'individually responsible' and that each would be liable for an 'individual court martial'. This was evidence that all along 'the DAAG was appealing to every man to act as an individual'. In addition, Captain Lee had given it as his opinion that 'the men were acting individually' and that both those men who went away and those who stayed were 'acting as individuals'. What happened on that parade was no different from 'certain spontaneous acts' by crowds at a racecourse or a football match, Quennell insisted. Surely nobody would suggest that those spontaneous acts were 'brought about by an agreement among the people present'.

As his argument gathered momentum, Quennell's tone became more confident: 'In my submission the evidence both of Captain Lee and Captain Williams is quite clear. These men, in their opinion, were on this particular parade given no opportunity to discuss matters amongst themselves. There is no evidence that they did so. The only evidence for the prosecution is that throughout the parade each man acted as an individual.

'There is this further factor to consider. The three orders given to the DLI were given while the non-DLI men were some distance away. The evidence is that those men could not hear what was happening. After the third order the men of the DLI were disarmed.'

By the time the DLI were disarmed, Quennell insisted, they had 'completed their offence under section 7(3)' and it was 'impossible to say, in the words of the charge, that they had combined together with members of regiments other than the DLI, who had by that time received no orders at all'.

Concluding, Quennell stated that there was 'no evidence before the court that at the time when these men were ordered to parade there was any combination or agreement between them to do anything'.

'Perhaps not,' Raphael replied, 'but is that not an inference which it is open to the court to draw from the fact that some 192 men in close proximity one with the other all refused to obey an identical order? Is not that some evidence from which the court may draw an inference of combination?'

'In my submission, the court ought not to draw any such inference,' Quennell countered. 'In the absence of evidence of agreement between the men the court should draw no inference either of combination or agreement. You could not in similar circumstances draw any inference of conspiracy.'

Major Raphael did not agree: 'You do not listen to conspirators agreeing to do the unlawful acts; you can only infer the conspiracy from the subsequent overt acts.'

Realising he was getting nowhere, Quennell decided to offer a simple illustration: 'In the language of conspiracy, supposing A, B and C are charged together with conspiring to defraud and the court is unable to come to the conclusion whether A conspired with B or with C but draws the inference that A did in fact conspire with B or C. Then there could be no conviction for conspiracy against A. There is authority for that proposition, of which I need not remind you.'

When asked by Major Raphael what case he was referring to, Quennell replied: 'It is the King against Thompson. I can give you the reference; it is on page 1,417 of *Archbold*, halfway down paragraph five. Perhaps I may take this matter a little further. Supposing each of the men in any one of these regiments who appear before you had got together and said: "We are not going to obey any order at all which divorces us from our division." Supposing each agreed, each regiment, and got together and said: "We are not going back to any division but our own." Could you say then that the Gordons and the Seaforths, for instance, combined together in a mutiny unless you could produce a scintilla of evidence that there was some combination between the two?'

Lost by this clever argument, Raphael replied: 'I am not sure if I understand that.'

Patiently, Quennell reeled off another illustration: 'Suppose the members of one family in a particular street in Liverpool determine amongst themselves that they will commit a conspiracy against the football pools and they go to the person in the football pools office who had charge of the opening or the reception of the letters. Suppose the members of another family in a different part of Liverpool do the same thing. In the absence of any evidence that the central pivot between the two groups had communicated between the two the intentions of the two separate groups, you could not, in my humble submission, possibly indict the two families with one joint conspiracy.'

At last Raphael was beginning to understand: 'I think that is clear. Come back to the illustration you gave before.'

Quennell did as he was bid: 'You have in a transit camp a certain number of men in seven or eight different regiments. You also have those regiments separated into two divisions. There is absolutely no evidence before the court that any two men spoke together about what they might or might not do if they got any particular order. There is no evidence that any particular regiment spoke to any other particular regiment, and there is no evidence whatever that either division spoke to the other.

'In my submission, assuming the prosecution could prove – which they have failed to do – that all the members of the Gordons, for example, got together and said, "We anticipate that tomorrow we shall receive an order to move off to 46th Division. That order we will not obey", and assuming the prosecution could prove that at the same time the men of the DLI also got together and said, "We are members of the 50th Division. Whatever orders we may get tomorrow to join the 46th Division we are not going to obey", in the absence of evidence that the DLI and the Gordons had some common link of communication, there would be no evidence of a combination between the two which would enable them to be jointly charged in a single charge. That is apart altogether from the point whether they could or could not in those circumstances be separately charged with joining in separate mutinies.'

It was clear from the glazed eyes of the members of the court that his complex legal argument was not hitting home, but Quennell went on undeterred: 'If the facts are those, suppose for the moment that the men of the DLI, having received three orders, and having failed to obey these orders, are disarmed and put under close arrest. Then so far as they are concerned the combination or agreement amongst them has come to an end and whatever orders were thereafter given to any other body of men could not possibly uphold a conviction against that second body of men for joining in a mutiny which had by that time already finished.

'Mutiny cannot, I submit, possibly be regarded as a continuing offence. If there be a point of time at which a number of men can be said to have joined in a mutiny, the moment those men are disarmed and put under close arrest the mutiny is at an end and no other people can join in it.'

Quennell's mental process then shot off on another tangent in an attempt to bolster this point. The footnote to section 7 of the *Manual of Military Law* did not seem to distinguish between 'joined in' and 'joined' a mutiny, he observed. 'If that be right and if my submission is accepted that mutiny cannot be a continuing offence and cannot possibly continue after a body of men have ceased to have any individual control by being in close arrest, that mutiny is ended and there is no mutiny at that moment of time which exists which any other body of men can possibly join.'

His arguments of submission laid before the court, Quennell made one last observation: 'The prosecution, having elected of their own volition to bring before you 192 men on a charge, the most serious known in military law, it is for them at the close of their case so to have established a *prima facie* case that you are satisfied that the defence ought to be called upon to make an answer. If the prosecution have not produced what is in your opinion a *prima facie* case beyond all reasonable doubt, then, in my submission, these men should no longer be left in peril on a charge of this nature.'[41]

On this stirring note he sat down, mentally exhausted. Although only a solicitor, with little experience of advocacy, Quennell had done his clients proud. But arguments that might succeed in a civil court necessarily carry less weight at a military tribunal during wartime. Legal niceties aside, the court was faced with evidence that proved that two groups of men had disobeyed the same order three times. These men had spent the previous four days in each other's company and it was almost inevitable that the court would assume that they had discussed their intention to refuse orders to join units other than their own.

As by now it was four in the afternoon, the court decided to adjourn until the following morning, at which time they would announce their finding on the second submission of no case. Before the court was cleared, Captain John Mitchell took the opportunity to speak to some of his defendants, in particular number 111, Corporal Hugh Fraser. Although a solicitor in civil life, Mitchell had served in Fraser's battalion – the 5th Camerons – for 15 months before being appointed as 152 (Seaforths & Camerons) Brigade staff captain. Indeed, he would later be decorated with the MBE for gallantry while serving with the 51st Division in Sicily. Consequently, his approach to the case was as emotional as it was professional, and he was apt to look on Quennell's efforts that day in the best possible light. 'Don't worry,' he told Fraser, 'there's no way you're going to be convicted.'

Chapter 7

Guilty

It was apt that the fourth day of the trial, Monday 1 November, fell on All Saints' Day, because by now many of the defending officers felt that their charges would need some form of holy intervention to prevent their conviction for mutiny. One more prisoner was temporarily spared the suspense. Number 169, Private John Pepler of the Seaforths, had been taken to hospital the previous evening, bringing the number standing trial down to 182.

Major Money was the first to speak, in response to Captain Quennell's submission of no case. He began by denying that 'at this stage' the prosecution needed to produce 'a *prima facie* case beyond reasonable doubt'. Instead, it was 'sufficient' to produce 'some evidence' to support the charge, and, in his opinion, the prosecution had done this. Despite Quennell's attempt to confine the charge to 20 September, the prosecution had produced evidence that would allow the court to 'infer' that the accused had combined to disobey orders before this date. Money then quoted from page 1,419 of *Archbold*, the *King versus Meyrick*: ' "Proof of the existence of a conspiracy is generally a matter of inference deduced from certain criminal acts of the parties accused, done in the pursuance of an apparent criminal purpose in common between them." ' This case, Money claimed, provided 'authority' for the court to draw such inferences 'from the acts on the part of the accused which have been proved'.

He then listed the 'acts': firstly, you could infer that there were 'mutinous acts' by the accused and others as early as 19 September by the necessity for Captains Lee and Williams 'to address various groups of men from the draft of 1,500'; secondly, the 'necessity for the parade' on 20 September, which was clearly a 'last resort'; thirdly, the 'necessity for reading to the two groups section 7 of the Army Act and the extract from the *Manual* relating to mutiny'; fourthly, 'the orders which were given were not individual orders' but 'collective'; fifthly, the DAAG's address to the men as a 'body' and his promise that 'as soon as circumstances permitted the men would be reposted to their own divisions'; sixthly, the address by the Cameron officer was 'an appeal to Scotsmen not as individuals but as a body; lastly, the evidence that the

119

'disobedience was collective', in the 'sight and hearing of every man'. All this, Money argued, was evidence 'that each man was drawing support and encouragement from the others; in other words, they were acting in concert'.

Money then turned to Quennell's challenge to the wording of the charge. If the words 'to resist lawful authority' and 'to disobey the orders of their superior officers' were synonymous then there was evidence to support the particulars of the charge, because 'provided the prosecution had proved disobedience it must also have proved resistance to lawful authority'. But, in his opinion, the words were not synonymous and the prosecution had to prove both. Evidence of disobedience had been 'clearly established', he said. The 'general course of conduct' of the men could only be described as 'resistance to lawful authority'. Evidence of such conduct were the 'addresses by Captains Williams and Lee to the men on 19 and 20 September', the 'parade on 20 September', the 'necessity for the reading of the section of the Army Act relating to mutiny' and 'the promise of the DAAG that as soon as circumstances permitted the men would be reposted to their own divisions'. This, Money argued, was 'abundant evidence of conduct on the part of the accused which clearly indicates their intention to resist lawful authority and their actual resistance to lawful authority'. Consequently, there was 'ample evidence to establish a *prima facie* case and the defence should be called upon to answer this charge'.[1]

His speech over, Money sat down. Before giving his own opinion, Major Raphael asked Captain Quennell if there was anything he wished to add. As there was nothing, Raphael began by summarising what he saw as the argument for the defence: 'It is conceded on behalf of the accused that there is evidence of the disobeying of lawful orders but it is contended that there is no case which ought to call for an answer. Firstly, it is said that there is no evidence of combination or agreement between the accused. Secondly, it is said that in any case there is no sufficient connection between the events in which the accused of the DLI took part and those in which the accused of regiments other than the DLI took part.'

Dealing with the first point, Raphael repeated the passage that Major Money had read from *Archbold*: '"Proof of the existence of a conspiracy is generally a matter of inference deduced from certain criminal acts of the parties accused, done in pursuance of an apparent criminal purpose in common between them."' This meant, Raphael explained to the court, that it was up to them to decide whether there was 'evidence from which the inference could be drawn that the individual acts of disobedience' amounted to a 'combination of persons acting in concert, in pursuance of an agreement arrived at between them'.

Raphael then moved on to the second point. It was true that 'orders were given to the two groups and given separately', but they were 'identical orders given to men who within a few minutes had been on the same parade together' and to whom there was 'some evidence from which the inference could be drawn of association or combination'. It was up to the court to decide whether this inference was justified.

Having clearly stated his opinion that the trial should continue, Raphael then made a show of giving the court an option: 'At this present moment the court are faced with the question: are they of the opinion, having listened to the arguments addressed to them on both sides, that there is a case sufficient to call for an answer from the accused? If so this case ought to proceed. If, on the other hand, they think there is no sufficient evidence which would justify them in drawing the inference of guilt, then it is open to the court to say that there is no case to answer. It is a matter entirely within the discretion and good judgment of the court.'[2]

After a brief conference, the court concurred with Raphael's opinion. There was a case to answer.

Now that the defence had to make a case, there were three options open to the accused, Raphael told them. They could give evidence under oath and then be cross-examined. They could make a statement not under oath, and not be asked questions, but this would carry less weight than evidence under oath. Or they could simply say nothing. In addition, they could rely on their defending officers to represent their case on their behalf, and they were entitled to call witnesses. At this point Captain Quennell asked for a brief recess so that the defending officers could consult with the accused. This was little more than show as the defence had already decided not to offer any evidence. The trial resumed 20 minutes later with each of the accused answering 'no' to the questions 'Do you apply to give evidence yourself as a witness?' and 'Are you calling any witness on your behalf?'

It remained only for the defending officers to give their summing-up speeches. Their original intention was to adopt the same format as the day before, namely Lieutenant Magnay addressing the court on behalf of Mulligan, Rae and DeLong, while Quennell made a closing speech for all. Major Raphael prevented this by arguing that as the accused were separately represented, each defending officer should make an address on behalf of his clients. The final format agreed on was that Magnay and Quennell would address the court first as planned, followed by the remaining defending officers.

Magnay opened by stressing the facts which, in his opinion, particularly concerned Mulligan, Rae and DeLong. Firstly, there was 'no evidence' which showed that 'these men were in any way concerned in the events before Captain Lee's parade on 20 September'. The 'only evidence' at all was that 'Mulligan and Rae were on one nominal roll'. DeLong, on the other hand, was not even on that, nor was there any evidence of his movements before Captain Lee's parade. Magnay then pointed out that all the men on parade on 20 September who were ticked off from the roll were on trial with the 'exception of Davies and Davison', about whom the prosecution had given 'no evidence'. This disposed once and for all the question of 'either of the three accused impersonating any other men whose names were then called out'.

The 'next concrete piece of evidence before the court' was the 'check-up in the prisoner-of-war cage' the following morning when 'DeLong, Mulligan and Rae were found to be present'. The 'inference' to be drawn was that 'between the parade when the second check was made by Captain Lee and the roll-call the next morning in the prisoner-of-war cage' these three men must somehow have joined the others. This could have been achieved on 'at least two occasions', firstly, during the 'considerable time' between the second roll-call on Captain Lee's parade and the departure to the prisoner-of-war cage. There was evidence that 'during that time the officers and the guard were engaged in checking the kits of the accused men', so allowing 'sufficient opportunity for the men to come among this group without either the officers or the guard noticing them'. In addition, there was an air raid. As it was normal for men to take cover in such an eventuality, this would have provided 'an even greater opportunity' for the three men 'to join the party'. The fact that these men were found in the cage the next day was 'not of itself sufficient evidence' for the court to find them guilty.

In conclusion, Magnay stated that to find the three men guilty the court had to be 'satisfied beyond all reasonable doubt' that they were 'present before 20 September, that they were present on that parade on 20 September', that they marched down 'to the beach and that they were in the cage the next morning'. In his opinion, the only part of that equation that had been satisfied was the latter. As to the rest, there was not 'sufficient' evidence to satisfy beyond reasonable doubt. On 'that ground alone' the three should 'be acquitted'.[3]

As Magnay had only spoken for three of his six clients, Major Raphael asked him if he would like to make an address on behalf of the rest. Magnay declined, saying he would like to hear what Captain Quennell had to say first. With that, Quennell rose. As the most experienced lawyer and the unofficial leader of the defence team, Quennell had volunteered to argue for all. Although others would speak later, his address was effectively the last hope for the accused. The failure of the submission of no case, and the decision to offer no evidence in defence of the charge, meant that the lives of the 182 men present in the courtroom literally hung by this gifted man's undeniable powers of persuasion.

He opened by repeating a simple fact: the accused were all 'first-class fighting soldiers'. Then came his argument. Even if there was, as the court had decided, a *prima facie* case to answer, there was a 'very great distinction' between this and 'a verdict of guilty'. Even if no evidence is called for the defence, it becomes a 'matter as a question of fact and not as a question of law for the court to say that they individually are satisfied beyond all reasonable doubt that these men are guilty'.

Quennell then reiterated his earlier argument that three 'ingredients' had to be proved to bring a verdict of guilty: the existence of orders, their being disobeyed, and a combination between the accused and other persons unknown. While the evidence clearly showed that three separate orders, all in the same terms, were given by Captain Lee on 20 September, there was nothing to prove that any other order was given to the accused before this time. 'The only evidence before the court of what happened on 19 September is the evidence of Captain Lee,' Quennell insisted.

To refresh the court, he then read extracts from the shorthand record of Lee's evidence: 'Question: Did you yourself take any action in regard to any men in the transit area on 19 September? Answer: Under instructions from the officer commanding the infantry wing I visited men of various regiments, speaking to them and advising them to leave. Question: What was the gist of what you said to them? Answer: The gist was that I advised them to obey the orders that had been given to them; that was to join either the 46th or 56th Division. Question: What was the attitude of the men you addressed? Answer: The men obeyed any other order but just did not wish to join other than their own division . . .'

Pausing, Quennell gave it as his opinion that this represented 'no evidence at all' against the accused: 'I should perhaps at the time the evidence was tendered have objected on the ground that it was inadmissible. I made a similar objection to exactly similar evidence given by Captain Williams. There is no evidence at all before the court that the men spoken to by Captain Lee, referred to in that evidence, are before you, and in the absence of that evidence I submit with confidence that it should be excised from the record. That is the only note of any event which had happened up to the 20th.'

Having tried to convince the court that the only evidence of orders being disobeyed was that referring to Captain Lee's parade on 20 September, Quennell moved on to the question of combination or agreement. His tactic was to deal in turn with each one of the facts that Major Money had alleged was proof of a conspiracy. 'The first point this morning was this: the mutual acts of the accused and others on 19 and 20 September before the parade. There is no evidence before this court, in my submission, of any acts of the accused before the parade on 20 September.

'Secondly, he raised this point: the necessity for a parade on 20 September, which he said was a last resort. In my submission, that is not an inference which the court should draw. There was a parade on 20 September and these men attended that parade. We have no evidence of anything which happened before except that some men had already left. There is no evidence before the court to show that these men had any order to do anything before they were ordered to parade on 20 September.

'He then mentioned the reading of section 7 of the Army Act. In my submission, that fact of itself is not one which entitles you to say that you are satisfied beyond all reasonable doubt that by subsequently refusing to obey three orders these men should be found guilty.

'The fourth inference was that the orders given were not individual; they were collective orders. I must again repeat that the three orders which are the necessary ingredient in this case are the three orders given by Captain Lee. As we know, they were given in two separate groups.

'His fifth point was the remarks made by the DAAG. We know from the evidence of Captain Lee that the observations of the DAAG were these: "The order has been given to you in all seriousness. Any person who acts in disobedience of that order will answer individually for his crime. Any man will then be the subject of an individual court martial."'

Quennell then pointed out that during cross-examination Captain Lee had admitted that he thought that both those who stayed and those who went after the address of the DAAG were acting 'individually'. This was a point which was 'vital to the defence', Quennell insisted, and one that should cause the court to bring a 'verdict of not guilty'.

Having dealt with the prosecution's inferences, Quennell returned to the question of the two groups on parade. The DLI group 'was disarmed and arrested before any orders were given to the non-DLI personnel'. If a mutiny existed, and the men of the DLI were 'guilty of joining in a mutiny in the terms of the charge', it was a 'separate and distinct offence'. At the moment of arrest, the offence was over and it was 'impossible for anybody else to join in'. If the court was going to draw 'any inference at all from the fact that there was a parade ordered on

20 September', it would have to be that 'all the men were inter-connected'. Yet, there had been 'no suggestion at all by the prosecution of any ringleader'. Furthermore, even if the DLI had 'combined together amongst themselves and had individually agreed with each other not to obey these particular orders, that would not justify a charge of mutiny involving the others'. The 'natural inference to draw' was that the men 'remained together in their own regiments'. In the absence of 'direct evidence that members of different regiments intermingled and in fact agreed and combined together', the court 'should not draw any further inference'.

To conclude, Quennell suggested that the court had to ask them-selves four questions. Firstly, what orders were given? In his opinion there were just three. Secondly, were the orders disobeyed? Yes. Thirdly, what evidence was there of combination or agreement? Fourthly, was there any evidence that the combination or agreement was to resist lawful authority and to disobey orders? Addressing the final question, Quennell reiterated the facts as he saw them: 'Whatever may have happened on 19 September, these men are paraded in the afternoon of 20 September, they are given orders and they are told to act individually. The only witness for the prosecution who deals with this parade says that in his opinion each man was acting individually. In the absence of any evidence to the contrary, I submit that the answer in cross-examination must be accepted by the court.

'In those circumstances, reiterating that it is for the prosecution to satisfy beyond all reasonable doubt, I submit that they have failed to do so and that a verdict of acquittal should be given.'[4]

With those final words, Quennell sat down. For just a second there was silence, all eyes on the court to see if their faces betrayed how they had received Quennell's argument. If the verdict was still in the balance, this was the moment of truth. Hardly a facial muscle twitched as the five members of the court – judges and jury – maintained a united front of blank expressions. Major Raphael broke the spell: 'Captain Taylor, do you address the court?'

Taken aback, Taylor rose reluctantly to his feet, admitting that he had not expected to be needed to speak. Of medium height and average build, without the arrogance that often comes with front-line duty, Taylor was an unprepossessing figure. As the only barrister among the defence team, it is surprising that he had not taken a more active role in the advocacy, content to let others like Quennell and Magnay take the initiative. Now, taken by surprise, he made no specific mention of the 17 Durhams he represented and did little more than repeat points made by Quennell, concluding with the assertion that all the court had to consider was 'the parade of 20 September' where the DAAG's speech that the men 'were all individually responsible' might have led them to conclude that you 'could not have individual mutiny'. But for this they might have 'gone'. Furthermore, the fact that some soldiers did respond to the DAAG's address was evidence that the men were acting individually. In summing up, Taylor said that the prosecution case was based solely on inference. That was fine only if they were 'certain overt acts you can draw inferences from'. In this case there were none, apart from disobedience to orders.[5]

It was Captain Bill Murgatroyd's turn next. Immaculately turned out in his spotless service tunic and glistening Sam Browne cross-belt, he certainly looked the part. After stating that he represented eight Gordon Highlanders, he pointed out that their silence should be interpreted 'as a preparedness to rest with absolute assurance on the evidence already before the court'. It was reasonable to assume, he continued, that the 'spontaneous statement made by one of the number of men now before the court', namely, 'It's not mutiny', was 'adopted by them'.

Next he repudiated the prosecution's suggestion that 'disobedience to a single order, however many times repeated, by soldiers who are willing to obey any other order given by their superior officers is necessarily mutiny'. If that was so, there would be no need for the warning on page 16 of the *Manual of Military Law* that 'all cases of insubordination, even on the part of two or more, should, unless there appears to be a combined design on their part to resist authority, be charged under section 8 or section 9'.

He followed this up with a simple rhetorical question: 'On the meagre evidence before them now can the court be content to accept that there is some evidence of a design to resist authority?' Rather, should not the court ask 'how easy it would have been for the prosecution to have brought absolutely concrete evidence of an order given in writing or verbally before the parade of 20 September if such an order had in fact been given to all the men in that camp', or if 'one had been put on the notice board'. How easy it would have been 'to call the particular individual who gave the order'.

Changing tack, Murgatroyd suggested that there was 'no real definition of mutiny in English case law, for the very good reason that Englishmen are not made that way'. Their allegiance to King and country was 'certain'. Such an allegiance could become 'marked in divisions as well as in nationality' and, in Murgatroyd's opinion, it would be a 'sorry day when divisional morale is put forward as a ground to support a charge of this nature'. As there was 'nothing whatever treacherous in the individual disobedience to this order', Murgatroyd concluded, the crime was 'not mutiny'.[6]

Lieutenant Gardiner, representing the other eight Gordon Highlanders, was next. Dressed similarly to Murgatroyd, but short and rotund, Gardiner looked an almost comical figure. Chosen for his law expertise, he knew none of his clients personally and his speech was short and devoid of emotion. 'An ingredient of mutiny must surely be the state of a man's mind,' he argued. 'I want you to consider the minds of these men.'

After a promising start, Gardiner's point lost some of its impact when his recollection of details went awry: 'We have heard in evidence from Captain Williams that at the time the DAAG was making his address someone . . . said to the DAAG, "This is not mutiny". That, I think, is a very cogent indication as to the state of soldiers' minds at that time.'

In fact, this was Captain Lee's evidence and was the reaction to the words spoken by the Cameron Highlander officer. Fortunately, Gardiner quickly recovered from his gaffe with these poignant words: 'You have heard in evidence that they were always of orderly demeanour, that at all times they conducted themselves properly, that they obeyed their officers' orders to fall in and march here and march there except for the three orders which are the subject of this case. Can it be said that mutineers would be so soldierly and so adherent to their military training as these men have at all times since this offence been?'[7]

Gardiner was followed by Captain Jimmy Kailofer, the defending officer for 21 members of the Durham Light Infantry, including all three sergeants. Wearing battledress but, like all the other front-line soldiers, without the comforting feel of a service pistol strapped to his leg, Kailofer felt a little naked. But as a solicitor who had served with the 8th Durhams for three years, who had fought alongside and knew personally many of his clients, he was determined to put the actions of the men in perspective. 'The court well knows that it may make use of its own military knowledge in determining the case and I think the court must therefore consider itself well aware of the very strong loyalty to the army, and in particular to their own divisions, which exists among men of the Eighth Army, and further, in the 50th and 51st Divisions,' he opened.

Consequently, the 'mere fact' that the men 'acted similarly cannot be any evidence of combination, as each man, considering the facts for himself, must quite easily have reached the same decision'. The failure of the prosecution to provide proof of criminal acts before the parade on 20 September meant that, other than the disobedience to one order given three times, there was nothing from which to deduce conspiracy.[8]

Taking over from Kailofer was his brother officer from the 8th Durhams, Captain John Wheatley. Although originally requested as a defending officer by men from his company, Wheatley had volunteered to represent the 15 members of the 9th Durhams. He began by pointing out that the evidence proved that when the men landed at Salerno there was 'considerable chaos of a type which is familiar to all soldiers who have been in transit'. He was sure that the members of the court would understand this as they all had recent active service experience. It was hardly necessary to remind the court, then, that it was 'likely that private soldiers in a party would be unaware of a certain set of conditions existing, a fact which would be known to officers, warrant officers and even to some of the more senior NCOs in charge of the party'.

In connection with this, Wheatley then asked why, if as the prosecution claimed a mutiny was in existence as early as 18 September, nothing was done for 48 hours. 'Surely the immediate reaction of anybody with a military sense of responsibility would be to take some action at once?'

Asking the court for their indulgence, Wheatley introduced yet another analogy: 'I submit that the prosecution have produced no evidence of combination or agreement proving that the accused acted in any other manner, in connection with their own incidents, than an audience would have acted had they been applauding, for example, Irving's entrance in one of the acts of *Hamlet*.'

Unfortunately, these useful points were undermined when Wheatley mentioned that the DAAG had said that 'each man would answer individually for his crime and in addition that each man would return to his own division', and that this caused the men to consider it worthwhile to commit an act of insubordination to get back to their units. In fact, the DAAG had said that only those who *obeyed* orders would be returned when circumstances permitted. Unaware of this gaffe, Wheatley signed off by emphasising that 'personal morale and general spirit' were big factors in 'helping each individual man to decide spontaneously that he was, if possible, going to return to his own division'.[9]

Next to rise was Lieutenant Howat, the Highland Division staff officer who had formerly served with the 7th Argylls. Recruited from his profession of solicitor in June 1940, he had spent four months in the ranks before being commissioned and knew all but three of the 22 Argylls on trial. Strangely, he was not wearing a kilt: either he had forgotten to pack it or he had decided, as a short man, that it did not best suit his figure. Instead this handsome, moustachioed officer was wearing dreary battledress. Sadly, he had little of originality to say. 'The prosecution,' he insisted, 'has absolutely failed to prove anything beyond individual insubordination on the part of these 192 men.' Other than using a handful of already much-used phrases such as 'good fighting soldiers', 'sure beyond the greatest possible shadow of doubt' and 'only one verdict possible', Howat was stumped for words and was back in his seat within a couple of minutes.[10]

Captain Samwell, MC, another member of the Argylls, took his place. Wearing the predominantly green and black kilt of his regiment – similar to and often mistaken for the Black Watch tartan – he looked every inch the noble Highland warrior. Perhaps understandably, as he had no law and much ground had been covered by the previous advocates, his words did not match his appearance. After telling the court that it would be 'tedious to reiterate what had already been admirably stated', he then proceeded to do so by asserting that the prosecution had failed to prove a criminal act prior to 20 September. Carrying on in the same vein for a couple of minutes, Samwell closed with the suggestion that the 'only possible verdict is acquittal'.[11]

If Howat and Samwell's speeches were brief, Lieutenant Edie's was no more than perfunctory. Perhaps, as he was defending just three men, he thought that was apt. Very tall, with a moustache whose pointed ends harked back to an earlier war, Edie was a typically brave combat officer. The third of the Argylls' trio, he had little to add. His three defendants were on the nominal roll, were present at the parade and disobeyed the three orders, 'but they did not mutiny', he assured the court.[12]

The curious figure of Captain Evers, the staff officer defending the Seaforths who had missed the beginning of the trial, was next to take the floor. Short, wearing the sand-coloured uniform favoured by staff officers in North Africa, he could not have looked less like a front-line soldier. Despite this, his short speech was colourful if nothing else. Reminding the court, it they needed reminding, that the key to the prosecution case was 'inference', he then pointed out that 'the greatest man who ever lived was crucified by an inference'. Not content with this biblical reference, Evers asked the court to engage in 'reverse philosophy'. Explaining, he described the accused as men 'belonging to divisions which will go down to posterity as immortal, having done deeds that will live for ever, glamorised in the press and living in the continuous spotlight of publicity and enjoying the plaudits of a world arena, possessing a divisional *esprit de corps* unique in the annals of military history'.

Taking all this into account, and using reverse philosophy, 'could you honestly,' he asked the court, 'make these men into criminals for taking the only step they knew of to preserve their divisional identities?' Evers concluding sentence was even more powerful: 'If on the evidence

before you you find these men guilty, we shall all be entitled to go back
to our units and to civil life and infer: "What a farce is our justice".'[13]

Evers had produced a hard act to follow, so it was fortunate that a
lawyer of the calibre of Captain John Mitchell was next. Born at Elgin
in 1907, and educated at Elgin Academy and Aberdeen University,
Mitchell had enjoyed a glittering academic career culminating in the
joint prize for the most distinguished law graduate. Then followed a
year's postgraduate study in international law at Harvard before joining
a firm of advocates in Aberdeen. Realising that his real calling was as a
solicitor, Mitchell soon switched to an Inverness firm, where he was
working when war broke out. It was for this reason that he joined the
Inverness-based Queen's Own Cameron Highlanders rather than his
home regiment, the Gordon Highlanders. Now, standing tall before the
court in the splendid blue and red kilt of the Camerons, he was spurred
by a determination to fulfil his earlier promise to Hugh Fraser.

He began by emphasising that the prosecution had 'deliberately'
chosen 'to bring a charge under section 7', that this implied 'a very
much higher responsibility of proof than a charge under section 9', and
that it was their duty to 'completely discharge the onus of proof'. His
clients did not deny disobeying orders, but there was no evidence of
combination. Instead 'the insistence of the DAAG' on the 'factor of
individuality' might have influenced the men to 'disobey individually'.

To establish this, Mitchell told the court, the defence had tried to call
the DAAG as a witness, but this had not been possible. He then moved
deftly to his key point: 'Should the court take the view that the facts
produced by the prosecution prove beyond all reasonable doubt that
there has been disobedience to a specific order or orders, and they do
not consider that there is sufficient evidence to justify disobedience plus
the amount of combination necessary to prove mutiny, then it is not in
law open to the court to record a special finding that these men are
guilty of disobedience.'

Describing the prosecution's charge as 'neck or nothing', Mitchell
was obviously pushing for a full acquittal. But he may have made a
mistake by pointing out that the court had only two options – guilty or
not guilty as charged. After all, the defence had repeatedly admitted
that their clients were guilty of disobedience and it was unlikely that the
court were going to be prepared to let them off scot-free.[14]

There were just two defending officers remaining, and neither took
much time. Captain Goldsmith, representing the East Yorkshires and
four of the Devons, said he was confident that when the judge advocate
had explained the finer legal points of the case, the court would find
insufficient evidence to convict the men.[15] Lieutenant Hammonds, the

nondescript Royal Engineer representing Private Swadkins of the Devons, simply stated that he wished to 'adopt entirely the speeches made by the previous defending officers', and that he agreed that the prosecution had 'failed to produce evidence of guilt'.[16]

Major Raphael then asked Lieutenant Magnay if he wished to add anything on behalf of his other three clients, and received the answer that the ground had been 'adequately covered' by the others. As the defence had completed their closing speeches and the time was just after 12.30, the court adjourned for lunch.

A little under two hours later the trial resumed. Before the court retired to consider its verdict, it was left to the deputy judge advocate, Major Raphael, to provide his summing up, much as a judge would do in a civil trial. His interpretation of the legal points that the defence had raised would be crucial in determining which way the court went. During the opening minutes of his speech, Raphael seemed to be fulfilling his role of impartial legal adviser: 'You have been told that this is an unusual, if not an unprecedented trial. It is to be hoped that it will remain an unusual trial, because from every point of view it must be regarded as a shocking thing that a large number of men, described – and no doubt rightly described – as first-class fighting soldiers, men of good character, should be here meeting a charge of this gravity.'

For a while, Raphael continued in the same vein: 'Although you are trying no less than 182 persons today, the law requires that you should give separate consideration to the case of each man. I know full well that that is easier said than done in a case of this sort. It means no more than this and no less than this: even though what is here charged is an offence of combination, it does not follow as a matter of law that because you convict one or more you must convict all.'

Yet, inevitably, Raphael's comments soon began to favour the prosecution. The defence, he said, had 'placed reliance on the fact that the refusal to obey orders was a refusal merely in respect of one order' while all others were 'obeyed punctiliously and with decorum'. In his opinion, such a refusal to obey one particular order could 'constitute conduct causing greater mischief than a general refusal to obey orders, because if a large body of men is taken to the scene of active operations and punctiliously carries out the orders given to them up to one moment, the subsequent refusal to act upon one order might cause as lamentable a situation as it is possible to imagine'. The scenario Raphael was referring to was unclear; his hostility to the case for the defence was not.

For a time, Raphael returned to a guise of impartiality. As they were taking part in a criminal trial, he reminded the court, the burden of proof rested with the prosecution. Consequently, they had to be 'satisfied beyond reasonable doubt' before bringing a charge of guilty. Such 'reasonable doubt' meant, he said, 'doubt which might influence you in the conduct of your ordinary daily affairs'. If there was such a doubt about any one of the accused, that person should be acquitted; if not, he should be convicted.

Turning to the crime of mutiny, Raphael described it as 'nothing more than collective insubordination', which was what the charge clearly stated. For the court to be satisfied that any of the accused had 'joined in an act of collective insubordination', that they had 'joined in that mutiny by combining together to resist lawful authority and to disobey the orders of their superior officers', they would first have to be satisfied that they had 'acted in combination with a purpose common to them all'.

If the terms 'to resist lawful authority' and 'to disobey the orders of their superior officers' were synonymous, there was no confusion. On the other hand, the court might feel that the terms meant that in 'disobeying the orders of their superior officers the necessary consequence was to resist lawful authority'. If this was so, then the court would have to be satisfied that the accused had 'joined together in an act of collective insubordination', as he had just described, before they could be convicted.

There was no doubt, he told the court, that Captain Lee's order had been disobeyed three times. Consequently, the court had to decide just one thing: was it 'satisfied that these persons combined together to disobey these orders'? Raphael than explained that 'combination' was the same as 'conspiracy', which meant 'an agreement by two or more persons to do an unlawful act'. In this case the 'unlawful act' was the 'disobeying of lawful commands of superior officers'.

Moving once more into partisan mode, Raphael explained how the defence had argued that there was no direct evidence of any such combination. In fact, one very rarely found, if ever, 'direct evidence of conspiracy', he said. Consequently, an agreement to do an unlawful act could be 'inferred from the acts of those persons said to be parties to that agreement'. Where one found 'practically simultaneous acts' one could be 'driven to the conclusion that those acts, so far from being the individual acts of each person responsible for them, spring from some common purpose, some agreement common to all of them'. What you have to decide, he told the court, is whether you are 'satisfied that the only possible inference to be drawn from the conduct of these men is that there was an agreement, a combination, between them to disobey the orders of their superior officers'.

Raphael then went on to dismiss the relevance of the DAAG's

comments that the men would be 'held responsible for their individual acts', saying that his words did not 'affect' the trial. Instead, the court were the sole 'judges of whether what in fact they did was a crime committed in combination', or whether, as the defence had suggested, it was 'no more than a number of individual acts of disobedience'.

Turning to the particular cases of Mulligan, Rae and DeLong, Raphael pointed out that although no one witness had been able to say that all the people who disobeyed the orders on parade at Salerno were on trial, given the number of men involved such a guarantee might be 'well nigh humanly impossible'. In the case of these three men there 'did appear to be some discrepancies', namely that 'their names were added to a list which did not contain them in the first place'. Whether this was sufficient for an acquittal was for the court to decide.

Yet, Raphael told the court, 'I feel it my duty to say in relation to those men that nothing would have been easier, if a mistake had been made in respect of the identity of those men, than for them to have gone into the witness box and given evidence about that matter.' The fact that they had not chosen to do that meant that the court were 'entitled' to ask themselves 'why'. While the burden of proof remained with the prosecution, he said, the court were 'entitled to say: "Is not the fact that these men, Mulligan, Rae and DeLong, were found with the others in the prisoner-of-war cage when the roll of those who disobeyed was ultimately taken evidence which by itself satisfies us that these men were men who themselves were a party to this act of collective insubordination?", if you are satisfied that it was an act of collective insubordination on the part of the others'. If a mistake had been made, he continued, 'nothing would have been easier for them to have come forward and explained what the mistake was'.

Moving on to Private Kemp, the man who changed his mind and asked to be able to join units at Salerno on 21 September, Raphael said that although his change of mind could only be regarded in his favour, it could also be argued that 'the offence had been completed by 20 September' and that 'any subsequent recantation could only affect the individual man by way of mitigation'.

This passage of Raphael's speech relating to Private Kemp was an example of how whenever he gave something to the defence with one hand, he quickly took it away with the other. More of the same was to follow. While informing the court that 'it would be safer in the circumstances to ignore' anything that was said by Captain Lee prior to the parade on 20 September, in deference to claims by the defence that there was no evidence to link the accused with Captain Lee's recollections of 19 September, he dismissed this issue as 'one small point' which he did not think had 'influenced the court to any great extent'.

Raphael was now moving towards his conclusion. The fact that only the prosecution had given evidence did not mean that the offence had 'necessarily been proved', he said. The case rested on one important question: 'Are you satisfied that these persons, or any of them, combined together to disobey the orders of their superior officers and to resist lawful authority? Put shortly, are you satisfied that this was mutiny? Are you satisfied that this was an act of collective insubordination?'

The defence, he reminded the court, had said that it was not mutiny because the acts were 'not the acts of persons' who were 'disloyal or treacherous'. Yet, he insisted, mutiny did 'not necessarily spring from treacherous motives or even disloyal motives'. Instead, it could 'equally spring from other motives, such as muddle-headedness, obstinacy or misguided loyalty to a wrong ideal'. If troops 'during a war, in the middle of important operations and not far from them, refuse to obey orders and refuse to obey orders in combination one with another, that of course is mutiny and it matters not what the motives may be'. Questions of motive could only be relevant in mitigation of sentence, he said.

After once again reminding the court that if there was reasonable doubt in respect of any one man he ought to be acquitted, Raphael ended his summing-up. It had taken almost exactly half an hour.[17] The time was now 2.45pm and the court closed to consider the verdict.

With the accused led away to sweat it out in the canteen, the five members of the court left the gymnasium and made their way to their designated retiring room, number 102, in the main school building. Once inside, the president, General Galloway, asked each in turn his opinion. As the junior member, Major William Harris spoke first. He had been dreading this moment of responsibility. 'It was ghastly,' he recalled years later. 'I had sleepless nights worrying about what to say, I kept recalling everything that had been said during the trial and I kept wondering what the hell I was going to do.' When it came down to it, various factors determined Harris's response: his experiences as a soldier, the deputy judge advocate's summing up and, possibly most importantly, his legal knowledge. The result was that he told the other members that in his opinion the action of the men during the parade of 20 September constituted mutiny. One by one they agreed. 'Then we dealt with each man individually,' Harris remembered. 'Although I admit that this was a difficult thing to do with so many defendants.'

After a recess of just over an hour, the court returned to the gymnasium to deliver their verdict. They had sent word ahead and the accused were already back in their places. The stomach-churning tension as they awaited their fate was far worse than anything they had experienced in numerous battles. Gone was their earlier confidence, sapped by the defence's decision to offer no evidence and the apparently biased nature of the deputy judge advocate's speeches.

Handed a piece of paper, Major Raphael read out the court's findings: 'I am instructed by the court to say that they find Number 5109764 Sapper W DeLong, Royal Engineers, not guilty of this charge.'

Excited gasps rose from the close ranks of the accused. Most were not familiar with court martial procedure and assumed this was good news and that they, too, might be exonerated.

'May DeLong be released, sir?' Raphael asked.

'Yes,' replied General Galloway.

'Major Money, have you any evidence to produce as to the remainder?'

Money answered that he had AFB122s – conduct sheets listing previous offences – for most of the accused. The significance of this was instantly grasped by the older hands and the few prepared in advance by their defending officers: conduct sheets were only required for purposes of sentencing; all 181 remaining defendants had been found guilty of mutiny. Unaware of this implication, the majority were bewildered by the proceedings. Why had judgment not been passed on them?

The reason was that only findings of not guilty were announced at trials. All guilty verdicts and sentences were subject to confirmation by senior officers and were announced later. Consequently, no verdict was equivalent to a guilty verdict. While confusion reigned among the accused, the officers dealt with the business of the conduct sheets as if nothing out of the ordinary had occurred, as if the largest-ever number of British soldiers had not just been convicted of mutiny. 'I propose asking Captain Daiches to produce those forms,' continued Major Money, referring to the AFB122s.

'I raise no objection,' Captain Quennell calmly replied.

Daiches duly took the stand and immediately informed the court that he was missing conduct sheets for 36 of the accused. At this point Captain Quennell requested an adjournment on the dual grounds that the defence had not had a chance to examine the sheets and that they needed time to prepare their speeches of mitigation. General Galloway agreed and at 4pm the court was closed until the following morning.[18]

Before they were led away, some of the accused – still confused by the sequence of events – were informed by their defending officers that they had been found guilty and that the only hope now was to get them as lenient sentences as possible. It was a devastating blow for men, mostly with spotless disciplinary records, who had served their country so well and whose only crime, they felt, was excessive loyalty to their units.

Chapter 8

'Do not, please, be too hard on them!'

The final morning of the trial – Tuesday 2 November – was a sombre occasion as the defending officers tried desperately, one by one, to offer some mitigation that would discourage the court from recommending the harshest sentence at its disposal: death.

The unreal, almost Kafkaesque quality of the courtroom drama was only heightened by the bizarre frequency of pale defendants, racked with dysentery, their trousers held up by hand, asking for and being given permission to visit the latrines.

Major Raphael opened proceedings by generously ruling that the character of all 36 of those whose conduct sheets were missing was to be taken as 'exemplary'. Quennell was then asked how he wished to proceed. He told the court that the defence would like to present the mitigation in two parts: first witnesses would be called, then each defending officer would make a speech.

Captain the Reverend Till, the padre for the 30th Beds & Herts, was the first witness to take the stand. He had seen the prisoners about three times a week since their arrival in Camp 209 and considered that their 'spirits' had been 'very high the whole time', he told the court in response to questions from Captain Mitchell.

Continuing, Till said that he had found their unit, division and army *esprit de corps* to be 'extremely high' and that they had demonstrated this by displaying their emblems and the names of the battles they had fought in outside their tents. On the matter of religion, Till stated that his Sunday services had been 'extremely well attended' and that the prisoners had requested a number of extra services during the week. When Private Dobson died, the prisoners started a collection to buy a wreath. As this was not possible, they 'asked me', Till said, 'to give the money to a British general hospital so that at Christmas time the men who were at the hospital might have special comforts as a sort of memorial to their friend who had passed on'. This, Till confirmed, had been done. He concluded his evidence with a general character reference. While 'the poorer type of soldier' often 'approached a chaplain with a view to having his troubles taken out of his own hands', not once had any of the men 'mentioned one word about the case' to him, leaving him to conclude that they were 'very good types of soldiers'.[1]

Company Sergeant Major R Green, the NCO who had organised the draft at 155 Camp and the star witness for the defence, was called next. As Captain Bill Murgatroyd had taken Green's 'proof of evidence' the week before, he was given the task of examination. After establishing that 155 Camp was a reinforcement depot for the Eighth Army and that Green was responsible for the infantry wing, Murgatroyd asked Green whether any of the accused had volunteered for a draft scheduled to leave by air about 10 days before the one to Salerno.

'I had so many applications that I could not give any special men's names,' Green replied. 'I do know one, Private Bell. There were many others whose names I do not know. I remember Private Bell's name because he came to me so insistently to ask me to let him go on that draft.'

Bell was one of Murgatroyd's eight defendants. On the question of normal procedure at the camp, Green admitted that most men arrived from 'hospital or convalescent depots'. They often asked where they would be sent on to, and the reply was usually that they would be returning to 'their own units'.

'So far as you are aware,' Murgatroyd asked, 'from your transit camp what proportion of men have gone back to their own units?'

'I should say that except for those in for transfer, 100 per cent,' came the reply.

Moving on to the Salerno draft, Murgatroyd asked: 'Did you know where this draft of 14 September was going to?'

Green paused before replying, as if assessing the impact of the bombshell he was about to deliver: 'Only by rumour. I heard nothing official except the fact that they were going to their own units.'

Going much further than he had been prepared to do when he gave his earlier statements to Murgatroyd, Green had provided the first solid evidence that the men had been deliberately misled. He had been told 'nothing official', in other words nothing by his superiors at the camp, *except* that the men on the draft 'were going to their own units'. He only heard of the true destination, Salerno, 'by rumour' and therefore was in no position to repeat this revelation to the draft. The decision by the camp authorities to disseminate a lie, for fear of how the men might react if the truth was known, had been partially revealed. Euphoric, Murgatroyd tried to hammer home the point: 'Could you say whether the camp staff who dealt with these men knew whether they were going to their own units or not?'

Unwilling to accuse directly his superiors of lying, Green was noncommittal: 'I could not answer that.'

It hardly mattered. Only a fool could believe that the commandant and senior staff of a transit camp would not be informed of the destination of one of their drafts. Asked whether the men left with any impression as to their destination, Green replied: 'I think the majority of them thought they were going to their own units.'

Satisfied with his *coup*, Murgatroyd turned to a visit by General Wimberley, the former commander of the Highland Division, to 155 Camp earlier in the year. Green said that Wimberley had told him that he 'wanted all Scotsmen who were not in the 51st Division to volunteer' to 'replace Englishmen' so as 'to make it an all Scottish Division'. The result was that the transit camp 'did not look favourably on applications by Scotsmen for transfer' from the 51st Division to the military police and other forces.

Murgatroyd then returned to the events of 14 September. After detailing the first 750 men shortly after 5pm, the rest were 'dismissed to their tents', Green recalled. When the order came for another 750, he 'sent runners, corporals and everybody I could get hold of who was in a responsible position to go round to the tents, the canteen, the beach and also to the dining rooms to get the men'. Stating that the second parade included members of both the 50th and 51st Divisions, Green gave it as his opinion that 'they were keen to get back to their units'. There had been a medical examination of the draft 'laid on for 2200 hours' but it was 'subsequently cancelled' and 'no reason was given'. Furthermore, there was in existence 'a GHQ order to the effect that a man leaving the transit camp' would be 'fully equipped up to the Middle East scale'. Despite this, some men left on the draft 'without bayonets', 'water bottles', 'bayonet frogs' and 'overcoats'. On the other hand, to Green's knowledge they all had ammunition.

'Have you seen any order at all, any GHQ order, governing transfers from these divisions,' Murgatroyd then asked, referring to the 50th and 51st. Only that 'men from Sicily who were ex-hospital would return to their own units,' came the astonishing reply.

'What order was that?'

'The order was signed by the adjutant of 155, which came from 02E,' Green explained, referring to the GHQ reinforcements section.

Murgatroyd's final question readdressed the issue of deception: 'If any man had asked you whether he was going back to his own unit from your transit camp, right up until the time that this draft left, what would have your answer been?'

'I would have said yes.'[2]

It had now been firmly established that the men had left 155 Camp under the impression that they were returning to their units. Major Money's decision not to cross-examine only underlined this point.

Captain John Wheatley, the defending officer, was examined next by Captain Quennell. A company commander in the 8th Battalion, the Durham Light Infantry, Wheatley told the court he had been abroad with his unit for 'about two-and-a-half years'. During this time he had got to 'know personally' about 12 of the accused, most of whom had served in his company, while he knew another six 'by sight'. His view of the 10 men who had served in his company in action was 'good', while the others, as far as he knew, had also given 'a good account of themselves' in battles. One of those he knew by sight was Private John McFarlane, number 9, who had won a Military Medal.

Asked by Quennell what he thought of the unit, divisional and army morale of these men, Wheatley replied: 'It was always extremely high, even before we came abroad, following on the action of the division in France before Dunkirk and through Dunkirk. Since the gradual collection of units forming the Eighth Army the morale has got higher still. In my opinion, for the invasion of Sicily it was perhaps at its highest level.'

Did he have anything to add? Only that he was 'unaware of any men' whom he knew or had come across 'out of the 75 Durhams' accused 'whose behaviour in action has been other than that of a reasonably high order'.[3]

As before, there was no cross-examination, allowing Captain Jimmy Kailofer to be called. He too was a company commander in the 8th Durhams, he told the court, and had been with the same unit for over three years. Of the 75 Durhams accused, he knew eight personally and at least two dozen by sight. Captain Quennell then asked General Galloway if he wished them to be identified. Before the president could reply, Major Raphael interrupted by acknowledging the defence's point that all 75 were of 'exemplary character who have fought well and done their duty properly'. This admission made any further detailed examination unnecessary, leaving Kailofer to finish by stating that he knew Sergeants Innes and Middleton 'very well', that he had 'seen them actually in action' and that they had 'fought in a first-class manner'.[4]

Then, for the one and only time during the trial, one of the accused – number 96, Private J Kemp of the 7th Argylls – took the stand. He confirmed that he had approached a sergeant in the prisoner-of-war cage at Salerno and told him that he was 'prepared to go to 46th Division', and that this was because he 'realised that in failing to obey Captain Lee's order' he 'had behaved improperly'. If he had been told that the military situation demanded his presence he would 'definitely' have been willing to go. Lieutenant Howat, the examining officer, then asked the attitude of the German prisoners in the adjoining cage at Salerno. Kemp answered that they 'made the British soldier feel highly inferior', that 'at every opportunity they sneered and laughed at us' and that 'they made us feel very unsatisfied with ourselves'. With that, Kemp's testimony in mitigation of his own action was over.[5]

Howat himself was the next witness, with Captain Samwell examining. Howat told the court that he was acquainted with all the Argylls except two of the three defended by Lieutenant Edie. In particular, he knew Privates Hodson, Green, Paterson and Middleton – numbers 81, 84, 91 and 94 respectively – as they had 'joined the army on the same day' as him in June 1940. Before being commissioned, he 'served with them in the ranks for four months' and 'got to know them very well and they always behaved and conducted themselves as good soldiers'. He also knew well Private Halloran, who joined soon after and he, too, was a 'good, well-behaved soldier'. Privates Middleton and Findlay (number 78) were both in action in the same company as him at El Alamein and both acquitted themselves 'like good soldiers'. As a closing comment, Howat mentioned that as he was the only legally-qualified officer on the staff of 154 Brigade all legal matters were submitted to him. Not once had he seen 'anything concerning any of the accused'.[6]

Howat and Samwell then changed places, and the latter opened by stating that he had been a member of the 51st Division for over six years. Within that division, he said, there was a very strong, unique *esprit de corps*, 'almost a religion'. On 'several occasions' he personally had been addressed by General Wimberley and other senior officers on the subject of divisional pride, while he in turn had addressed his men in the same terms. On one particular occasion he did this on the orders of his CO, the legendary Lieutenant Colonel Lorne Campbell, VC, DSO. 'I addressed the men on the subject of their duty when away from the battalion for any reason,' he told the court. 'It was their bounden duty to ensure they were not inveigled into joining any other unit and they were to leave no stone unturned to return to their own unit as soon as they were fit to do so. This I did on the orders of my commanding officer.'

On the question of acquaintance, Samwell said that with the exception of the three 1st Battalion men he knew all of the Argylls accused personally. 'Every one of them has served in my company at one time or another during the desert campaign.'

'Are all these men of whom you have spoken good fighting soldiers,' Howat asked.

'Every one of them,' Samwell replied. 'In fact, one of them, Private

Cranston, was one of the ones who was with me at El Alamein. On the third night he attacked with me. His section commander was killed and he took over the section. After that his platoon commander and all the remaining NCOs in the platoon were killed or wounded, and he took over and commanded the platoon. He was wounded just a little later than I was and for quite a time he took charge of the situation. Private Wilson was also throughout that show with me, and Privates Carr and Cooper were in my company during the advance on Tripoli and subsequently in the battles of Akarit up to Enfidaville up to Sicily. All these men have at no time given me any trouble. They have always obeyed any order that I have had occasion to give them and they have behaved as real fighting soldiers.'

Highly emotional now, Samwell concluded by saying: 'I should be very proud to have every one of them back in my company at the earliest opportunity.'[7]

The final witness was Captain John Mitchell. He was staff captain for 152 Brigade of the 51st Division, he told the court. The brigade consisted, as it always did, of the two most northerly Highland regiments – the Seaforths and the Camerons. The policy before embarkation was 'that by consent of very high authority, Scotsmen from almost every other division then in the United Kingdom were transferred to the 51st to make up as far as possible the Scottish strength'. Furthermore, this policy was 'very much' continued after the arrival of the division in the Middle East. Mitchell could remember, in the course of his duties as staff captain, issuing orders on behalf of his brigadier to the battalions 'that men would at the earliest possible moment after evacuation from a unit, for any reason, advise their unit of their destination before posting in order that every possible application could be made to secure their return'. He had, he said, 'personally handled hundreds of such applications'.

'Were the men fully aware of this policy?' Lieutenant Howat asked.

'A great many men to whom I have spoken at one time and another were, without exception, aware of this. I know that orders to acquaint the men with this situation were issued to me on behalf of my commander in accordance with orders from higher authority.'

Questioned about his particular knowledge of any of the accused, Mitchell replied that he wanted 'to testify from personal knowledge to the consistent good character' of seven Cameron Highlanders – one of whom was Corporal Hugh Fraser – and one Seaforth Highlander, Private Robert Thompson. Furthermore, as a staff officer of the brigade, he recognised many of the other Seaforths and on every occasion he had had contact with them their 'character' had been 'without reproach'.[8]

With the evidence of the witnesses concluded, Captain Quennell told the court that he and the other officers defending members of the 50th Division would make their mitigation speeches first, followed by those representing the 51st Division. Before opening, he handed in as exhibits a pile of forms containing the conduct records, battles fought and particulars of wounds of the 181 convicted soldiers.

Launching into his speech, Quennell reminded the court that, in Major Raphael's words, the 181 men had been convicted of an 'act of collective insubordination'. There were 'two classic reasons for imposing punishment', Quennell said. To prevent the guilty party from doing the same thing again, and to deter others from committing the same offence. In addition, 'the question of uniformity of sentence' should be taken into account when considering punishment.

Quennell then once again referred back to Major Raphael's closing speech. While he agreed with Raphael that both motive and the proximity of the crime to a combat area were irrelevant in considering a verdict, they were 'of the highest importance in reaching a decision as to sentence'.

'It will be within your knowledge,' he told the court, 'that the news on 20 September was better. So far as these men were concerned, as early as 17 September the newspaper headlines were "Good news from Salerno". There had been a crisis, but that crisis, so it was stated, had passed.'

The men 'disobeyed one order and one order only' and their motive for doing so was 'obvious', Quennell said. 'Their minds were actuated purely and simply by divisional spirit. If the order had been "March off and go to the 50th Division", who in this court doubts that they would have obeyed that order with alacrity?'

Returning to the question of uniformity of sentence, Quennell pointed out that 'throughout the course of this war people in England in various industries, in defiance of legal and lawful orders from those entitled to give them, have gone on strike' and so 'committed an act of collective insubordination'. Two strikes had occurred at almost the same time as the events of 20 September, 'two acts of collective insubordination for which no punishment was awarded'. The government had often stated that 'every person, whatever his occupation', was 'equally in the front line', and this should be taken into account when considering sentence, Quennell said.

'If the factors I have adduced appeal to the court,' he concluded, 'then I ask the court by tempering justice with mercy to pass such a sentence as will restore these men to their rightful place as fighting soldiers of the 50th Division.'[9]

Captain Kailofer was next, and he began by saying that all the men he represented had 'been in action at one time or another with the 50th Division', while some had joined the division 'before the war' and had been 'through France' and 'all the actions in the Middle East and Sicily'. Sergeant Innes was one such man, while Sergeant Middleton did not have a single offence on his conduct form. Furthermore, he said, the 'only evidence' that the court had of the sergeants addressing the men was 'after the DAAG had spoken to them'. According to Captain Williams, 'several men went off before the third order was given'. The 'inference' to be drawn, he concluded, was 'that the sergeants were attempting to persuade the men to go off, whatever their own individual views on the subject were.' The remainder of the speech simply reiterated Quennell's point about the comparison between civil and military strikes.[10]

Kailofer was followed by his fellow battalion officer, Captain Wheatley. His first point addressed the previous records of his men. Not one conduct sheet, he said, had an offence within the last 12 months, the length of time that GHQ Middle East had ruled that convictions be recognised. Furthermore, each one of his clients had fought in at least one major battle during that time, while five had fought in 'every action' in which the division was involved 'since the initial breakthrough near the Belgian frontier'. On the latter occasion, one man had been 'placed by the acting battalion commander in command of what was left of his company, which was 11 men'.

Since arrest, the behaviour of his clients – 'as testified to by every witness who has appeared' – had been 'exemplary'. They had had 'many opportunities for escaping' but not one had been taken.

As far as conduct in battle was concerned, he could not 'remember any occasion whatever' when the 12 men who had served in his company had been 'called upon to do some act or other to which they have not responded or performed as well as could be expected'.

Finally, in Wheatley's opinion, 'no greater result of any acid test of loyalty to any person or body of persons could have been produced than the reason why the men, wrong though it may have been, committed this act of refusing to fight for any formation other than their own'. The 'popular impression of mutiny' was 'something very different from the acts of the accused', argued Wheatley, and 'no evidence' had been produced 'to show they said "I will not fight"'.[11]

Completing the mitigation for the members of the Durham Light Infantry was Captain Taylor, the lone barrister. After pointing out that the award of the Military Medal to one of his men, Private C Sollis, spoke for itself, he insisted that none of them were motivated by cowardice.

After all, some had fought at the beaches of Dunkirk, some from El Alamein to Sicily.

Historically, the British Army was not 'prone' to mutiny and, consequently, it was 'unnecessary' to impose harsh sentences to ensure that it would 'never recur'. His 'experience as a colonial magistrate had led him to conclude that it was enough to let the district know that they 'could not commit offences with impunity'.

Realising that a little flattery would not go amiss, Taylor stated that the men had only behaved the way they had because 'there was no real soldier present at the time'. Addressing General Galloway, he continued: 'I feel certain, sir, that had you been there this thing would never have occurred. This is not so much the fault of these men as the fault of those who were in command. These men have committed this crime through misguided loyalty perhaps and they have committed it on account of inefficiency from above.'[12]

Captain Goldsmith was next to speak and, like his earlier performance, he said nothing to inspire his defendants from the East Yorkshires and the Devons with confidence. Largely reinforcing earlier arguments, he finished his brief address by stating his confidence that the court would take 'a humane view' of the offence in view of the 'unstinted service that these men have given to their country during four years of war'.[13]

With Sapper DeLong acquitted and on his way back to his unit in Italy, Lieutenant Magnay had just five men to speak for in mitigation. He began by drawing attention to the fighting record of Private Mulligan, a regular soldier, which since 1935 appeared 'very favourable even when compared with the splendid records of some of the men that you have before you today'. Magnay then referred to two sick reports he had submitted, which showed that Mulligan and McCarron (one of his two privates from the Cameronians) were 'not fighting fit' at 'the time these men sailed from Tripoli'. In spite of this, Magnay said, 'they were glad to go, as the rest of the men I represent were glad to go, because their divisional morale was at its highest'.

Magnay then turned to the specific case of Mulligan and Rae. He had, he told the court, endeavoured to obtain 'independent evidence which would have shown that these two men were in hospital at Salerno after their arrival on 16 September until some time on 20 September'. He mentioned this, he said, in case the court had accepted the prosecution's argument that the mutiny was in existence before 20 September. Furthermore, he asked the court whether his enquiries could be followed up because he was sure that there was 'some substance in them' and that they 'would undoubtedly be a very great mitigating circumstance'.

Speaking on behalf of all his clients, Magnay stated that 'when they arrived at Salerno they all thought they were returning to their old units and divisions' and 'their morale was then at its highest'. The result was that they were faced with a choice between 'higher loyalties' such as to family, country and religion, and 'special' more 'recent loyalties' such as to unit and division. The fact that they chose the latter was, in Magnay's opinion, because an 'ordinary soldier with those fresh loyalties continually kept before him tends to allow higher loyalties to slip into the back of his mind, and when a higher loyalty conflicts with an immediate loyalty he may quite wrongly, but without any malice and entirely in good faith, come to the wrong decision'.

Like Captain Taylor, Magnay argued that had the situation at Salerno been 'handled tactfully by men used to man management and if the true situation had really been put before these men, not one of them would have been found in court today'.

Furthermore, he said, none of the 'usual attributes of mutiny' – lawlessness, disorder, dishonesty – were present in this case. These were men who had been addressed by Churchill and told that it was enough for them 'to say they had marched and fought with units of the Desert Army'. Only by returning them to their units could the court discover whether this 'fighting spirit' remained.[14]

Next up was Lieutenant Hammonds, the Royal Engineer. If his summing up had been terse, his mitigation was almost non-existent. The man he represented was from the Devonshire Regiment, he told the court, and, as his case in no way differed from the remainder of that regiment, he wished 'to endorse everything that Captain Goldsmith has said on their behalf'.[15]

The first defending officer to speak for men from the 51st Division was Captain Murgatroyd. Unlike many of his colleagues, he referred directly to Sergeant Major Green's crucial evidence, stating that Green 'could not have left any other impression on the court's mind than an absolute conviction that every man of the 50th and 51st Divisions who left the 155 Transit Camp on 15 September thought he was returning to his own unit.

'Would the court,' Murgatroyd implored, 'in deciding the penalty in this case try to put their minds in the same condition as the minds of these men, who, having left their divisions think they are returning to them, and think that right up to the last moment, when, like a dash of cold water, comes the order of which we have heard.'

Continuing, Murgatroyd briefly outlined the battle history of his men, all remaining seven of whom had fought in at least three major desert battles. Considering such high fighting morale and their soldierly bearing since arrest, the court could do no better service 'than to restore them to their units at the earliest possible moment'.[16]

Lieutenant Gardiner, representing eight men from the 5/7th Gordons, was next, and like Murgatroyd concentrated on their military record. 'With few exceptions, they fought at El Alamein, and from El Alamein through to Sicily,' he began. 'Among them is a boy of 19, Nicklin. His record of service starts at El Alamein, he fought at Marsa Brega, El Agheila, Wadi Zem Zem, Mareth, Wadi Akarit, Sicily – a veteran soldier at 19 years of age. I mention him because he is very representative of all these Gordon Highlanders.'

Given the fact that 'loyalty to division' had been 'instilled into them throughout their military career', it must be 'easy for you to understand their impulsive act of disobedience upon the receipt of an order which they had never expected', Gardiner stated.[17]

Captain Evers then spoke for the remaining 21 Seaforth Highlanders. As he was not legally qualified, he told the court, his appeal would be to their hearts rather than their heads. His clients, all first-class soldiers, had 'been through hell'. He continued: 'The bulk of these men are civilians who have taken up arms in defence of ideals that have been inculcated into them since the day they were born. Do not, please, be too hard on them for seeking in a civilian manner to right what in all conscience they considered was an injustice. Let them, of your charity, soon be restored to their rightful place in the struggle for the preservation of all they hold dear and for which purpose they have left their homes and their loved ones.'

Evers concluded his eloquent appeal with a paraphrased quotation from Shakespeare's *Merchant of Venice*: 'The quality of mercy... is twice blessed; it blesseth him that gives and him that takes.'[18]

A difficult act to follow, but Lieutenant Edie did his best. As his three men were all from the 1st Argylls and he was from the 7th, he could not speak as to their military character, he said. Yet the court was in possession of conduct sheets with 'no entries on them whatsoever' and schedules of service from which 'they will be able to draw their own conclusions as to the individual characters of the men'. For his part, he was sure that they were 'good soldiers' and could give 'excellent service to Great Britain in the future'. They certainly were not 'Yes' men and he, for one, would 'prefer to have a man of character rather than a fellow who always says "Yes, sir" and does what he is told'.[19]

Although representing nine members of the 7th Argylls, Lieutenant Howat told the court that as he knew all the Argylls bar two his remarks would 'of necessity apply to the Argylls in general and, to a certain extent, to all the soldiers of the Highland Division'. Referring to Major

Raphael's summing up, he repeated Captain Quennell's point that while motive was not relevant to the verdict it was to the sentence.

'Why did these men mutiny?' Howat asked rhetorically, before providing the answer: 'I submit that the offence was committed because their ideals were so high that they could not bring themselves to forsake those ideals. I put it even higher. The forsaking of those ideals in the men's minds would have amounted to treachery which their consciences would not permit them to commit.'

Reminding the court that Captain Samwell had testified that the *esprit de corps* in the Highland Division was 'almost a religion', Howat continued the analogy: 'To these men ... General Wimberley is their military god and the sign "HD" is the altar at which they worship. So much so, that to ask a soldier of the Highland Division to fight with another division is, in my mind, akin to asking a Hindu to worship Mohammed. Such a thing is unthinkable. Remove the Highland men from their Highland Division and you have torn them from their military altar and cast them out into utter darkness.

'With this belief within them, established by years of service with the Highland Division and tempered in the field of battle, these men eventually found themselves on the Salerno beaches. There, after considerable delay, they were ordered to proceed to another division. Their natural reaction was that they stood dumbfounded – such a thing was unthinkable. Therefore the offence was committed. Although as a soldier I cannot do otherwise than disapprove of the disobedience of these men, I cannot but admire their divisional pride.'

Had one of their 'own officers' been at Salerno, or, failing that 'had even a little understanding been shown, this offence would never have been committed', Howat assured the court. The evidence that 'certain officers prior to 20 September advised soldiers to go to the 46th Division' was no more than a 'miserable confession of weakness'. It was 'neither necessary nor customary to advise a Scottish soldier to fight'. If they had been marched 'straight into battle' they 'would have acquitted themselves like men'. Instead, they were 'left in a field at Salerno for two-and-a-half days, like so many sheep that were lost, crying in the wilderness'. The result was a 'Shakespearean tragedy in which the principal players were the DAAG X Corps and Captain Lee'.

Whereas inside prison the men would be of 'no use in bringing about the downfall of a system which we have sworn to beat into unconditional surrender', in the field 'they may help to sway the balance in our favour as they have helped to do before in many battles'. Appealing to the court as soldiers, Howat asked: 'Which will it be?'[20]

Captain Samwell, representing the remaining 7th Argylls, was given the unenviable task of emulating Howat's magnificent speech. Remarkably, he all but succeeded, making up for his lack of law with raw emotion. Like Howat, he told the court that he was speaking on behalf of all the Argylls and the Highland Division in general. 'I am not a legal man,' he began. 'I am here solely as company commander of 10 of the men concerned in this trial. They asked for me personally and I am very proud that they did. I was brought at certain inconvenience to defend them. Never in my life have I been so proud of having to defend men.'

They were, he stated, the 'last types of men one would expect to find convicted here in a court of this kind on a charge of mutiny' as they were 'some of the finest soldiers that our Empire has ever produced'. The court could 'put them up against a wall and shoot them' or it could 'give them a lesser punishment', but neither would remove the 'stigma' of conviction.

So why did these fighting soldiers 'disobey one, and one only, order?' Samwell asked.

Both Howat and he, in his earlier evidence, had given the reason. 'I only wish,' he said, 'it had been possible to produce General Wimberley here today as further corroboration of those facts. For four years and more it has been the studied policy of the 51st (Highland) Division to ensure that every possible effort on every possible occasion should be made to ensure that all men of that division remained in that division.'

Every man of the division, he said, had 'been addressed over and over again by their superior officers from their divisional commander downwards and told it is their bounden duty to remain in the division'. On one occasion, owing to a similar mistake to this one, when 'some of the men got detached from the Highland Division', General Wimberley 'went back to Egypt in a special plane to see that the mistake was immediately rectified, and it was rectified'. In Samwell's opinion, some of those men had 'committed practically the same crime' as that of which his own clients had been found guilty.

'What went through their minds' when they were told at Salerno to join unfamiliar divisions? Samwell asked. '"Under no circumstances must you be inveigled into getting detached from the Highland Division." I have said that to the men, my commanding officer has said that to the men and General Wimberley has said it to them.'

His voice rising with emotion, Samwell concluded: 'In all seriousness, gentlemen, not only as a defending officer but as a soldier and a British citizen, I consider that the fact that this case was ever allowed to arise is a smudge, first and foremost, on the officers concerned at Salerno, but more than that, it was a national disaster. Not that it is too late to rectify that. I can only appeal to the court to ensure that these fine men are released at the earliest possible moment so that they can resume the vital job from which they have been taken and which they were so excellently carrying out. Our country and our army need these men and need them right away. If there had been more of them this war would have been over.'[21]

Following Samwell, and rounding off the speeches in mitigation, was Captain Mitchell. He began by talking about past records. All his 22 Cameron Highlanders, he said, had fought in 'between one and nine' battles, 'an average of four or five for each man'. Of the conduct sheets, 17 had 'no entries or one inconspicuous entry'.

Mitchell then felt it necessary to refer to one man in particular, number 119, Private D Anderson. 'The name of this man,' he said, 'did not appear on the avalanche [ship's] roll deposited by the defence; it did appear on the purple roll deposited by the defence, although later deleted in pencil. The point I wish to make is that number 119 was not in fact detailed by 155 Camp to join this draft but did so voluntarily, attaching himself to it. I suggest this is a special factor which the court should consider.'

Speaking for all his defendants, Mitchell asked the court 'to bear three things in mind'. Firstly, that 'the disobedience was restricted to one particular occasion only'. Secondly, that when the men sailed they were unaware of their destination and were 'under the impression that they were rejoining their units'. Consequently, there was 'bound to have existed a certain amount of mild resentment at the maladministration at the transit camp'. Thirdly, almost without exception the men were in the Sicilian campaign and were evacuated 'by reason of wounds or sickness'. There was no suggestion from the prosecution that the offence they committed originated in 'treachery or cowardice'. If the men were 'actuated by a misguided loyalty to a right ideal', this was a 'mitigating factor of some importance', he argued.

Concluding, Mitchell stated: 'I think it is right to suggest that had these men been put in the picture, as is now almost universally done throughout the British Army, this offence would not have occurred.'[22]

Fortunately for the defence, their most convincing speech – a combination of righteous indignation and careful argument – had come last. Falling just short of accusing the officers of 155 Camp of deliberately misleading the men, Mitchell had lain before the court the key to the whole incident. Without this deception, he implied, it would never have happened. But would the court see it like this? Would Mitchell's words be enough?

The president, General Galloway, gave no clue as he wound up the proceedings: 'The court is closed for the consideration of sentence. The sentence to be awarded by this court, being subject to confirmation, will not be announced but will be promulgated later and the proceedings in open court are accordingly terminated.

'Before I go I wish to say this. I am fully aware of the fact that the orderly and quiet conduct of the proceedings in this court has rested largely in your hands. Your conduct in the court, which is what I have been concerned with, has been excellent and I thank you. I also wish to record my appreciation of the manner in which the officers both for the prosecution and the defence, each of whom has had a duty to perform, have performed that duty.'[23]

With those typically British words, Galloway brought to a close the biggest trial for mutiny in the history of the British Army. The lives of all 181 convicted men were in the balance.

Chapter 9

Sentenced to death

A wave of conflicting emotions washed over the defendants as the members of the court and the deputy judge advocate left for Room 102 to decide on the sentences. Relief that the five-day ordeal was over and hope that the court would accept the arguments in mitigation on the one hand, depression at the verdict and fear of the ultimate punishment on the other.

Thus preoccupied, many did not hear the order to form up outside the gymnasium where their escort was waiting to return them to their camp, and it had to be loudly repeated. With some weak from illness, others forlorn and hangdog, the men were a pathetic sight as they shuffled along, their bearing a far cry from the previous Friday when, with uniforms immaculate and heads held high, they had so impressed the sergeant major from the Welsh Guards. Next to leave were the prosecutors, almost embarrassed to remain alone with the men whose valiant efforts they had thwarted at every turn.

The defending officers stayed seated, reflective, as if suddenly aware of the awful responsibility that had been placed on their shoulders, wondering if they had done all they could. Regimental men like Samwell and Wheatley were bitter at the shoddy way their veteran soldiers had been treated by 'chairborne' staff officers from Tripoli onwards. Lawyers like Quennell and Magnay were angry with the prosecution for failing to abide by either the spirit or the letter of their 'Agreement', and with the deputy judge advocate for repeatedly dismissing what they saw as relevant legal points. Had they made a tactical error by not calling Sergeant Major Green and at least some of the defendants to give evidence before the verdict? Or was the die cast from the outset? They suspected the latter. Murgatroyd broke the brooding silence. 'I've got a camera. How about a group photo outside?' he suggested.

As the defending officers emerged into the sunlight, leaving behind the depressing makeshift courtroom for good, it was as if someone had lifted a weight from their shoulders. The sentences were still to be decided but many would be long gone from Constantine before they were announced. As Murgatroyd showed an Algerian bystander how to take the picture, the officers formed into two ranks in front of the gymnasium's main entrance: the shortest, like Gardiner, Howat and Taylor at the front; Quennell, Edie, Mitchell and others behind. The picture taken, Samwell asked all the officers to come for a farewell drink that evening in the bar designated as an officers' mess in the Casino Hotel. He was also planning to invite Captain Daiches, he told them, to settle a few scores.

* * *

After more than four hours' deliberation, with the advice of the deputy judge advocate weighing heavily, the court finally agreed on the sentences. The three sergeants were to be shot, the corporals were given 10 years' penal servitude, the lance corporals and privates seven years. The one exception was Private Kemp, who was given five years; the fact that he had offered to join 46th Division on 21 September had obviously counted in his favour.

Given the flaws in the case for the prosecution and the powerful mitigation that had been offered by the defence, these were draconian sentences out of all proportion to the offence. If the men had been involved in an armed uprising they could hardly have been given harsher penalties.

When Captain Lionel Daiches, the assistant prosecutor, heard the awards he was shocked:

> Under the circumstances of the mitigation that was put forward by the defence, I personally felt that the sentences passed by the court were harsh. Even Major Money thought so.

Clearly, the British Army's legal system was operating under its usual slogan: 'For the sake of example'. Whatever the grievances, whatever the circumstances, it simply could not allow a large group of men, veterans or no, to get away with disobeying orders in a combat zone. Yet, according to Captain Daiches, 'if the object of the exercise was to issue an awful warning to the troops, it completely failed in its purpose because the details of the trial were kept so secret'.

Major William Harris, a member of the court, attempted to justify the sentences during an interview with me in 1993:

> I can't tell you how appalling this whole procedure was. To sentence people to death is an appalling thing, especially when one saw perfectly good, honest men. But what was one to do; they were mutineers. There wasn't an officer. The sergeants were the most senior there, therefore they were more responsible than any others and they had to be awarded the

harshest penalty. One very important point is that those people who did go and fight, they went into a hell of a bloodbath and a lot didn't come back. I'm sure this fact weighed in our minds when we decided on the death penalty.

One factor that Major Harris forgot to mention was the advice of the deputy judge advocate, Major Geoffrey Raphael. A Metropolitan Police magistrate for 20 years after the war, Raphael built a reputation as a hard-liner to be feared. Bill Murgatroyd remembers him simply as the magistrate equivalent of a 'hanging judge'.

The sentences decided, the task of the court was over. The fate of the prisoners was now in the hands of Lieutenant General Sir Humfrey Gale, the senior British officer at Allied Force headquarters in Algiers, whose duty it was to review the findings and sentences and then decide whether to confirm them or not. The members of the court would soon return to their units, but none would easily forget the mental strain of sitting in judgment on their fellow soldiers. That evening, Major Harris wrote a hurried letter to his wife. Part of it read:

> Just come back from the final day at a Court Martial. Don't mind admitting that it has been absolute HELL & has upset me considerably. Wish I was in a position to tell you all about it – one day I will. Never did I think that one would have such an awful cold-blooded responsibility – but after the court had deliberated for some 4 to 5 hours, am completely satisfied that justice & the right decisions were come to. At the moment feel mentally whacked – sleepless nights etc.[1]

While Harris was writing his anguished letter, the defending officers were taking care of some unfinished business in the bar of the Casino Hotel. One officer who did not attend the farewell drink on the evening of the final day of the trial was Captain Bill Murgatroyd. He explains why:

> I was asked by Samwell and the others if I wanted to go to the officers' club where they were going to deal with Lionel Daiches for the prosecution going back on the 'Agreement' and not giving us enough time to get the witnesses we wanted. I knew they were going to take the mickey out of Lionel, who they had invited along, so I didn't go. I heard about what happened afterwards. Apparently, they gave him a drink, took his trousers off and turned him loose in the middle of Constantine, leaving him to find his way back to his room. He complained to the garrison commander and all the officers involved were put on parade the following morning. They got off with a warning.

Captain Daiches' recollection of this humiliating episode is, not surprisingly, less forthright:

After the trial there were some very unpleasant scenes between me and some of the defending officers. Samwell and Quennell asked me to join them for a drink in the officers' club. There, Samwell in particular became extremely offensive. He called me a 'chairborne' officer who was only there to put the law into motion without having regard to the realities of war. In general I got the impression that the Eighth Army defending officers felt the whole case had been engineered by lily-livered, white-kneed staff officers of the JAG Branch who were living on the fat of the land while all the Eighth Army boys were doing the fighting. My view, of course, was that this was a load of rubbish.

* * *

In the early hours of 3 November, the three sergeants were taken by a heavily-armed guard from the compound in the Legion of Honour Wood to a deserted hut, where they were informed that they were to be shot. Unlike penal servitude and lesser penalties, death sentences are always communicated to prisoners before confirmation so as to allow them time to petition for clemency.

Still in a state of shock, the sergeants were then driven non-stop for more than 100 miles to 1 Military Prison and Detention Barracks on a hillside overlooking the Algerian port of Bône. Death Row consisted of three small cells, bare except for single iron beds. As they were led in, the sergeants could not help but notice the chilling sight of strait-jackets and handcuffs hanging on the wall outside.

Their first night was particularly torturous. Unable to escape from his awful predicament in sleep, Wally Innes tossed and turned, conjuring visions of being shot by his own platoon. He could not stop thinking about his wife, Elizabeth, and his young boy, Brian, now three, whom he had last seen as a chubby baby more than two years before and might never see again.

The following morning the three sergeants were visited by Captain Hugh Quennell. The other defending officers were on their way back to their units, but Quennell had volunteered to remain behind to draw up the petitions against sentence. Horrified by the sergeants' sentence of death with no recommendation to mercy, and realising there was no time to lose, he had borrowed a jeep and driven straight from Constantine. After speaking to each sergeant for more than an hour, making notes on any point he considered important, and telling them not to give up hope as there was a good chance that their sentences would be commuted, Quennell left.

That same day the five full corporals – four from the Durham Light Infantry and one, Hugh Fraser, from the Camerons – were also separated from their comrades in the Legion of Honour compound and taken to a nearby detention centre to await the announcement of their sentence.

On 7 November, just five days after the end of the trial, Colonel Edward Russell, otherwise known as the 2nd Baron Russell of Liverpool, deputy judge advocate general and the senior legal officer in North Africa, was sitting in his spacious office in the Hotel St George, serving as Allied Force headquarters in Algiers, when an orderly handed him a sealed envelope. It contained two documents from Captain Quennell: one was a general petition appealing against the verdict on behalf of all, with an appendix appealing for the commutation of the sergeants' death sentences; the other was a supplemental petition opposing the verdict on behalf of Privates Mulligan and Rae. Russell's task was to take these two petitions into account before advising his superior, Lieutenant General Gale, on the matter of confirmation.

The first petition, on behalf of all, asked that the finding of guilty be reversed on three main grounds: firstly, that the deputy judge advocate in his final summing up 'failed to direct the court at all upon one of the defences raised'; secondly, that the deputy judge advocate in his final summing up 'misdirected the court in law'; thirdly, that 'the verdict was against the weight of the evidence'.

To back up these points the petition then summarised the 'only material facts proved before the court'. This was in effect a chronological list of events. The most important of these points were that 'approximately 1,500 men embarked on three cruisers from Tripoli on 15 September 1943 for an unknown destination'; 'on 18 and 19 September 1943 various bodies of men who had disembarked at Salerno from three cruisers were despatched to 46 Division and 56 Division Personnel Transit Areas'; 'at approximately 1600 hours on 20 September 1943 there was a parade of the 300 men then remaining in X Corps' Transit Area'; 'the parade was an orderly one and there was no talking'; 'the parade was divided into two' and 'anything said to one group could not be heard by the other'; the DAAG 'stated that any man acting in disobedience would be subject to an individual court martial' and that he would 'have to answer personally for his crime'; after the sergeants had been spoken to by the DAAG, and they in turn 'had spoken to the men of the Durham Light Infantry, some of the men obeyed the previous order given by Captain Lee; after the non-DLI parade had been dealt with, the two were 'formed up together and marched away in close arrest'.[2]

On the basis of these facts, the petition then listed the grounds for opposing the verdicts, firstly concerning the deputy judge advocate's failure in his summing up to direct the court upon one of the defences.

The defence submitted, it stated, that even if the prosecution's case 'amounted in law to an offence under section 7(3) of the Army Act', the 'men of the Durham Light Infantry had by the time they were disarmed completed their offence' and so 'it was impossible to find that they combined together with members of regiments other than the Durham Light Infantry who had by that time received no orders at all'.

The defence also submitted on the authority of *Rex v Thompson* 'that even if the court came to the conclusion that men of individual regiments had come to some agreement amongst themselves, in the absence of any evidence of a connecting link between the various groups of regiments, they could not infer combination'.

It was 'conceded' by the deputy judge advocate, the petition continued, that a conspiracy could not be proved unless 'one conspirator common to both' had 'communicated the intentions of one group to the other'.

That defence was 'first made in submission to the court that there was no *prima facie* case to answer', the petition stated. Yet 'in his statement of that submission', the deputy judge advocate 'dismissed' it with the words 'it is true that the orders were given to the two groups and given separately. They were, however identical orders given to men who within a few minutes had been on the same parade together, as to whom there is some evidence from which the inference could be drawn of association or combination.'

At this point, the petition stated, the court had heard evidence from both Captains Lee and Williams that they had both on 19 September 'addressed certain groups of men whose identity they could not establish, advising them to obey any order and go to 46 Division'. Exception was taken by the defence to this evidence, but 'some of it was recorded'. In contrast, the 'only admissible evidence before the court was that the men had been ordered to parade at a certain time and they had paraded'. There was 'no evidence of the purpose for which the parade was called' and it was 'separated' into two groups 'before any indication was given to any single man of the purpose for which the parade was called'.

In summing up, the deputy judge advocate 'advised the court that it would be safer to ignore anything said by Captain Lee prior to the afternoon of 20 September 1943 when the formal parade took place'. Yet, 'despite having given that direction as to the evidence', the deputy judge advocate 'made no reference at all in his summing up to the submission of the defence that if any crime had been committed it was two mutinies and not one'.[3]

Next, the petition moved on to the second ground, namely that the deputy judge advocate misdirected the court in law in his final summing up. If it was held that 'there was no obligation' upon the deputy judge advocate to direct the court in his summing up 'that there were in fact two mutinies and not one', the petition contended, then his direction 'was in fact a misdirection'.

His only direction to the court at any time during the trial was 'during the course of the summing up on the submission that there was no case to answer' when he said that 'there is some evidence from which the inference could be drawn of association or combination' between the two groups.

Yet, the petition stated, the deputy judge advocate did not in that direction do three things: firstly, he did not 'draw the attention of the court to the evidence from which he suggested they could infer association or combination' between the DLI and the non-DLI regiments; secondly, he did not 'point out to the court that pursuant to the authority of *Rex v Thompson* in the case of a combination alleged between A, B and C, A could not be convicted of conspiracy unless the court could say whether A conspired with B or with C'. It was 'not sufficient' to conclude that 'A conspired with B or with C without being able to fix the identity of A's co-conspirator'; thirdly, while he 'rightly pointed out' that 'proof of conspiracy could only be adduced from inferences, he failed to point out that in this particular case there was no evidence at all before the court of any events after the arrival of the men at Salerno and prior to the formal parade on 20 September 1943 except evidence that of the original 1,500 men who arrived, 1,200 had moved off'.

Concluding the second ground for reversal of the verdict, the petition stated that the case for the prosecution – the disobedience to the three orders of Captain Lee given to two separate parades – 'forced the court to take the conclusion that the accused were acting pursuant to a pre-arranged agreement'. Yet the evidence before the court was that 'the men had been told by the DAAG X Corps to act individually, that each man would have to answer individually for his crime' and 'would be subject to an individual court martial'. Furthermore, Captains Lee and Williams had both stated that after the DAAG's speech 'the men who left appeared to be acting individually and in their opinion, there being no opportunity for talking the men who remained also acted individually'.[4]

The third ground for reversal of the verdict, that it was against the weight of evidence, was effectively a summary of the previous two. The court had 'no evidence at all', the petition stated, 'of any order given before 20 September 1943 even though there was plenty of opportunity open to the prosecution to get any such order if it had been'. In consequence, the 'only evidence was that 300 men were ordered to parade for a purpose which was not disclosed to them, that the parade was orderly'. There was 'no talking and no connection between the men', particularly not between 'men of the Durham Light Infantry and men of other regiments who formed a separate parade'.[5]

The first section of this petition ended with a request for the points of law raised to be 'submitted to the Law Officers of the Crown' on the grounds that the deputy judge advocate general, Lord Russell of Liverpool, had advised on the case before the trial.

The second section or appendix, the appeal by the three sergeants against their death sentences, contained nine points. Firstly, it quoted the deputy judge advocate in his summing up: 'You have been told that they all stand here upon the same footing and that there are no ring-leaders ... It is quite true that there is little material upon which you could discriminate between one and the other'. Secondly, there was 'no evidence' that the sergeants 'endeavoured to persuade' any of the accused 'not to obey orders'. Thirdly, after being spoken to by the DAAG the sergeants 'tried to persuade some of the men to obey the order already given, as a result of which some did obey that order, even before the further order of Captain Lee was given'. Fourthly, 'there were present on parade approximately 10 officers, the senior being a major'. Fifthly, the 'reasons for inflicting any punishment are to deter the offenders, to deter others from the same offence', but there should also be 'uniformity of punishment for the same degree of offence'.

Sixthly, the sergeants' motive 'was solely idolatrous devotion to divisional morale sponsored by the regimental officers, their divisional commander and the commander of the Eighth Army'. As it would be 'impossible to believe' that the sergeants 'would commit the same offence again', it was 'unnecessary to pass an exemplary sentence either to deter them or to deter others'. Seventhly, the sergeants have been found guilty of 'an act of collective insubordination', yet contrary to the law 'frequent industrial strikes have taken place' in Britain without punishment. Lastly, the sergeants submit 'that having proved them-selves worthy of marching and fighting with the Eighth Army as first-class soldiers of the 50th Division they should be preserved to continue in that sphere of leadership in which they have so excelled in the past'.[6]

The supplemental petition on behalf of the two Black Watch privates was, not surprisingly, a shorter document. Its first point was to summarise the evidence before the court in relation to the identity of all the accused: Mulligan and Rae's names were on the 'original ship's roll' of 'approximately 1,500 men who embarked from Tripoli'; their names did not appear on the comprehensive roll, prepared at X Corps' transit area, because until 20 September they were, 'as was well known to the prosecution', in a 'field ambulance unit, situated about four miles from Salerno'; their names also 'did not appear' on the 'purple' roll, 'prepared from the comprehensive roll after Captain Lee's parade on 20 September'.

Secondly, the 'alleged offence must have been committed near Salerno, between 17 September and 20 September'.

Thirdly, there was 'no evidence' that Mulligan and Rae 'were with the other accused' during this time.

Fourthly, the only evidence concerning these two 'was the undisputed fact that they were found to be in a POW cage, along with the other accused men, on 21 September'.

Fifthly, other evidence was, 'by inference, in favour' of Mulligan and Rae because it showed that their names were not 'called out, or ticked off', when the roll was called by Captain Lee either before or after the parade; when Lee checked the names he had double ticked on a newly-prepared roll, the purple roll, their names were 'not included' on it, and were only 'added when they were found in the POW cage' the following day; the original number of names on the purple roll 'was 192', including those of 'Privates Davis [*sic*] and Davison who disappeared after the parade'; by the disappearance of these two, 'the number was reduced to 190, corresponding to Captain Dallenger's rough count of 191'; the 'final count in the POW cage on 21 September disclosed 193 men which, it is submitted, proves conclusively that three men, namely DeLong and the petitioners, joined the parade after Captain Lee's parade and after Captain Dallenger's count'.

Sixthly, the 'inference which the prosecution sought to draw was that' Mulligan and Rae must have 'been on parade with the other accused because they were found with them' on 21 September. To have established this, the prosecution 'should have affirmatively proved that there was no opportunity for any men to join or leave the body of men' after they were arrested and before the roll was called the next day. No such evidence was produced. Other evidence 'showed that there were at least two occasions' when men could have joined or left the accused body of men: the 'period of some hours' when they were 'awaiting the order to march to the Salerno beach', during which time the men were walking about having their kit checked, a complete watch was not kept, and there was an air raid and everyone took cover; and while they were marching to the beach and a shell exploded, causing everybody 'to take cover'.

Furthermore, 'if the check had been as effective as the prosecution tried to show', why were Davies and Davison not in the cage on 21 September. The presence of Mulligan and Rae in the cage was 'not evidence, *per se*, that they had committed the offence charged, and in the absence of any other evidence, the court was wrong in law in holding that there was a case' for them 'to answer'. Lastly, in his summing up the deputy judge advocate did not 'adequately' direct that the prosecution had not proved their case 'beyond all reasonable doubt', nor did he 'draw the attention of the court to all the factors' which should have forced them to conclude that Mulligan and Rae 'joined the accused men after the the orders of Captain Lee had been given'.

Finally, the court acquitted Sapper DeLong, 'whose special defence on the question of identity was, in all material particulars, identical with that of the petitioners', and it was 'contrary to natural justice that one man should be acquitted and others not acquitted on the same facts'.[7]

The following day, 8 November, Lord Russell of Liverpool wrote a secret memo to Lieutenant General Gale with his opinion of the proceedings, the two petitions and his advice on confirmation. He dealt first with the defence's objection on day one that the charge was not particularised. Field general court martials, he wrote, were different to general court martials in that a special set of rules of procedure applied to them. One such rule, number 108, stated that a charge 'may be made briefly in any language sufficient to describe or disclose an offence under the Army Act'. In Lord Russell's opinion, 'the prosecution were entitled to rely upon the provisions of Rule 108', and the subsequent charge 'both disclosed and described' such an offence, while the accused, 'all of whom received a copy of the summary of evidence, cannot have been in any way prejudiced or embarrassed by want of particularity'.

Next, Russell dealt with the two petitions:

> It is true that, in his summing up, the judge advocate did not specifically refer to the point raised by the defence that the true view of the matter was that the men of the Durham Light Infantry had, by the time they were disarmed, completed their offence ... and that it was impossible to find that they combined together with members of [other] regiments.

Yet, the case of *Rex v Thompson* was 'no authority' for the proposition that combination could not be inferred 'in the absence of any evidence of a connecting link between the various groups or regiments', he stated, because 'the reason for the quashing of that conviction was on the ground that the special finding of the jury was in fact no finding at all'. If the jury had 'found that A had conspired with B or had conspired with C, the conviction of A would have been good in law'. Instead, 'the jury found that A had conspired with either B or C but they could not say which'.

The deputy judge advocate 'had dealt with this aspect of the case' both in his advice to the court on the submission of no case and in his summing up, on the latter occasion asking, '... are you satisfied that the only possible inference to be drawn from the conduct of these men is that there was an agreement, a combination between them, to disobey the orders of their superior officers'?

Concluding, Russell gave it as his opinion that 'there was sufficient evidence, in the fact that all the accused on parade disobeyed the order given by Captain Lee, to enable the court to infer that this disobedience was the result of a combination between all the accused', and that 'it was not necessary for the prosecution to have established express evidence of a connecting link between the various groups or regiments'.

Moving on, Russell dismissed the second ground of the petition by simply stating that 'the advice given to the court by the judge advocate on the submission as set out above was adequate and right in law'.

Dealing with the third ground, Russell admitted 'that there was no evidence of any order given before 20 September', but the court had been 'advised by the judge advocate that it was open to them, having regard to the uncontested evidence that all the accused on parade disobeyed the order given by Captain Lee, to draw the inference that this disobedience must have been in pursuance of a common agreement'.

'In my opinion,' Russell wrote, 'there was evidence from which the court, in the absence of evidence for the defence, might properly draw such an inference and convict the accused on this charge.'

Then Russell addressed the request that the points of law raised in the petition be submitted to the Law Officers of the Crown:

> I am instructed by the Judge Advocate General that it is my duty and responsibility as his deputy to advise before confirmation of all cases submitted to me irrespective of whether I have advised before trial, and that I should do so in this case unless you or I, for special reasons, consider it desirable to submit the proceedings to him before confirmation.[8]

With those words, Russell perfunctorily, and unfairly, dismissed the points raised in the first part of the general petition and ensured that no more qualified legal officer would get a chance to consider them.

The memo then dealt with the sentences of death passed on the sergeants. While it was true that 'there was little material in the evidence upon which the court could discriminate between the accused as to their responsibility', it was 'open to the court to pass a heavier sentence upon the three sergeants' as 'they were the three senior non-commissioned officers on the parade'. To back up this opinion, Russell quoted from page 61 of the *Manual of Military Law*: 'A NCO should, as a rule, be more severely punished than a private soldier concerned with him in the commission of the same offence'. The court had also stuck to this principle, Russell stated, by awarding 'a heavier sentence' to the corporals than the privates. What he failed to mention was that for the court to be consistent, they should have awarded the privates lesser sentences than the lance corporals.[9]

Lastly, Russell turned to the second petition. In his opinion, he wrote, 'there was evidence before the court which entitled them, in the absence of any explanation by the petitioners at the trial, to find these accused guilty of the charge'. Also, 'there were different considerations in the case of Sapper DeLong', whose name 'did not appear' on the ship's roll, the roll of the 1,500 infantry soldiers who were sent by sea to Salerno. These two points were the only comments Russell made about this petition. Despite the flimsiest of evidence, which could not possibly have secured a conviction in a civil court, Russell had effectively pronounced the convictions of Mulligan and Rae as 'safe'.[10]

Russell concluded his memo with these words:

> I am of the opinion that no legal grounds are disclosed in either of the petitions for withholding confirmation in the case of any of the accused. The sentences awarded are in accordance with law. In my opinion these proceedings may be confirmed.[11]

Mercifully unaware of Lord Russell of Liverpool's advice to General Gale to confirm the death sentences, bringing their execution by firing squad ever nearer, the sergeants were nevertheless reaching the end of their tether. A decision, any decision, on their fate was better than the endless hours of torment alone.

Exercised once a day at different times, they were unable even to gain solace in each other's company. Their only conversation was with the guards, but the latter had quickly made their hostile feelings known. In a friendly gesture, Wally Innes had agreed to lend his watch, a present from his father, to a guard for the evening. He never saw it again. Gradually, though, as they heard the full story, the guards became more sympathetic. One, asked by an anxious Innes whether the army would inform his wife that he had been executed for mutiny, so condemning her to live with the shame of his 'crime', replied: 'No, they will say you've been killed in action.'

About a week after arriving at Bône, the strain proved too much for one sergeant. As he was being brought in from exercise his eye caught the strait-jackets and handcuffs and he cracked. 'What are they going to do to us with these?' he screamed, struggling with his guards, his anguished cries continuing long after he had been bundled back into his cell. It was only after a friendly guard agreed to pass messages of support from the other sergeants that the man calmed down.

Finally, during the morning of 16 November, the suspense was ended. One by one the sergeants were taken to the office of the prison commandant, Major Winter. On account of his seniority, Wally Innes went first. Sitting behind Winter's desk was an officer he did not recognise: Major Flowers, the DAAG of North Africa district, whose duty it was to promulgate, or announce, the decision of the confirming officer. Not bothering to introduce himself, Flowers told Innes to take a seat opposite him. It was all too familiar. Almost sick with apprehension, his heart thumping as if it would break through his ribs, Innes sank into the chair.

In front of the officer was a sheaf of papers, and without further ado he began to recite from them. It was a transcript of the prosecution evidence against the mutineers, and it was plainly his heartless intention to read out every word before announcing whether or not the sergeants' appeal for clemency had been accepted. After being forced to endure this torture for some time, Innes interrupted: 'Excuse me, sir, could you not tell me what's on the back page?'

'It's my duty to read every page out,' came the callous reply.

At last, after some 20 minutes of this gratuitous torture, Flowers reached the last paragraph of the last page: 'You have been found guilty of mutiny and sentenced to death. General Gale has confirmed your conviction but has seen fit to commute your death sentence to 12 years' penal servitude and reduce you to the ranks.'[12]

Flowers looked up. Relief flooded across Innes's face, quickly replaced by anguish. He had escaped death only to serve what amounted to life behind bars with hard labour. It was hard for him to decide which was worse.

Despite Lord Russell's advice that the death sentences should stand, Lieutenant General Gale had decided to temper justice with mercy, with the proviso – in accordance with General Alexander's wishes – that the first two years of imprisonment would be served in North Africa. It was a dubious concession.

The day before, Flowers had visited the corporals. Up until then, kept in solitary confinement, Hugh Fraser had whiled away his time reading the New Testament and polishing his mess-tin until it must have

become, in his words, the 'shiniest in the British Army'. Brought before
Flowers, he was told that he had been found guilty of mutiny, reduced
to the ranks and sentenced to 10 years' penal servitude.[13] Fraser recalls:

> I could hardly believe my ears. Ten years in prison was something I could
> not comprehend. Until that time my most serious misdemeanour had
> been seven days' confined to barracks for being in bed after reveille,
> oversleeping in other words. Before I could come to my senses, however,
> I was hurried away and taken to the prison in Bône where the sergeants
> were being held.

That same day, Flowers visited the compound in the Legion of
Honour Wood. Although the convictions and sentences of all but two of
the inmates had been confirmed, Flowers did not go to inform them of
this as the formal promulgation had been set for a later date. Instead,
Flowers went to tell the two Black Watch privates, Mulligan and Rae, that
their convictions had not been confirmed by General Gale and that,
consequently, they had been acquitted. As with the sentencing of the
sergeants, Gale had rightly dismissed the advice of his chief legal officer
and had relied on his own amateur judgment that their identity at the
parade was unproven.[14]

Before the sentences against the lance corporals and privates could be
promulgated, a chance visit to North Africa by the adjutant general, Sir
Ronald Adam, turned the whole case on its head. Adam – the most senior
officer in the British Army after General Sir Alan Brooke, the chief of the
Imperial General Staff – arrived in Bône by air from Italy during the
evening of 17 November for a routine inspection of military installations.
He was met by his deputy, General Gale. By an amazing coincidence, one
of the places they were scheduled to visit the following day was the military
prison in which the sergeants and corporals were being held.

Inevitably, during the visit, the topic of the mutiny was raised and
Gale told Adam that he had recently confirmed the convictions in all
but two cases. Already aware of the controversy surrounding the posting
of Eighth Army veterans to reinforce Fifth Army units from a conversation with General Alexander during his visit to Italy, Adam took the
opportunity to look into the case in person. Gale had no option but to
turn over all the relevant papers to his superior.

During the Second World War, Adam was a man almost unique in
such a high military position. While most officers of his rank had
concluded from their experience of the previous war that iron discipline was the only way to achieve maximum fighting efficiency, Adam
was more flexible in his approach to crime and punishment. Oddly,
there was nothing in his background to explain such liberal leanings:

the son of a baronet, he had gone straight from Eton to the Royal Military Academy. An artilleryman during the First World War, winning a DSO in the process, his administrative talents enabled him to rise quickly through a series of staff appointments in the inter-war years. By 1938 he was deputy CIGS, a year later a corps commander in the ill-fated BEF, and finally, two years on, adjutant general. Such impeccable military credentials masked his true nature. Only after retirement from the army in 1946 was he able to give his liberal sympathies free rein. After the war he was, among other things, a member of the National Association of Adult Education, the National Institute of Industrial Psychology and the Miners' Welfare Commission. He was also director-general of the British Council, chairman of UNESCO (United Nations Educational, Scientific and Cultural Organisation) and principal of the Working Men's College.

It was doubly fortunate for the mutineers that such a man had both the opportunity and the authority to intervene. Only in Algeria for two days, he did not have long to study the papers, but it was long enough for him to decide that the blame for the incident at Salerno lay with others and that all the sentences should be immediately suspended. In a letter to General Montgomery, five months later, he described the case as 'one of the worst things that we have ever done'. Continuing, he explained that initially he had 'put a good deal of the blame' on Alexander and 'his having no proper administrative staff to deal with these matters'. It was when he discovered that the men had arrived at Salerno 'after the crisis was already over', that he 'arranged with AFHQ that all sentences should be suspended'.[15]

Typically, Adam's decision was not immediately acted upon in all cases, and, even when it was, not in the spirit with which it had been reached. It was almost as if the authorities in North Africa could not bear to let mutineers off scot free.

The convicted lance corporals and privates had to endure a nerve-wracking 25-day wait in the Legion of Honour compound before hearing news of their sentences from Major Flowers on 27 November. Of the 181 men originally found guilty of mutiny, eight were corporals and sergeants, two had since been acquitted and three had recently fallen ill and been taken to hospital. This left 168.

Called on parade, they were addressed first by Major Flowers: 'Number 2991406, Private J Kemp, you have been found guilty of mutiny and sentenced to five years' penal servitude. The rest of you have been found guilty and sentenced to seven years' penal servitude.'

There was a deliberate pause as Flowers allowed the announcement to sink in. Private Robert Thompson was stunned, as were many others. After what seemed like minutes, but was in fact just seconds, Flowers continued: 'Except in the case of Private ——, who has already served a period of penal servitude, all sentences have been suspended on condition that you agree to join units of the Eighth Army fighting in Italy.'

A wave of relief swept through the three ranks of prisoners, bar the one exception. For some this was tempered with disappointment that despite all that had happened they would not be rejoining their own battalions, but most were pleased that the 'authorities' had finally seen sense. Such generous thoughts did not last long.

A second officer stepped forward and spoke. 'By refusing to join units at Salerno and joining in a mutiny you have disgraced yourselves. Fighting in Italy will give you a chance to retrieve your lost honour, but you should realise that any misdemeanours committed between now and the end of your time in the army will lead to the immediate reimposition of your sentences.'

The identity of this officer has never been discovered. Some of the men thought they recognised him from the trial, and that he was either a member of the court or the deputy judge advocate. Whatever his identity, the effect of his speech is not in doubt. The men were outraged.

Private Edwin Scott, like all the others, was stung by the implication that his actions at Salerno had been cowardly and did not feel that his honour had ever been called into question. Far from it. If anything, honour and principle had caused him to disobey orders. Furthermore, it was next to impossible not to commit some form of misdemeanour in an army ridden by petty regulations, and it occurred to him that it was only a matter of time before the sentences were reimposed.

The same thoughts were whirling through Private Archie New-march's mind. 'If the words had been calculated to humiliate,' he later wrote, 'they could hardly have been more effective. The sense of being understood had gone and the feeling of being part of a cause, for reasons that seemed good and proper, evaporated.'[16]

In his report to the War Office, written in January 1945, army psychiatrist Lieutenant Colonel Main summed up the catastrophic effect of these words on the men's morale:

> This speech dashed their hopes, and later discussion of it created alarm. They recalled that 'the least thing' they did in the future would immediately mean seven years' penal servitude. Few understood that full reinstatement would be possible and some believed that a 'suspension' meant only postponement and that they would eventually be called to serve the sentence.
>
> A minority hoped that 'the Eighth Army' might mean their own units,

but many brooded on the prospect of going to a strange unit with a reputation of mutineer and where they would be 'at the mercy' of any NCO or officer. Pessimism grew; as mutineers they would be given the most dangerous jobs; any slip would mean seven years' penal servitude; and slowly the opinion formed that this was not a fresh start.

They comforted each other with indignation and agreed now that they had fought for a noble principle. The army had supported them – their sentences had been suspended – and yet somehow they were worse off than before. They had been insulted, called mutineers, and been told to retrieve their honour. Clean conduct sheets were ruined, penal servitude was almost unavoidable, and they felt trapped and indecisive.[17]

Chapter 10

Cannon-fodder

Within 24 hours of learning that their sentences had been suspended, the 167 fit lance corporals and privates were on their way to join Eighth Army infantry battalions fighting in Italy. Escorted by an armed platoon from the 30th Beds & Herts, they left Constantine during the morning of 28 November on a train bound for Philippeville, the Algerian port from where the emergency reinforcements for Salerno should have sailed in September.

Left behind was the former convict whose sentence had not been suspended because he was seen as a persistent offender. Taken away to a military prison to begin serving his time, he was later joined for the same reason by one of the men who had missed the original trial. Also remaining in North Africa were the three convicted men who had fallen ill – Privates Holmes and Wade from the Durham Light Infantry, and Private Kemp of the Argylls. On return to fitness, they too would be sent to units in Italy.

Three of the 10 men who had avoided conviction because they were not well enough to attend all of the court martial – Privates Devaney and Merrikin of the East Yorkshires and Johnson of the Gordons – had since recovered and were awaiting a second trial. The remaining seven – Privates Atterton, Little and Ball of the Durham Light Infantry, Privates Middleton and Pratt of the East Yorkshires, and Privates Baudains and Pepler of the Seaforths – were still in hospital.

Thanks to General Gale's petty-mindedness, the sergeants and corporals remained in Bône military prison under the impression that they would serve out their sentences. On account of their rank, and to teach them a lesson, Gale had decided to let them experience the horrors of life in a military prison for a month before informing them of the suspensions.

Arriving at Philippeville, the men took leave of their escort and were immediately loaded on to a troop ship bound for Taranto on the heel of Italy. Unguarded, but confined to a lower deck, they were visited shortly before sailing by a young Royal Artillery officer, Lieutenant Lionel Munby. Called up in the summer of 1940, Munby had already served in the ranks of a Territorial gunner regiment for two years when, as a sergeant, his CO recommended him for a commission. It was a natural, if belated, promotion given that he was an Oxford University graduate and a qualified teacher. On the other hand, he came from a background of left-wing intellectuals, both male and female, and would not have considered himself typical officer material.

He had been training as an officer when his regiment departed for North Africa, and his colonel had asked him to try to rejoin the regiment or at least the division. After being commissioned, he was posted to North Africa as an unattached reinforcement. A period kicking his heels in various Algerian transit camps came to an end when he and a number of other officers were ordered to report to an Eighth Army reinforcement camp in Italy. His ship happened to be the same one transporting the mutineers.

Once on board, Munby was told to report to the officer in command, who asked him if he would take charge of a large body of troops without officers. It was a happy coincidence for the mutineers that their 25-year-old 'minder' was well aware of unit loyalty, as he was himself trying to rejoin his original unit and was bound to be sympathetic to their plight. Munby recollects their first meeting:

> I went down to the relevant deck and walked in. Most were sitting or lying on the floor. I could tell immediately that they were veterans because they were tanned, which we reinforcements officers weren't. Also I noticed that their uniforms were worn, not like the new issue we had, and that several of them had badges of rank which had been taken off; you could see where the stripes had been because the khaki wasn't so faded. They sat to attention, and I said: 'I've been asked to take charge of you for the two days on this boat. Who is the senior NCO?' There was a gale of laughter and one man explained: 'Sorry sir, we ain't got no NCOs.' So I said: 'Well, we've got to make do for two days. Now we can't operate in such a big group, collecting grub for example, so are you prepared to act as though you have the ranks you once had?' 'Oh yes, sir,' they replied. And they did. They all sorted themselves out and behaved with perfect discipline.

As the voyage progressed, Munby had long conversations with the veterans in an attempt to discover how they came to be travelling to Italy without officers or NCOs. The more he heard, the more his curiosity gave way to indignation. He recalls:

> They were all very, very disgruntled and disheartened. I gathered from them that they had been told they were going to join their own regiments again. Some had been brought out from hospital before they were completely fit, but because they thought they were going back to their

own units they were happy. When they got to Salerno, nobody tried to explain anything to them. They told me that they had been perfectly willing to go and fight, and that their only crime had been loyalty to their units.

They kept saying things like, 'Why didn't they call our commanding officers back from Britain,' and, 'These bloody First Army people, they were just getting their own back. It's a dirty trick. We weren't the villains. We were just trying to get back to our regiments, which is what we'd always been told to do by our commanding officers.'

This particular cross-section of soldiers had clearly proved themselves in Africa as fighting soldiers; I had been in the ranks long enough to realise that this produced an enormous loyalty to your comrades. Also, the ordinary soldier had a very strong sense of natural justice and, while he could put up with a lot, there were certain things he would not accept.

I could quite believe their claim that, at the trial, they had been discriminated against by First Army men. My own division, which I later rejoined, had been in the First Army in North Africa but was transferred to the Eighth Army for the fighting in Italy. The First Army felt that their efforts in Tunisia had not been properly recognised, while arrogant Eighth Army men got all the laurels. There was an enormous amount of bitterness between these two armies.

On disembarking at Taranto, Munby was congratulated by the ship's captain, who told him that his troops were the best-disciplined group he had had on board. By now, Munby was determined to do all he could to help men he felt had been grievously wronged. Assuming that they, like him, would be posted to new units from the transit camp at Taranto, he reported to the camp adjutant and told him that he would soon be receiving a group of soldiers who were the most disciplined he had come across in his two-and-a-half years in the army. In his opinion, he said, they had been badly treated and he hoped the adjutant would do the best he could for them.

It was all to no avail. Anxious about security and keen to get them in the front line as quickly as possible, the authorities had arranged for them to be taken by rail to the Eighth Army's No 2 Corps reinforcement unit at San Basilio, a small settlement some 20 miles north. This was to be the first stop *en route* to an advanced transit camp at Foggia, about 120 miles up the east side of Italy.

Despite Munby's humane treatment of the men aboard ship, their morale was steadily declining. During the voyage, other troops had learnt of their convictions and had refused to speak to them. This, more than anything, forced them to accept that they would never be able to escape the label of 'mutineer'. Censure from the military authorities was one thing, alienation from their fellow soldiers was quite another. They reasoned that things would be just as bad in their new units. In such an atmosphere, constantly reminded of their past, they asked themselves how they could expect to avoid committing misdemeanours that would bring an immediate reimposition of their sentences.

Lieutenant Colonel Main summed up the men's feelings at this time in his report to the War Office:

> They began now to dislike the group they were with – its reputation was too unpleasant – and sub-groups with smaller loyalties rapidly formed. Friends recalled to each other that they had not acted as a group at Salerno, but only as homesick members of various units. Group allegiance turned into a longing for their own battalion communities.[1]

This was certainly the case with the three pals from the 5th East Yorkshires – Privates Archie Newmarch, Fred Jowett and Charlie Smith. Angry and resentful at their treatment, without mail from home for over two months, and anxious about the future, they had decided to stick together, come what may.

Late that evening, 2 December, the train carrying the mutineers screeched jerkily to a halt, throwing its passengers into confusion. In the inky-black December darkness its driver had missed the small rural station that served No 2 Corps reinforcement unit and was forced to reverse back up the track. As the men detrained, they were grumpily ordered to fall in by NCOs with Tilly lamps and together they marched off to the camp, a large tented area surrounded by wire.

Awake well before dawn after a good rest, Archie Newmarch felt unusually refreshed. It was still dark, but his appetite was aroused by the smell of breakfast being prepared. Anxious to be one of the first, Newmarch awoke his two companions and the three of them joined the already sizeable queue for the morning meal. Minutes later, by chance, Newmarch overheard a whispered conversation between two officers. He recalls:

> One officer said to the other, quite quietly but it was loud enough to be heard: 'The group of men that arrived last night are mutineers. They are going to send them up to the front line and keep them there because they want to get rid of them.' I could hardly believe my ears. I wasn't the only one who heard, and soon the news had spread through the camp like wildfire. Up until this point, not one of us had gone absent. But this was different. It was difficult enough not to commit an infringement in the army, which would have brought our sentences back, but now we felt they were trying to do away with us.

During their meal, the trio angrily discussed the implications. Against their better judgment they agreed to wait and see what reception awaited them in their new unit before taking the drastic measure of doing a bunk.

On hearing the same rumour, Percy Aveyard of the 9th DLI, the former lance corporal now reduced to private, went straight to see the camp commandant:

> I told him that I wanted to go back to North Africa and serve my time. I didn't see how I could avoid committing an offence and then having my sentence reimposed, so I may as well have started it then. Anyway, we all suspected that when we got to the front line we would be given tasks that would make our survival very unlikely. The officer replied: 'I've got my orders. You're to go up one way or the other.'

From this point on, Aveyard was determined to go absent at the first opportunity, and he was not alone. Others requested postings to their own units and were inevitably turned down. They were told that the rules about men with long service in particular units did not apply to them, nor did the camp standing orders that all men should receive training before being sent up the line.

Worried about the obvious disaffection among their new intake, the camp authorities wasted no time in detailing them to front-line units. That afternoon they were despatched by train for the advanced transit camp at Foggia. It was during this journey that many 'jumped ship', taking advantage of the train slowing on bends and hills. Among them was Percy Aveyard, who went with three other men from his battalion.

The majority, though, were still on board when the train pulled in to Foggia station. News of the absconders had been signalled ahead and the men were not surprised to be met on the platform by three ranks of 'red caps', who escorted them to a huge tented encampment at the north of the town.

There they were met by an officer and a sergeant major of the camp staff, who gave them a roasting for being so scruffy. They were still in the same faded khaki drill they had been wearing since Tripoli, a stark contrast to the olive battledress worn by the other inhabitants of the large camp. This was rectified after a roll-call, when they were sent to company stores and issued with full battle equipment: rifles, bayonets, entrenching tools, water bottles, steel helmets, battledress, greatcoats, shaving gear, mess-tins, eating implements, groundsheets, blankets, trunks, valises and hold-alls. It was a far cry from the equipment they had been sent to Salerno with.

Fully kitted, and feeling less conspicuous, the new intakes would have been more hopeful about the future but for one omission: no ammunition. Clearly, they were not to be trusted until they were back in the front line. Such 'special treatment' continued when they were directed to tents on the extreme perimeter, despite the fact that there were many empty ones in more central positions. Suspicions about deliberate segregation were confirmed when no one came to speak to the new arrivals. Gradually, their earlier depression returned. Would they ever be allowed to forget their convictions?

Among those most downcast were Archie Newmarch, Fred Jowett and Charlie Smith, in the tent nearest to the gateway. They had been lucky enough to be posted together to the 1st Green Howards, a Yorkshire unit whose sister battalions they had fought alongside in the 50th Division. They would join the next draft of reinforcements sent from the camp to the battalion, fighting in the front line further north. But their treatment since arriving in the camp had confirmed their worst fears. At best they would be treated like pariahs in their new unit, at worst they would be kept in the front line until they were killed, they concluded. The only alternative was to go absent.

After some discussion, they decided to try and reach a port from where they could stow away on a boat back to Britain. If this failed and they were caught, they reasoned, their suspended sentences would be reactivated and, with luck, they would be sent home to serve their time. Either way, they would have a chance of telling their parents and MPs the true story. Backed up by their copies of the summary of evidence, with which they had all been issued before the trial, they hoped to mount a public campaign to get their convictions repealed. In any case, they reasoned, seven years in prison was preferable to death.

The plan finally agreed upon was to leave before reveille, while it was still dark. Fred Jowett was having a last cigarette before turning in, his two mates already asleep, when a shadowy figure walked into their tent. 'Who the hell are you?' Jowett asked.

By way of response the interloper lit a match, illuminating his youthful face topped by the black beret of the Royal Tank Regiment. 'I'm from the other side of the camp,' he replied.

Suspecting he had something of importance to say, Jowett woke Newmarch and Smith with sharp digs to their ribs. With a succession of matches the visitor was managing to keep his face visible. 'What's he want?' asked Newmarch, drowsily.

'They're all talking about you lot,' replied the visitor, jerking his thumb over his shoulder towards the main body of the camp.

'What are they saying?'

'That you're mutineers.'

'What else?'

'That they're sending you all up the line tomorrow.'

'And?'

'They don't know, but nobody wants anything to do with you.'

The visitor then told them that he was called 'Tankie', that he had been on a charge and wrongly convicted, and that he suspected they were going to go AWOL and wanted to tag along. Careful not to admit their intentions to a complete stranger, Newmarch ended the conversation by saying that they were tired and wanted to go to sleep. Tankie left.

Taking it in turns to rest while the other two sat up to ensure they did not oversleep, the night seemed interminable. Shortly before 5am, as planned, they got up, carefully stacked their rifles, left most of their kit, and set off wearing just battledress and greatcoats. Skirting round the town of Foggia, they plunged into open countryside, heading south. As dawn broke they were huddled together for warmth on a railway embankment when they noticed a squat figure 50 yards away, moving towards them. It was Tankie. It turned out he had kept watch on their tent through the night, and when they made their move he had followed. They had no option but to let him join them.[2]

By 7 December 1943, when Newmarch, Jowett and Smith took off, a sizeable proportion of the 167 lance corporals and privates shipped back to Italy had already gone absent, and more were to follow. In his 1945 report to the War Office, Lieutenant Colonel Main attempted to explain what lay behind the mass desertions:

> Personal morale as well as group morale was low, and though viewpoints about the injustice of their humiliation and the failure of their stand to get back to their divisions were exchanged, the unity of the group had gone and each man was taking stock of his position. Most men believed they were to be given a dangerous job, and there was even a small rumour that they were to be deliberately used as cannon-fodder. In their gloom, some saw penal servitude as the only alternative to death in a strange, hostile unit and few argued against such a deduction. Whatever else, seven years in prison was inevitable. It was also the least they could hope for.[3]

* * *

Back in North Africa the authorities were trying to ensure that those who had been too ill to attend the original trial did not go unpunished. By 9 December, seven had recovered sufficiently to be arraigned before a second tribunal in Constantine: Privates Little, Atterton and Ball of the Durham Light Infantry, Merrikin and Devaney of the East Yorkshires, Baudains of the Seaforths and Johnson of the Gordons.

No record exists of these proceedings. Johnson, however, later turns up in Italy, but there remains a question mark as to how Privates Merrikin and Ball came to fight and die in the Normandy campaign. Either the battalions they were drafted to in Italy were switched to Britain in time for the Normandy landings or, surprisingly, they were sent back to their old units. Certainly, Commonwealth War Graves Commission records state that Merrikin died on D-Day, 6 June 1944, with his original unit – the 5th East Yorkshires.[4] As for the three men who were not well enough to attend either court martial – Privates Middleton and Pratt of the East Yorkshires and Pepler of the Seaforths – it seems they were never tried. They were very lucky.

About a week before Christmas the heartless torment of the former sergeants and corporals was finally brought to an end. One by one they were taken before the prison commandant, Major Winter, and told that their sentences would be suspended if they agreed to join units fighting in Italy. As with the privates and former lance corporals, it was stressed that any future infringements, however minor, would bring the reimposition of their sentences.

Elated by the news, but still doggedly determined to rejoin his regiment, Wally Innes asked: 'Do I go to the Durham Light Infantry, sir?'

'You go where you're sent,' came the curt reply.

Hugh Fraser's reaction on hearing that his sentence had been suspended could not have been more different. Horrified by even his short time in a military prison, he was prepared to go anywhere, do anything, not to be sent back. He recalls:

> Having had a spell in prison there was no way I was going to misbehave in the future. At first I was breaking rocks with a sledgehammer, overlooked by armed guards. This didn't last long and I was soon given more menial tasks, but it made me realise that I was in prison for a long time and I was going to get a hard time. I learnt some useful tricks there, like how to improvise a cigarette by rolling some fluff from an army blanket in toilet paper, but the worst thing was having to mix with the other prisoners. Men were in there for desertion, murder, rape and robbery, and, by picking up prison slang, I found myself being dragged down to their level.
>
> Letters from the prison were censored, and I wasn't allowed to say why I was there or for how long. I wasn't married then, but I hate to think how my parents must have felt at that time. My father had gone through the First World War, and been gassed. It must have been heartbreak for them.

At the beachhead I had refused to go to another unit, and I had been told I could've been shot. Now, when they told me I was being transferred to another unit, I agreed. After that time in prison I would've gone anywhere.

Within days the former NCOs were with their new units in Italy. Wally Innes was posted to the 6th York & Lancasters, a 46th Division unit that had recently been transferred to the Eighth Army along with the rest of X Corps. Hugh Fraser went to the 1st York & Lancasters, Captain Lee's battalion. It was as if the army was unwilling to let them forget.

At first things went well for Innes in his new unit. Ronnie Serginson, then a 19-year-old lance corporal and Innes's immediate superior in the anti-tank platoon, remembers the veteran former sergeant as 'a great bloke, a happy-go-lucky fella who had forgotten more about army life than I would ever know'. It was not just Innes's combat record that endeared him to his new comrades. Serginson recalls:

> Wally stopped me making a fool of myself. At the time we were up in the mountains. There weren't any tanks there so we had the job of humping stuff up and down the mountains on mules, but we carried a lot. This was every day: rain, snow or sunshine. Mostly we were living on hard tack and bully-beef. We had lice, scabies, crabs, the lot. We had been fighting since the Salerno landings, in and out of the line, and we were sick of it. One day I was sitting there and I said, 'I've a good mind to piss off, I'm bloody sick.' And it wasn't only me that felt like that, neither. But at the time Wally stopped me by saying, 'Ronnie, there's always somebody worse off than yourself.' 'How's that?' I asked. 'Look down that hillside,' he replied. There were seven Guardsmen lying in a row, dead.

But while Innes was trying to forget the past by getting on with serving his country, the army was doing its best to refresh his memory. On 28 February 1944, orders were posted that the 6th York & Lancasters was being pulled out of the front line, prior to a period of rest and recuperation in Egypt. The exceptions were all mutineers, most of whom had previously served with the Durham Light Infantry: they included Innes, former Corporals Yorke and Carr, and Private Billy Holmes, one of the three men who had missed returning to Italy with the main body because of illness. Innes later recalled this incident:

> The sergeant major says, 'Have you read orders.' I said: 'No.' 'Well read them.' So I went to read the orders, the standing orders, and there was our names, ranks, numbers up on the board, telling us that we had to stop there and wait 'til the next regiment came on up. Now I thought this was well out of place. No British person would do that to any other one. They

were using us for cannon-fodder. In my opinion, they didn't want one
bloke who was on that mutiny charge to go back. They wanted us all dead,
and that's my honest opinion. So I told them, I said: 'I'm going back with
you's, or I'll not be here in the morning.' I never said no more. At two
o'clock in the morning, I took my shaving kit, towels, soap, toothbrush,
and off I went.[5]

Ronnie Serginson confirms Innes's version of events:

When we were pulled out to go to Egypt, Wally and the others were left
behind, which was wrong. We got the impression that they wanted to see
them off; they were an embarrassment and the army wanted to see the
back of them. We all played hell but what could we do? Some of the junior
officers complained about it but they couldn't do nothing – these orders
came to our CO from high up, he didn't give them. He must have been
told, 'Leave these fellas behind. They're to get no rest, nothing.'

Shortly after we left, Wally deserted. If our battalion had stayed in Italy,
he wouldn't have gone; or if he had gone with us to Egypt he would have
been quite happy. He said: 'Righto, I've done my best but now they've
done the dirty.' He wasn't the only mutineer that deserted; many of the
others did too.

* * *

Billy Holmes was one, going absent with Innes. They were just two
among many mutineers who were given reason to believe, once they had
arrived at their new units, that the army was trying to do away with them.
Private John McFarlane, MM, posted to the 2nd Lancashire Fusiliers,
quickly became disillusioned when he and other mutineers were
repeatedly put on dangerous night patrols. For him it was a confirmation of his worst fears. On 15 January he went absent, but returned
within twelve hours. It was a mistake. Singled out as a troublemaker, his
relations with his fellow soldiers deteriorated. As if a belief that he was
being unfairly victimised was not enough, he was expected to fight in
horrendous conditions of mud and snow. Nearing the end of his tether
he applied for leave. Inevitably he was turned down, and on 23 February
he went absent again, this time for good.

Private Edwin Scott and nine other DLI mutineers thought they were
in luck when they were told they would be joining their 16th Battalion,
albeit a unit in the previously spurned 46th Division. Unfortunately, the
circumstances of their arrest at Salerno were known in their new
battalion and they were quickly singled out for special treatment. In his
first three days in the front line Scott recalls being repeatedly put on
night-fighting patrols. The final straw was when his company was

relieved and he and the other mutineers were told they would have to stay. Convinced that the authorities wanted him dead, he and a fellow mutineer, Harry Glassman, went absent.

Private Ray Whitaker of the Argylls was also posted to a unit from his own regiment – the 8th Battalion. But gradually he too felt he was being victimised. Relieved with his battalion after a spell in the front line, Whitaker was picking his way down a narrow goat-track when he slipped and fell. He recalls:

> As I was getting back up, this officer that I had had a few run-ins with before came up and said, 'You're on report.' When I asked what for he replied, 'Drunkenness'. So I was sent up in front of the CO and punished. When I came out, the RSM said to my company sergeant major, 'Watch this man, he's got seven years hanging over him. First chance you get, send him back here on a charge and we'll have him doing his sentence.' I replied, 'I'll give you a good chance, I'm going to pack it in.' It was obvious that they were going to do their best to get my sentence reimposed. Because I had been done for mutiny they thought I was an agitator, a troublemaker. That's when I decided to go absent. I had been with the 8th Argylls for about four months by this time.

Of course, there never was a general conspiracy to see the mutineers killed off in the front line. At worst, some unit commanders received instructions that certain mutineers, such as the sergeants, were not to be given leave. If men were victimised by either officers or men in their new battalions it was because they were known to be convicted mutineers, from which it was often deduced they were cowards. Yet for every man who was singled out, another was given an opportunity to prove himself.

Private Robert Thompson was one. He and fellow mutineer Charlie Keir, a mate from the 5th Seaforths, were sent to their regiment's 6th Battalion. Thompson was lucky enough to know a handful of his new colleagues, one of whom had served with him as an apprentice bricklayer. Although it was known that Thompson and Keir were mutineers, they were accepted into their new company. Once it was clear that the past would not be held against him, Thompson was determined to keep his nose clean.

The Italian campaign was particularly brutal, with the Germans offering stiff resistance all the way up the peninsula. Much of the fighting was in mountainous regions with harsh weather conditions. Without the friendship of his fellow soldiers it is unlikely that Thompson could have seen it through. It was this support that gave him the strength to survive the hazardous night crossing of the River Garigliano when Charlie Keir was badly wounded, and the infamous blood-baths of Monte Cassino and Anzio that followed. After reaching Rome, the 6th Seaforths were switched to the new north-western front opened by the D-Day landings, and Thompson went with them, fighting on until the German surrender on 7 May 1945.

As Hugh Fraser had already spent more than a month in a military prison, he was even more determined than Thompson not to put a foot out of line in his new unit, the 1st York & Lancasters. The absence of discrimination against him by his new colleagues helped. He recalls:

> I used to go on lots of night patrols, but so did everyone else. I wasn't going to rock the boat, and if I'd been ordered on more patrols I would have gone. I don't think I was treated any worse than the other soldiers in the battalion. They were mostly a nice bunch of lads and they accepted me for what I was.

Yet, despite equal treatment, Fraser remained bitter and made few friends. In some ways it was a relief when, on night patrol at the Anzio beachhead in April 1944, he was badly wounded by a hail of machine-gun bullets that tore a hole across his chest. If he had not been turning at the moment of impact, the bullets would have hit him face on; as it was they only narrowly missed his heart. Hauled to safety by his officer, he was told by an NCO at the casualty clearing station that he was 'the luckiest man alive'. After a long period of convalescence he was regraded B1 (unable to wear equipment), transferred to the Royal Army Service Corps and saw out the war as a clerk at GHQ 2nd Echelon near Naples.

Amazingly, while at GHQ he was going through a correspondence file relating to September 1943 when he came across a telegram referring specifically to him. It was from the CO of the 5th Camerons, Lieutenant Colonel Monro, and requested that Corporal Hugh Fraser be returned to his unit at soon as possible. Fraser was stunned by this discovery. At about the same time he had been refusing to join any other unit but his own, his CO had been working towards the same end. The irony was too much. Finally, in July 1946, Fraser was demobbed. On his release papers the camp commandant of GHQ 2nd Echelon wrote: 'I feel sure that Fraser will give complete satisfaction in his civilian duties and have no hesitation in recommending him to any future employer.' In some ways, his rehabilitation was complete.

Not every mutineer who stayed with his new unit was as lucky. Private Herbert Crawford of the 5th East Yorkshires was drafted to the 1st Green Howards, the same battalion as Archie Newmarch's group. Crawford's experience with the Green Howards tends to confirm their decision to go absent rather than join. Bullied and victimised, repeatedly chosen for the most dangerous duties, such as night patrols, and continually at the front, Crawford met his nemesis at Anzio when his legs were smashed by mortar fire. A delay in treatment led to gangrene and both limbs had to be amputated above the knee. His war was over. In the eyes of the authorities, his honour had been redeemed. He would have preferred his legs.

One by one the mutineers who had gone absent either gave themselves up or were arrested. Archie Newmarch's small group lasted less than a week on the run. Given a roof by Italian peasants for the first couple of nights, they were turned in by a farmer who took them for Germans. Fortunately, they managed to convince the Americans who came to arrest them that they were British soldiers on their way back to their units – which was half true anyway – and they were allowed to continue in peace. At Brindisi this fabrication was again swallowed by a British railway transport officer, and after a welcome meal they were put on a train to Taranto. It was there, though, that they lost heart. Without food and money they considered the chances of stowing away on a ship to be minimal. If they gave themselves up, they reasoned, they were bound to be returned to a British prison, from where they could set about clearing their names. This belief was based on the erroneous assumption that a term of penal servitude had to be served in British jails. In fact, a maximum of two years could be served abroad. Unaware of this, the group turned themselves in.

After an unpleasant month in Taranto jail they were taken to the Eighth Army Court Martial Centre at Campobasso, where they were put into a large room containing a number of other former mutineers also awaiting punishment for going absent. Towards the end of January, Newmarch, Jowett, Smith and 14 others were taken before the commandant and told that, instead of being tried for their new offence, their suspended sentences would simply be reactivated. But if any were prepared to go back into the front line, he would put in a good word for them. Asked individually, only one said he was willing. The rest were taken off to begin their seven years in custody.

During the following month the trio escaped twice, the first time on 13 February – Newmarch's 21st birthday. Both escapes were prompted by harsh prison regimes and were half-hearted attempts to get home. Both ended in recapture. After their second escape, and to ensure they would not go again, they were sent to the imposing 56th Military Prison in Brindisi. It was from here, in early May 1944, that Newmarch was able to write to his parents for the first time in five months. Not able to include any details about his sentence, he hoped that the address alone would prompt his parents to make enquiries. With no response, he tried again on 24 May. The letter read:

> My Dearest Mother, Father and family,
> For reasons unknown to me I have never had a line from you whatever. 'Why!' For this very word has me puzzled. Maybe you think me of a bad type for being in the above address. 'I'm Not', some day, when this feud is all over and I return home, I can and will explain. Words fail me here, but I want you to think of me as the very same lad, son you waved goodbye to a long while ago.
> While I lay on my bed I often think (very deep thoughts too) of what each one of you in turn is doing at that very moment. Old faces, even memories come back. I feel free, happy. Then the scene changes and I realise where I am and the most touching part is as to why I am receiving not even a line from you. It often makes me wonder.
> There's a very old adage, it goes like this: 'One's best friend is one's mother.' It looks very much to me as though I have no friends. Time will not permit much more to tell you, so I will close by saying: Have faith in me, for I will not let you down.
> Cheerio and Keep your Head up.
> From your Ever loving son,
> Archie.[6]

In fact, although Newmarch's first letter took slightly longer than normal to reach England, his mother had received it and sent a reply by 18 May. It was her first news of her son's predicament. As recently as 6 May she had written to the officer in charge of infantry records in York, asking about her son's whereabouts. The reply of 11 May stated: 'Private Newmarch is now serving with the Green Howards, and so far as is known in this office is in good health.'[7]

Newmarch's letter to his mother of 24 May was the last from Brindisi. When next he wrote, on 10 June, it was from the brutal 50th Military Prison in Egypt, where he, Fred Jowett, Charlie Smith and a number of other mutineers had been taken. He was allowed to tell his mother that he had been sentenced to seven years' penal servitude, but no more. By this time, though, his mother was already making enquiries through official channels that would eventually lead to a full-blown campaign to clear the names of all the Salerno mutineers. She would continue this fruitless quest for the rest of her life.

Edwin Scott, too, only managed a week on the run. After hitching a ride with an American truck-driver to a small village near Naples, he and Harry Glassman soon ran out of money and decided to give themselves up to MPs. Telling them that they were from the Lancashire Fusiliers, they were amazed to be told that a battalion of that regiment was billeted nearby. Taken to rejoin 'their' battalion, they were doubly shocked when 'their' CO, on hearing the whole story, agreed to let them stay. For the next few months they were content, Scott ending up as the regimental sergeant major's right-hand man, helping to get ammunition up to the front line. Eventually, though, they were tracked down by the authorities and informed by their sympathetic CO that they would have to serve out their original sentence. Taken to the military prison in Naples, they were surprised to find many other mutineers, including former sergeant George Middleton.

Wally Innes's brief absence was ended when he and Billy Holmes were arrested near Naples by the army's detective arm, the Special Investigation Branch (SIB). Expecting his sentence to be reimposed, Innes was lucky. After months of detention and a number of interviews with high-ranking officers, he was given a second chance. Recognised as an experienced, first-class soldier, he was offered a posting to a battalion of his beloved Durham Light Infantry and jumped at the chance. This time round, accepted by officers and men alike, he served with distinction until demobilisation in March 1946. In his soldier's release book his military conduct was described as 'very good', while his testimonial read: 'A good hard-working soldier. Clear and reliable. Should do well in civilian life.'

After just 11 days on the loose, John McFarlane and his companion were arrested in Naples after being duped by a man they took for a fellow runaway. He turned out to be a member of the SIB in disguise, on the look-out for deserters. McFarlane recalled:

> We were sitting having a cup of coffee in a place called the Churchill House when this guy came over and sat down beside me. We got into conversation. I looked at him, saw his battledress was all tattered, his two tapes were hanging off his arm. I said: 'Well boy, you're on the run anyway.' So everybody tried to kid everybody on that they were on leave. During the course of the conversation he says to me: 'Are you a Durham?' I says, 'Aye.' 'There are a lot of Durhams down at our place if you want to come down and meet them.' 'Just the job,' I says. We had no money or nothing and thought we would get a meal at least with them. So we walked down the street and he walked us right into the jail.[8]

McFarlane's suspended sentence was put into operation on 6 April, and within weeks he had joined Newmarch and the others in the 50th Military Prison in Egypt.

Percy Aveyard and his three mates managed to stay at large for an incredible five months, by living and working with an Italian family and cadging supplies off the Americans. As with McFarlane and his mate, their period of freedom was ended by an informer. Technically deserters rather than absentees, in that their intention to stay on the run seemed to be permanent, they were lucky to avoid a court martial for this new, serious offence. Instead, like the others who had only been absent for a matter of days, they had their suspended sentences reimposed and eventually ended up in Egypt.

Undoubtedly the most resourceful of the mutineers who did a bunk was little Ray Whitaker. At first he and his two partners, neither of whom were mutineers, made a living buying cigarettes from NAAFIs in the Foggia area and then selling them at a profit to Italians. They even managed to draw pay from some units by filling in the missing spaces on each other's paybooks so it would look as if they were still serving. Eventually they got hold of a pick-up truck and drove to Bari, where they were arrested trying to sell stolen army blankets. Taken to the court martial centre at Campobasso, they escaped before being re-sentenced.

For the next five months Whitaker survived by illegally trading in olive oil. As the withdrawing Germans had taken most vehicles, the warehouses in the south were full of oil that could not be moved. Whitaker simply bought up oil in Bari, took it by stolen truck to Naples and sold it for four times as much. At one stage he teamed up with Alec Johnson, the man who had missed the original court martial and had been re-tried with six others in December. Their partnership ended when their truck was stopped by the American SIB in Naples and they tried to make a run for it. Johnson was caught and pistol-whipped; Whitaker escaped. But the diminutive Yorkshireman finally ran out of luck on 2 October 1944. Stopped at an American MP road-block in the town of Corato, near Bari, he tried to escape by drawing a pistol. He recalls:

> As I did so the two MPs dropped and started firing into the cab. I tried to start the truck but some others opened up with tommy-guns, hitting the engine. I started firing back with both my pistols until I quickly ran out of ammunition. How I wasn't killed I don't know. I was hit in the thigh and I only managed to get out and hobble a short way before they arrested me.

After recovering from his wounds, Whitaker was in Bari prison waiting to be court martialled when, incredibly, he was visited by Hugh Quennell, the officer who had led the defence team at the mutiny trial. Then working for the JAG Branch as a permanent court president, Quennell told Whitaker that because of his previous involvement he had been given permission to defend him on the new charges. But before Quennell was able to plan his defence, he was posted and replaced by another officer. Found guilty of five charges, including desertion, robbery and attempted murder, Whitaker was given concurrent sentences totalling six years' penal servitude. In one of the great anomalies of the British Army's legal system, Whitaker's earlier suspended sentence was ignored and he ended up with a sentence shorter by one year than those men who had simply gone absent. He began it in Naples' prison.

According to Lord Russell of Liverpool, who claimed to have kept a 'careful record' of the subsequent activities of the mutineers, almost a year after the original trial 75 of them 'had either been convicted by court martial for desertion in the face of the enemy or were actually, at that very moment, in a state of absence without leave'.[9] Thus, of the 185 or so men found guilty of mutiny and detailed to unfamiliar units in Italy, more than 40 per cent decided that deserting or going absent without leave was the only solution to their fears for the future, both real and perceived. Given that all these men were veterans, and that few of them had any previous record of wrongdoing, it seems safe to conclude the the army's attempt to rehabilitate the men after the suspension of their sentences was an unmitigated failure.

While the experience of some who were happily accepted into their new units is evidence that there never was a general conspiracy to do away systematically with the mutineers, a fear of and subjection to discrimination in particular units was the major factor behind the mass desertions. As it turned out, just 13 mutineers were killed in action between December 1943 and the end of the war, including Harry Merrikin, who was serving with his old unit. But this figure does not take account of those permanently disabled, like Herbert Crawford, and it may well have been higher if those men who felt they were being unnecessarily exposed to danger had not gone absent.

Chapter 11

'One of the worst things that we have ever done'

Unaware that the mutineers were absconding from their new units in droves, the British contingent at Allied Force headquarters in Algiers spent the early months of 1944 trying to put a lid on the whole Salerno 'affair'. On 15 February, General Sir Henry Maitland Wilson – Eisenhower's recent British replacement as Supreme Commander, Mediterranean Theatre – turned down a supplementary petition against sentence on behalf of the men convicted in both trials. 'I can find no reason which would justify interference with the sentences as confirmed and promulgated,' Wilson wrote. 'The petitions fail. Future action regarding the sentences depends in each case upon the subsequent behaviour of the individual men concerned in action and elsewhere.'[1]

Like General Gale before him (now back in Britain with Eisenhower, preparing for the Normandy landings), Wilson was heavily influenced by his chief legal officer, Lord Russell of Liverpool. On 22 December 1943, Russell had penned a memorandum containing his advice on what to do about the new petition. 'You will probably consider that there are no grounds for further consideration of the sentences at this stage,' he wrote, 'but that any further remission or commutation should be considered ... in the light of the conduct in action of each individual soldier.'

To support this advice, Russell pointed out that the petitioners had erroneously claimed that when they were ordered to join 46th Division they were not told 'that the military situation was in any way serious'. In fact, he wrote, it was clear from a statement given to the prosecution by Major Ellison, the DAAG of X Corps, 'that the urgency for reinforcements was made known to all the men who were addressed by the corps commander'. This statement was not used as evidence during the trial, Russell wrote, because there was no documentary proof – such as a roll-call – that could have proved the attendance at the speech of all the accused. 'However,' he continued, 'it would not be improper for a superior military authority reviewing these statements to take into consideration the terms of the corps commander's address if satisfied that the petitioners must have been present on that parade.'[2]

Attached to Russell's note was a copy of Major Ellison's statement listing the main points of General McCreery's address of 19 September. McCreery had 'pointed out that the campaign had been so far very hard for the infantry in the line, and that it had been operationally necessary to ask for reinforcements urgently', Ellison wrote.[3] The fact that these words could have been correctly interpreted by the reinforcements to mean that they had been, but were no longer, urgently needed, was not appreciated by either Russell or Wilson. The sentences had been suspended and any further remission would depend on future performance. Of course, many had already gone absent by this date and, in the circumstances, the likelihood was that the authorities would see this as both confirmation of their 'bad' character and justification for the original convictions.

Not everyone in a position of authority, though, was working against the mutineers. Early in 1944, soon after rejoining his unit in Britain, Captain Samwell wrote to Major General Douglas Wimberley, the former commander of the Highland Division, in an attempt to enlist his help on behalf of the mutineers. Years later, in his memoirs, Wimberley wrote of Samwell's initial contact:

> Owing to his court martial oath of secrecy, he was unable to tell me about the actual incidents which led to the men being court martialled, but it seemed they had been suddenly landed at Salerno, in Italy, in the previous September to act as urgently-needed reinforcements for other divisions. In his letter to me he wrote – 'These men acted from a perhaps distorted, but none the less completely genuine motive of loyalty to their division.' He also pointed out to me, with truth, that I had often told the officers and men of the 51st when in North Africa, that if wounded etc and sent to the base, they should not allow themselves to get drafted to other divisions, but should see that they came back to us. It appeared that a number of them had asked Samwell to ensure that I was told, at home, what had happened to them, so that I could try and help them in their troubles.[4]

Feeling in some way responsible for what had happened, Wimberley immediately began using his contacts in the War Office to make enquiries. But, as he later admitted, he 'found it an extremely difficult matter to get the true facts, as being wartime, the whole affair was hushed up by the military authorities'. Furthermore, he had not even been with the Highland Division when the incident happened and was in 'no strong position ... to obtain any information'; the official line was that it was none of his concern. Gradually, however, by unofficially approaching officers and men of the Highland Division, and using other private sources, he built up a remarkably accurate picture of what had happened. He later wrote:

It appeared that nearly one hundred of our men, on leaving various base and transit camps in Africa, by sea for Sicily and Italy, had applied, and understood that they were being sent back to us, in Sicily, about Messina. Then they were suddenly switched to Salerno, some 200 miles up the west coast of Italy, where a landing had recently been effected by the 10th [*sic*] Corps. On arrival they were at once told that they were urgently required to provide battle reinforcements for various British regiments, who were, at this time, fighting hard near the beaches. As regards our ex-Highland Division soldiers, the men of one Highland Regiment had, luckily, one of their own regimental officers with them, whom they knew. He spoke to them and explained matters, and in the case of that regiment all was well. The Jocks of the other Highland regiments had, it seemed, none of their own known officers with them. They were harangued by various strange officers, and even, I believe, by the corps commander himself. They remained, however, stubborn and mulish that they only wished to get back to their own divisions, as 'Jocks' and 'Geordies' certainly become, when they think they have been mishandled and let down. No doubt, they had among them, some real 'bad hats', as were to be found in wartime in every regiment and division, but a lot of them, I soon discovered, had been excellent soldiers, who had fought with us in many battles, had been wounded in action, and some of them had, when with us, been decorated for gallantry in battle.[5]

By July 1944, Wimberley had collected a good many hearsay accounts, including one from a Highland officer he knew well who told him, he later wrote, about the 'specific case of a good soldier' he had interviewed. Although not named in Wimberley's memoirs, this officer must have been on the defence team because, having returned to Britain, no other divisional officers would have had an opportunity to speak to the mutineers. The most likely candidate is Captain John Mitchell, a brigade staff officer who would have had frequent contact with General Wimberley when he was commanding the division. It follows from this that the soldier was one of Mitchell's defendants, probably Hugh Fraser, who was highly thought of within his battalion. Certainly, Wimberley's record of the account given to him fits exactly with Fraser's own recollection:

> This particular soldier had been told, it seemed, at a transit camp in Africa, that he was being sent back to the Highland Division, and, instead, he was suddenly and unexpectedly landed on a Salerno beach and told he was to join an English regiment . . . in a strange division, in action.[6]

While Wimberley was trying to piece together a case that might force the War Office to act in favour of the mutineers, General Montgomery, their former army commander – then in London in charge of the 21st

Army Group due to land in Normandy – took it upon himself to tell his side of the story. On 10 April 1944, Montgomery wrote to General Sir Ronald Adam, the adjutant general. Unaware of Adam's earlier involvement in the case, Montgomery had chosen him because he was the army's senior administrative officer and a good friend. Addressing Adam by his nickname of 'Bill', Montgomery wrote:

My Dear Bill

I think you should know certain facts about the Courts Martial that took place over the refusal of men of 50 Div and 51 Div to serve in other Divisions in Italy. Of these, the case of Private J T Petitt [*sic*] has been represented officially from here.

2. As far as I know the basic features of the case are as follows:

(a) Reinforcements were urgently required for British Divisions in the 5th Army on the Naples front.
(b) Charles Miller could not find enough men from their own reinforcements, so he ordered up certain men of the Eighth Army from my depots in Tripoli.
(c) Before taking action as in (b) he did not consult me, nor did he consult Alexander. If I had known what was to be done I would have said 'No'. Alexander would also have said 'No'; I am sure of this as we discussed it together afterwards.

3. You know well what happened. The men refused to go into battle, which is of course quite inexcusable – and cannot be condoned.

4. But when soldiers get into trouble it is nearly always the fault of some officer who failed in his duty. The real culprit in this case is Charles Miller, now MGA, Southern Command.

5. I know Charles well; he was a dismal failure in Africa and in Italy, and in my opinion is unfit to be a Major-General i/c Administration. He is quite unable to face up to a big problem; he tries to bypass it, and leaves it unsolved; in the end, the resulting confusion is appalling, and was so in Italy. However, all this is not my business, but I thought you might like to know my views.[7]

Four days later, Adam replied, explaining his own involvement and expressing his surprise that most of the blame lay at Miller's door:

My Dear Monty

Your letter of 10th ... I was in on this case and incidentally dealt with it when I was over in North Africa. I think it is one of the worst things that we have ever done. I did not know, however, that Charles Miller was the chief culprit. I am afraid I had put a good deal of the blame on Alex and his having no proper administrative staff to deal with these matters. In actual fact, on enquiry, I find that the men had arrived after the crisis was already over and I arranged with AFHQ that all sentences should be suspended.

I have not yet seen the case of Pettit, but will go into it.[8]

As his letter makes clear, Adam had suspected all along that the sending of Eighth Army veterans to reinforce Fifth Army units at Salerno was an administrative cock-up. But Montgomery's assertion that General Miller had taken such action without consulting Alexander who, if he (and Montgomery for that matter) had known, would have stopped him, was a revelation. The most celebrated general in the British army had stated that, although their actions could not be excused, the men at Salerno had got into 'trouble' because an officer, Miller, had 'failed in his duty'. If Adam had been sympathetic to the plight of the mutineers in November, he was even more so now that the identity of the 'culprit' was clear in his mind.

By late summer 1944, confident that he had gathered most of the facts, Wimberley wrote to General Oliver Leese – Montgomery's successor as commander of the Eighth Army. As well as giving a lengthy account of the mutiny and its aftermath, Wimberley stated that the case was very much on his conscience and asked Leese to find out what had happened to as many men as possible. At around the same time Wimberley went to see Sir Ronald Adam at the War Office and, unaware of Adam's earlier involvement or Montgomery's recent intervention, was surprised to be given a 'very sympathetic hearing'. Anxious to exploit Adam's interest, Wimberley quickly followed up his visit with a letter, saying that while 'there were probably "bad hat" ringleaders mixed up in the affair', the majority were motivated by mistaken loyalty. He continued:

> All my information is to the effect that plenty of the men concerned were first-class material, who have suffered chiefly owing to their breeding and their upbringing, and by being true to what was, in their mistaken opinion, a course of action which they considered was loyalty to their pals, their old officers, and their old Division. I feel a big responsibility towards these men of the 51st, as their old Commander, and I should be most grateful if you could now see your way to check up where all the men under suspended sentence are now serving. And in the case of those who have done their duty properly, ever since the trial, consider now the annulment of their sentences.[9]

Six weeks later, in October 1944, Adam replied. His branch had taken over the case and was in the process of tracking down all the men concerned so that each case could be 'individually reviewed', he wrote. Wimberley had played his part, but his indefatigable effort to see justice done was now over. He later wrote:

> There was nothing more, unfortunately, that I could do to help my old comrades but the words written me, about that time, by that fine old regimental soldier, General 'Wiggie' Thomson, Colonel of the Seaforth Highlanders, remain with me to this day, when he wrote me, and with complete justice – 'You are sad about it, as I don't wonder. The very spirit which led them to such heights, has been the downfall of these men. They look to you to mitigate the results. Something worse than a blunder, a crime was committed in North Africa which, from your information, high-placed officers in Italy could not assuage.'[10]

A veteran of the Sudan campaign of 1898 and a former CO of the 1st Seaforths who had risen to command a division in the First World War before his 40th birthday, Lieutenant General Sir William 'Wiggie' Thomson was well qualified to make such a judgment. For such a celebrated soldier to describe the treatment of the men as nothing short of criminal is indicative of the strength of feeling to which the case gave rise among serving and ex-Highland Division officers.

Disturbing news soon reached Adam that many of the mutineers had deserted or gone absent from their new units, and on recapture had had their suspended sentences reimposed. Furthermore, in deference to General Alexander's original request – that the first two years of any sentence be served in the theatre – many were languishing in prisons in North Africa while only a handful, including John McFarlane, had been returned to Britain.

Adam had hoped to be able to quash the original suspended sentences on the grounds of continued good service. But while this criterion was fine for those who had remained with their new units, it would not suffice for those who had not. If these new offenders were to be given remission, it would be necessary to show that the motives behind the original disobedience were genuine if misguided, that the maltreatment of the men did not end with the court martial, and that, in this way, the absences were linked to the original sentences. To find out one way or the other, Adam decided to arrange for an army psychiatrist to interview each man separately about his thoughts and motives before and after conviction. But first all the men had to be brought back to prisons in Britain.

It was mid-November 1944 when Archie Newmarch received word at 50th Military Prison in Egypt that he and the other mutineers were going home. For him it was not a moment too soon. Malnourished by a poor diet, ravaged by relapses of malaria, bullied by the guards and tortured by the unfairness of his predicament, he was a shadow of his former self, on the verge of a mental breakdown. One incident shortly before he left amply illustrates what he was up against. Reported by a guard for talking on parade when he was neither talking nor on parade, Newmarch was taken before the prison governor. Scanning his record and noticing his conviction for mutiny, the governor asked what he would do if he could relive that part of his life again. 'I'd do exactly the same again, sir', Newmarch replied. Almost speechless with anger, the governor called him a 'bloody bolshie' and ordered him to be taken away. For this 'offence' he was given two days' punishment diet, consisting of 48 hours in solitary confinement with six ounces of dried bread and a cup of water twice a day.

By early December, most of the mutineers who had absconded were in British prisons: Archie Newmarch, Charlie Smith and Percy Aveyard were among a group in Walton, Liverpool; Fred Jowett, 'Cushy' Mills and Edwin Scott were part of another in Barlinnie, Glasgow; John McFarlane and Ray Whitaker were in Perth and Durham respectively.

Once reunited with their families, the mutineers were shocked to discover that they were not the only ones who had suffered for their stand. From the date his suspended sentence was reactivated, John McFarlane's wife was notified that she would have to return her army allowance book which represented her share of her husband's pay. With two young girls under five to care for, she was destitute. There was no welfare state as such then, and Maureen McFarlane was forced to accept emergency relief of £1 12/- a week from the local council, all of which had later to be repaid. As she later recalled, it was 'grim' trying to bring up a young family on such meagre money. McFarlane was more explicit when he later spoke of this:

> That was the thanks I got from the British Army. I never even got the Welcome Home fund, I never got no medals, campaign medals, which I didn't worry about, I still don't worry about . . . But the persecution of my family was the worst, the worst. Talk about Germans and Jews, we did it; only we did it underhand. They persecuted innocent people the same as the Germans did, only the Germans did it openly. We didne . . . They made a wife and two kids suffer for my doing. And I still say they can shoot me yet. It broke me.[11]

Other families were in the same boat. Where a mutineer had a wife and children, like McFarlane, life was particularly hard. But many parents also relied on a voluntary allowance from their sons' pay and they too were affected. Percy Aveyard's mother was one, and her suffering was not solely financial. After writing to her from Walton, Aveyard was aghast to receive a reply saying that he could not be her son because he had been dead for over a year. Later, his filial credentials re-established, he discovered that the army had written to her on 28 August 1943, stating that he had died from wounds received in Sicily![12] As a consequence, she was asked to return her allowance book comprising seven shillings a week of her son's pay. Aveyard had written home earlier that year from the 50th Military Prison in Egypt but for some reason the letters never arrived. For almost 15 months his heartbroken mother had assumed that he was dead. It is hardly surprising that her initial reaction to a letter from 'beyond the grave' was one of disbelief. But for the mutiny, Aveyard would have been in a position to put the record straight much sooner.

The army psychiatrist chosen by the Sir Ronald Adam to conduct the psychological investigation of the men was Lieutenant Colonel Thomas Main of the Royal Army Medical Corps. Born in South Africa in 1911, the son of a ship's carpenter from Newcastle upon Tyne who had gone out to the then British colony to find work, Main was just three when his father went to war and his mother returned with him to England. The beneficiary of the best education Newcastle could offer – the Royal Grammar School followed by the university – Main qualified as a doctor in the mid-1930s and began to specialise in psychiatry. By 1939, when he was called up for wartime service, he was working at the Gateshead Mental Hospital and, logically, was posted to the Psychiatric Department of the RAMC.

During the previous war, the army had not recognised that desertion, refusal to obey orders and a myriad of other capital military offences were often committed by men suffering from 'shell-shock' and other combat-related nervous disorders. All this changed in the inter-war years when the Army Psychiatric Department was formed and the death penalty was repealed for all offences bar mutiny and treachery. Main was one of this new breed of specialist army medical officers whose job it was to identify and alleviate the psychological pressures of war.

Given a general outline of the events at Salerno, Main was asked to produce a report outlining the 'operative moods' within the group both before and after the mutiny. By investigating the 'emotional events' that caused the men to disobey orders and led to many having their sentences reimposed, he hoped to be able to make a general evaluation about their motives.

Throughout December Main traipsed from one prison to the next, privately interviewing each mutineer for about half an hour. A tall, strikingly-handsome man with prematurely grey hair that only added to his signal appearance, Main was not a figure his subjects would easily forget. Nor, indeed, would they forget the content of his interviews. Already interested in psycho- or Freudian analysis (he would practise it after the war), he used its 'dream interpretation' technique to assist his enquiry. Archie Newmarch's experience was typical:

> One evening after 'lock-up' I was taken without explanation to a small office. Inside was a distinguished-looking guy, sitting behind a large desk. For a while he continued to write. When he did look up he didn't explain who he was, he just started asking questions. At first they seemed pointless. Then he moved on to my personal war experiences. 'Do you dream about the war?' 'Yes.' 'Bad dreams?' 'Yes.' 'Are you in action?' 'Yes I am.' 'Are you in attack or in defence?' At this I began to laugh. But the questions continued: 'Do you have any phobias or tendencies?' 'Do you have any ill effects or headaches?' Then he moved on to the mutiny, asking me questions about before, during and after the court martial, allowing me to give my own personal account. He finished by asking whether I thought the court martial was fair and whether if I could relive that part of my life I would do things differently. To the first I answered: 'It was all cut and dried before we went in.' To the second: 'I'd do exactly the same again.'

On 9 January 1945, Colonel Main submitted his report – entitled *General Matters in the Salerno Mutiny* – to Sir Ronald Adam. In the preface he described it as a 'general statement on the emotional events which preceded the mutiny, and which subsequently led to certain men having sentence reimposed'. Nevertheless, Main continued, the statement had to be accepted with caution because it was not easy to build up a 'general picture of the operative moods within a group' from 'individual medical interviews' where only 'subjective information is gained'.

Notwithstanding this qualification, Main's evaluation of the information he received was wholeheartedly in favour of the men. Over six pages of typed foolscap, he charted the emotional events before and after the mutiny. Five extracts, plucked from various parts of the text, suitably summarise the report:

> The draft which set out from Tripoli was firm in the belief that it was formed to reinforce the 50th and 51st Divisions. The RSM [*sic*] at 155 Transit Camp had told many so at a parade the previous evening, and had sent runners round the camp in the early morning telling late arrivals that any man who wanted to join the 50th or 51st Divisions should join the draft . . .
>
> [The] draft consisted mainly of men willing or glad to face whatever the future might hold for them in these divisions . . .

[Those] with the highest divisional morale and a combative family spirit grouped themselves together in the decision to refuse all divisions but their own. They believed at the time that their actions were soldierly and that they were content to wait, in the belief that a senior official would sooner or later support them . . .

The verdict of guilty was felt to be as unjust as their defending officers had suggested in their final speeches. The sentences were read out on a parade and then immediately suspended and it seemed to them for a moment that the 'authorities' had, after all, backed them against incompetent transit officers. But these feelings were short-lived for they were immediately given a speech about what suspension meant, with warnings for the future, and were told that they were going to the Eighth Army as a chance to retrieve their honour! This speech dashed their hopes . . . They recalled that 'the least thing' they did in the future would immediately mean seven years' penal servitude. Few understood that full reinstatement would be possible and some believed that a 'suspension' meant only postponement . . .

The plans for rehabilitation of the men after the first sentence was suspended were not wholly successful; the opportunity to restore and stimulate morale was not taken, and this led to a rapid failure of discipline.[13]

Given the scale of desertion and absenteeism that followed the suspension of sentences, it could be argued that this last comment, which served as Main's sole conclusion, was something of an understatement. Certainly, Robert Ahrenfeldt, a fellow army psychiatrist and author of *Psychiatry in the British Army in the Second World War*, thought so. After paraphrasing Main's report, he gave his own conclusions:

In fact, it may be said that the whole of this pitiful incident was a tragedy of errors. In the first place, the men were misled from the very beginning; secondly, there was a complete absence of clear direction, precise information, or firm leadership, throughout; thirdly, there was a total disregard (whether avoidable or not) of well-established group loyalties in experienced fighting men of previously high morale; and finally, when the trouble was well under way, the men were further demoralised – it would seem almost beyond repair – by the humiliation and degradation they suffered; it should not be forgotten that these experienced British soldiers, who together had been through previous battles and campaigns, were subjected to ridicule by German prisoners of war, and to the contempt of their comrades in arms. Incidentally, in this instance as on other occasions, the absence may be noted of any effective procedure to enable men to express collective grievances. The effect of these serious errors in man-management and leadership was a gradual disintegration first of group morale, and then of individual morale. The consequences

of ignoring certain basic principles essential to morale proved disastrous.[14]

While Main's view of the events surrounding the mutiny was not quite
as forthright as Ahrenfeldt's later interpretation, it did absolve the men
of any 'treacherous' motive and blamed their subsequent re-offending
on the army's failure to 'restore and stimulate' their 'morale'. This was
enough to convince Adam that those still held deserved to be released
early and those who had remained with their new units deserved to have
their suspended sentences remitted.

With the war nearing its conclusion, though, the War Office decided
to wait before acting on Adam's recommendations. The intention was
to suspend the sentences a second time on the condition that the
prisoners made up for the army service they had missed while behind
bars. Yet to do this during wartime was considered to be courting more
trouble.

As the prisoners sat out the remainder of the war amid rumours of
their imminent release, an outbreak of publicity about the mutiny in
April 1945 ensured that the issue remained high on the political
agenda. First, on 17 April, questions were asked in the House of
Commons by John McGovern, the Independent Labour MP for
Shettleston, who had been alerted to the plight of the mutineers by
'Cushy' Mills's uncle, one of his constituents. Would the Secretary of
State for War, Sir James Grigg, 'state the cause of the mutiny', he asked,
and could he say whether he had 'reduced the sentences' of those
involved?

Part of Grigg's written reply was both inaccurate and incomplete:

> A party of reinforcements refused to join the units to which they had been
> ordered. It was impossible at the height of battle, which was at its most
> critical stage, to send them to their own specific units or normal
> formations, and the men concerned refused to obey orders to join the
> other units where they were most urgently needed. Except in two cases ...
> the sentences were suspended immediately or within a few weeks in all
> cases and the soldiers were despatched to Eighth Army units as reinforce-
> ments.[15]

In fact, as already noted, the battle was not even 'at its most critical
stage' when the men arrived on 16 September, let alone when the
mutiny occurred four days later. If it had been, it would not have taken
two full days before any men were detailed to join front-line units. Some,
it appears, did not receive a firm order to move until the parade on 20
September. The truth is that the worst stage of the battle was over by 16

September, making it possible for the matter to have been thoroughly investigated and the men returned to their 'own specific units'. Adam confirmed this in his letter to Montgomery of 14 April 1944, when he stated that 'the men had arrived after the crisis was already over'.

In addition, while correctly stating that the sentences had been suspended, Grigg failed to mention that a large number had since deserted or gone absent from their new Eighth Army units, had had their sentences reimposed and were being held in British prisons.

Inevitably, the exchange was reported in the national newspapers and read by many of the relatives, including Edith Newmarch, Archie's mother. She immediately wrote to McGovern, who used the opportunity of the annual debate on the Army Act on 20 April to read out the letter to the House:

> Thank God someone has taken this case up. The reply by Sir James Grigg is a deliberate lie. The men have been in prison the whole time and are still there.
>
> All these men were recovering from sickness, some not fully recovered, including my son, suffering from malaria, and Private Merrikin of Hull, who was so ill he had to be carried back to hospital on a stretcher.
>
> They were told they were to join their unit and on disembarking at Salerno they were ordered to join a different unit altogether.
>
> They were ordered to pick up their kit and join the 46th Division. The men did not move and the order was repeated. My son was sent to Liverpool prison last November after being in prison in Africa and has now been moved to Wormwood Scrubs . . .
>
> They are decent brave lads who would have fought anywhere with their old unit. My son's name is Archie Newmarch.[16]

Reacting to the letter, Arthur Henderson, Financial Secretary to the War Office, told the House that McGovern did a disservice to the relatives of the men by raising the question and by giving particulars which were not completely accurate.[17] On the second matter he had a point. Contrary to what she had written, Mrs Newmarch was perfectly aware that her son had not 'been in prison the whole time' and that, instead, his sentence had been suspended but later reimposed because he had gone absent from his new unit. Sir James Grigg had stated this in a letter to Lieutenant Commander Braithwaite, Mrs Newmarch's MP, the previous July and he had forwarded the letter to her.[18] On the other hand, Grigg had not admitted to the House that many of the mutineers were in prison, and she may have been referring to this when she accused him of lying.

Henderson continued his reply by admitting that 'a proportion of those released on suspended sentences committed a second offence'.

They were subsequently tried, he said, 'not on the old charge, but the new charge – absence without leave or whatever it was – and court martialled, convicted and sentenced to whatever period of imprisonment was applicable to their case'.

Once again, the official explanation was inaccurate and misleading. Apart from Whitaker and possibly one or two others, the men who went absent or deserted were not tried a second time. Instead, their original mutiny sentences were reactivated. Either Henderson was not aware of this or, more likely, the War Office was unwilling to admit the truth because it would have directly linked the ongoing prison terms to the original conviction and so bolstered the arguments for early release. When McGovern then asked why the information about a second offence had not been given to the parents, Henderson replied that the less publicity the better from the parents' point of view. However, the cases of those men who had committed a second offence were being reviewed by Sir James Grigg, he said.[19]

If the War Office had been having second thoughts about the early release of the mutineers, this exchange indicated that any failure to act would almost certainly lead to an unwelcome renewal of debate within Parliament and the media. Consequently, when the war in Europe ended on 7 May, the War Office began making arrangements to free those still held. One condition was attached: the men would have to agree to a period of extended service in the army based on both their time spent in prison and their date of mobilisation. Not surprisingly, almost all the prisoners agreed to these terms and during the summer and autumn of 1945, the exact day depending on their period of absence and their behaviour in prison, most were released.

One of the first was Archie Newmarch. On 24 June 1945 he was 'tarring' out the latrines in Wormwood Scrubs when he was told that, after more than 18 months behind bars, he was to be freed. Escorted by a sergeant from the Green Howards, the regiment he should have joined in Italy, Newmarch was taken to a holding battalion in Bridlington, East Yorkshire, where he was delighted to find his old mates Fred Jowett and Charlie Smith. The former had been released from Barlinnie, the latter from Camphill on the Isle of Wight. Two days later, after being medically classified A1, kitted out, inoculated and vaccinated, they were told by the commanding officer that they were being sent back to their old unit, the East Yorkshires, and would serve an extended military service of between 19 and 28 months. By the beginning of November all three were overseas: Newmarch with the 30th Northumberland Fusiliers in Malta; Jowett with the 2nd East Yorkshires in Palestine; Smith with the 1st East Yorkshires in India.

Ten months later, back in Britain on leave, Newmarch collapsed. A mental and physical wreck, he was admitted to Northfields – the army psychiatry hospital in Birmingham. After five months' treatment he was discharged from both the hospital and the army, mentally much improved but physically well below minimum requirements with the lowest possible grading of C3. Fred Jowett saw out his army service in Palestine and was finally discharged in October 1947, after an extra 27 months' service. Because he had been in the reserved occupation of agriculture before the war, Charlie Smith came back from India in August 1946 and was discharged two months later.

Another released from prison in June 1945 was John McFarlane, MM, but he never was reunited with his beloved Durham Light Infantry. Instead he was posted to a transit camp in Stranraer and there served out the remainder of his military service as a member of the police staff!

Percy Aveyard got out around the same time but was returned to his original regiment. Sent to Singapore with the 2nd DLI in January 1946, he was finally demobilised in October of that year with the rank of corporal.

When 'Cushy' Mills was released towards the back end of 1945, he was immediately returned to the battalion he had first joined in 1931 as an 18-year-old – the 2nd Seaforths. With it he completed his 22 years of regular service.

Not freed until Christmas 1945, Edwin Scott was sent to a holding battalion at Bedlington, Northumberland. Luckily, he knew the regimental sergeant major there from before the war, and with this warrant officer's protection he was able to avoid foreign service until demobilisation in August 1946.

Ray Whitaker, in prison in Durham, was also offered early release around this time. To qualify, he was told, he would have to agree to join the Pioneer Corps and serve abroad building roads. He refused:

> I had had enough of the army and its discipline. I didn't feel I could buckle down to it. Anyway, it wouldn't have been easy joining a new unit with all the charges I had against my name. So I decided to stay put. I finally got out in October 1947, after serving three years of my six year sentence.

Chapter 12

The human cost

While none of those involved in the Salerno mutiny lost their lives as a direct result of their convictions, most suffered immense psychological damage. The hardest hit were those who felt driven to re-offend by the treatment they had received in their new units, preferring lengthy terms in prison to their status as military pariahs.

Archie Newmarch is a prime example. An idealistic youth who went away to war believing in the slogans of democracy, peace and justice, he left the army a bitter and confused man, family loyalty his one remaining value. Even the campaign medals relating to the action he had seen before the mutiny – the 1939–45 Star and the Africa Star with 'Eighth Army' clasp – were denied him. *King's Regulations* at the time stated that any medals forfeited as a result of conviction for mutiny could only be considered for restoration if 'a minimum of three years' service has been rendered subsequent to release ... provided that no offence has been committed during such service as would normally disqualify the individual from the award of an "Exemplary" character on discharge' or 'when the individual is promoted to sergeant or higher rank'.[1] As Newmarch's character assessment on discharge was only 'Fair', on account of his absence in Italy, and his rank was only lance corporal, he did not qualify. Instead, he received just the Italy Star, for his brief service after the mutiny, and the ubiquitous War Medal. Such erasing of official recognition for services rendered before the mutiny seems spiteful and continues to be a bitter bone of contention for Newmarch and others.

When released from the army psychiatric hospital in February 1947, Newmarch was two stones under weight, listless and suffering from a nervous disorder that manifested itself in hypochondria, depression and aversion to company. While, over the years, these physical and mental afflictions eased, his preoccupation with the perceived injustice did not. In his opinion, this obsession with clearing his name 'rankled and festered like a growing cancer' and indirectly caused the break-up of his marriage.

In 1959, Newmarch was one of a number of mutineers interviewed by George Pollock of the now-defunct *Reynold's News* for a series of articles that told, for the first time, the version of events in the words of the participants. In 1966 he and others formally petitioned the Queen for a pardon from the conviction for mutiny. It was forwarded to the Ministry of Defence and inevitably turned down. In 1982 he took part in a BBC documentary entitled *Mutiny* – screened on 23 February – which strongly supported the stand of the mutineers. A month later, as the campaign to clear the mutineers gathered momentum, three opposition MPs asked John Nott, the Secretary of State for Defence, if he would 'consider recommending a pardon for, and the restoration of medals' to those found guilty of mutiny. Jerry Wiggin, Under-Secretary of State for the Armed Forces, provided a written answer:

> The existing Ministry of Defence records have been researched and there is no evidence that those who were found guilty of mutiny in 1943 by a field general court martial were not fit or were misled about their destination as vital reinforcements for the Salerno campaign. The disciplinary proceedings were reviewed by the Solicitor-General in 1947, who found they had been properly conducted, had fulfilled the requirements of justice, and that the proceedings were legally in order. The review took place well after the war and I do not believe there are any grounds now for reopening the case. Medals forfeited by those found guilty of mutiny can normally only be restored when at least three years of further exemplary or meritorious service has been given.[2]

A week earlier, in a letter to John McFarlane's MP, James Hamilton, Wiggin had made the same point about there being no evidence supporting the mutineers' claim that they were misled:

> There is nothing either in the contemporary proceedings of their trial or in subsequent official records held by this Department to suggest that they set off for Salerno under any illusions whatsoever as to their eventual destination.[3]

* * *

This book, however, contains evidence that proves both that the men *were* misled and that many *were not* fit.

Undeterred by the Ministry of Defence's brusque attempt to close the case once and for all, and physically reinvigorated by a blood transfusion in 1986, Newmarch remains determined to continue his crusade for justice until the end.

Fred Jowett's health, too, was seriously affected by the mutiny and its aftermath. In 1981, aged just 58, he was forced to retire from his factory job at Reckitt and Coleman's with a nervous disability. He recalls:

> I used to shake so much that when I gave someone tea there would only

be half in the cup by the time it got to them; I was always breaking down and crying at work. I went to see a psychiatrist and he attributed it to the mutiny, to the blitzes and to the length of time I spent in solitary confinement.

In 1989, recovered from his shaking, Jowett belatedly applied for his campaign medals. Surprisingly, as well as the Italy Star and the 1939–45 War Medal he was also issued with the Africa Star with Eighth Army clasp that, technically, he was no longer entitled to and which had been denied to Newmarch. Encouraged by this success he again contacted the medal office to ask about the General Service Medal with a 'Palestine 1945–48' clasp. The officer who took his call said that a mistake had been made with the first issue of medals and if he pressed for the Palestine medal he could lose them all. Jowett agreed to let the matter rest, and was surprised to receive the GSM with clasp in the post a few days later!

Charlie Smith went back to working the land, but did not last long. Snubbed by his local authority – which, on hearing about his conviction, had decided not to honour him along with the other war veterans – and taunted by his work colleagues, he was forced to move away from his native Skelbrooke. After years of back-breaking work – first down a pit, then on the motorways – he died in 1986 at the comparatively young age of 64. His wife never forgot his treatment at the hands of former neighbours and, against the wishes of many of his family, insisted that his remains be buried not in Skelbrooke but near their last home in Rose Hill, Lancashire.

Resuming his job as a bricklayer in Ryton, Newcastle-upon-Tyne, Edwin Scott took many years to come to terms with his experience. He shied away from all associations and clubs, unwilling to be under obligation to anyone or anything. His uncle, a freemason, wanted him to join the 'Brotherhood' but he refused. It was just as well. Resentful, he became abrupt and aggressive if ever the mutiny was mentioned. Nightmares about the court martial, and about being in action, persisted for a time. Now he just wants to forget.

Ironically, despite all he had been through, Percy Aveyard could not readjust to civilian life and tried to re-enlist in 1952, aged 28. He was turned down by the Bradford recruitment office without an explanation, on instructions received from the officer in charge of infantry records in York. Despite his excellent service after release with the 2nd Durham Light Infantry in Malaya, which led to his promotion to corporal and caused his brigadier to remit the remainder of his suspended sentence, his conviction for mutiny was still held against him. Later, in 1962, he managed to join the Royal Engineers as a Territorial but was discharged three months later, once again at the insistence of the officer in charge of infantry records.

Wee John McFarlane undoubtedly had to suffer the most petty and unnecessary wrong done to a mutineer in the post-war years when the War Office wrote and demanded the return of his Military Medal. This was not, they later explained, for his mutiny conviction but for his absence while under suspended sentence. Like Newmarch and others he also forfeited the Africa Star with the Eighth Army clasp and the 1939–45 Star, but for him they mattered little. What tortured him was the fact that the War Office had taken away his gallantry award, as if the heroic act which had earned it had never happened. Initially tempted to ignore the demand, he was forced to give in to threats:

> They wrote for it. They told me that I was still on suspended sentence, which I thought was another warning that I could go back into prison if I did not send this medal back, because my sentence actually finished in '51 or '52. They told us that if I got into any trouble during that time at all, I could still be recalled and put back into prison to serve the remainder of my sentence.[4]

Originally a man well-suited to military service, proud of his unit and its achievements, McFarlane retained an undiminished hatred towards the army for the rest of his life. Such was its force that he used to tell his three sons that if they were ever called up he would maim them before letting them serve. He died in 1987, heartbroken by the confiscation of his Military Medal.

Ray Whitaker became, arguably, the most tragic victim of the mutiny. A cocky, likeable rogue who never took kindly to discipline and who was, perhaps, too willing to let his fists do the talking, he earned by his conviction a 'bad boy' reputation that he could not, or would not, throw off. When handled cleverly, as he was by the officers of the 7th Argylls, his qualities of fearlessness and loyalty came to the fore. When handled badly, as he and others were before and after the mutiny, his unruly, dangerous nature took over. Always close to the precipice of wrong-doing, he was pushed over the edge by the perceived injustice of the court martial. Thus, his immersion into serious crime in Italy was a way of showing two fingers to the authorities that had so badly let him down.

Following his release in 1947, Whitaker soon found himself drawn into the world of petty, and later more serious, crime. His own explanation is that he tried to start afresh, but that he was victimised by

the police on account of his mutiny conviction. A more likely explanation is that he retained a righteous indignation against authority and
found it difficult to ignore his brief success as a criminal in Italy. Perhaps
inevitably, given his character, he entered a vicious circle of crime, each
petty offence drawing a disproportionate sentence which only angered
him to re-offend. When I interviewed Whitaker in March 1993 he was,
aged 71, on bail, charged with offences relating to drug smuggling.
Since 1947, he has spent more than 30 years in prison for a variety of
offences. 'Everything that has happened to me since the war is linked
to my conviction for mutiny,' Whitaker insists. It is hard not to agree.

Of all those who were lucky enough, or determined enough, to see
out the war with new units in Italy, Hugh Fraser was one of the most
successful in refusing to allow his conviction to destroy his life. Although
completely rehabilitated within the army by 1946, evident in his glowing
reference, he still had practical reasons to be bitter. His wartime
gratuity, which should have related to his service from 1939–46 and
would have been a substantial amount, was instead only based on his
service since the mutiny. In the same way, while those who had been
called up with him in 1939 were demobilised in 1945, he missed a
number of demob groups and had to wait another year. But he did not
let this get him down and, after a brief return to his pre-war occupation
as a swimming instructor, he applied to join the police force. Subcon-
ciously, perhaps, he was determined to remain on the right side of the
law. Fraser recalls the last hurdle before he was accepted:

> I had an interview with the chief constable in Aberdeen, and felt obliged
> to tell him that I had been in some form of trouble before – namely
> convicted for mutiny and a spell in prison. He just smiled and said: 'Don't
> do it again.' There is no rhyme or reason about this. He could easily have
> seen this as a reason to reject my application. One of the jobs I had as a
> policeman was to vet the new applicants. I had to submit reports saying
> that some weren't acceptable because of some very minor indiscre-
> pancies. They were very strict then, and many were turned down. And yet,
> there was me, a convicted mutineer, and I was accepted. There's no logic
> in that.

Fraser spent 29 years with the Aberdeen police, receiving a long-
service medal after 25 years and retiring with the rank of inspector. He
had come a long way. Still convinced about the rightness of his stand at
Salerno, he has just one regret:

> Given the same circumstances, I would do the same again. It was purely
> and simply a matter of principle; I'm not being boastful, but I've always

had strong principles. I feel no shame or stigma about what I did. The conviction didn't affect me one way or the other; I just got on with my life. I'm not interested in pardons, but what I would like to see, more than anything, is for John McFarlane's Military Medal to be returned to his wife. It is a sin to take back a gallantry medal after it has been awarded. It broke his heart, and the hearts of his wife and family.

Wally Innes, like McFarlane, died before achieving his life's ambition – in his case a free pardon. Despite being demobilised in March 1946 with a 'very good' military conduct assessment, he never received his campaign medals. The awful experience of Death Row, and the knowledge that many saw his stand at Salerno as cowardice, turned this previously happy-go-lucky man into a moody, inward-looking soul, willing to fight anyone who questioned his personal integrity. His second wife, Hannah, recalls:

> Many times he told me about being on Death Row, waiting to be shot, and I wondered how he survived it. He was always upset when he talked about it. He did this a lot after he got ill. All he wanted was his name cleared; that's all he lived for. He couldn't let it go. My daughter used to say, 'Mam, Wally's gone through, just leave him.' We just left him to get on with it.

Yet, despite his bitterness, Innes did not recoil like so many others from all contact with his military past. In 1982 he was given a Gold Award for 25 years' meritorious service to the British Legion in his home town of Birtley, Newcastle-upon-Tyne. Also in that year, following the screening of the BBC documentary *Mutiny*, he appeared live on *Newsnight* with William Harris, QC, one of the five men who had sentenced him to death. It was one of the most dramatic confrontations in the history of television. After the introductions, Peter Snow, the presenter, went straight to the heart of the matter. 'Do you stand by the verdict and the sentence you handed down 39 years ago?' he asked Harris.

'Undoubtedly,' came the confident reply. 'I would like to say, Mr Snow, this is a very traumatic evening for me – and I'm sure it is for you,' he added, nodding towards Innes. 'But I would like to say, here and now, you can well imagine the appalling stress this was, the agonising decision that was placed upon us. It was our duty to take all the evidence and decide was it mutiny or was it not. And we decided it was.'

'Can I just get this clear,' Snow replied. 'You're saying that you believe that Mr Innes, sitting here, should have been shot 39 years ago?'

'I do.' said Harris.

Innes, unable to contain his anger and contempt, loudly interrupted:

'Well let me tell you something. I was at Dunkirk, come all the way from Dunkirk. And I was at the desert when we were surrounded. I was there at Mersa Metruh when Makinshaw got his VC. I was two years in the desert, I didn't just come up when the Coldstream Guards came up, I was there when you came up. And we travelled right from Alamein right to the top of Algiers, over to Sicily, half way through Sicily, Primosole Bridge where we lost 500 men out of three battalions . . .'

'It's absolutely ghastly,' Harris muttered.

Undeterred by the interruption, Innes continued: 'And then we've got to be humiliated by . . . Well, you say you weren't no armchair soldier but the rest of them were. If I had any relations to go through that, my advice would be: "If you get prosecuted, make sure that them buggers have been in the front line, because if they haven't been down your pit they don't known what a pit's like. And it's the same at the front line."'

Embarrassed by this emotional outburst, Harris tried to mollify Innes: 'First of all may I just say . . .'

'Excuse me for losing my head, like,' Innes interrupted.

'No, no. You're perfectly entitled to do that. Of course I know the wonderful reputation that those two divisions had in which you were. Marvellous, absolutely marvellous. Alas, it was my job, with the officers, to say: "Was this mutiny?" Now as you know well, as an old soldier, mutiny really is something . . .'

'It's a dirty word,' Innes retorted.

'A dirty word,' Harris agreed. 'Now if we made up our minds on the evidence, as we did, that it was mutiny, there is really only one answer, at least that's what the court said and I agree with it. Because we must maintain absolute discipline in an army, and once any soldiers – officers or men – feel they can get away with it, the rot sets in.'

'But would you not accept that there were, in this particular case, the most extraordinary mitigating circumstances, as we've seen described in this story?' Snow interjected.

'Maybe mitigating. The fact remains that there was a mutiny.'

Switching interviewees, Snow asked: 'Can I be clear, Mr Innes, is it not a fact that what you did was, whether you like it or not, technically mutiny and there was very little that the judges could do?'

Innes replied: 'We were tricked into a mutiny. We were told we were going back to our own units. Had our own units been there . . .'

Snow interrupted with another question: 'Was what you call a trick sufficient reason for you to have been let off that charge, pardoned of that charge?'

'Well I couldn't say. I mean a man sentenced to death, commuted to 12 years' penal servitude and suspended all within 11 weeks. It was a mockery to authority, it was a mockery to them fellas,' Innes responded, pointing at Harris.

Asked by Snow what he would like to see happen now, Innes replied: 'I'd like to see that little box, with the official statement in, open to the public. Let them see, let them judge. We've put our cards on the table. Let them put their cards on the table. I'll tell you something else I'd like to see: half of these soldiers didn't get their medals; they fought and they didn't get their medals. Biggest disgrace. McFarlane, MM, hero one minute, coward the next.'

Snow's last question was to Harris: 'With the benefit of hindsight, do you think these men should be pardoned?'

'I fear not,' was Harris's predictable reply. 'I must stand by the ruling of the court which I thought then was right, and if it happened today I'm afraid I would say exactly the same thing.'[5]

Sadly, Innes died in July 1989, four years before the Ministry of Defence saw fit to grant his wish and release the court martial papers relating to the Salerno mutiny. These documents – published for the first time in this book – represent the last realistic hope for a free pardon. For most of the mutineers it is already too late.

Chapter 13

A pardonable offence

The conviction of 186 men – and the sentencing of three of them to death – for mutiny at the Salerno beachhead in 1943 ranks as one of the greatest iniquities in the history of British military justice.

The iniquity is evident in the trial, where the defence was forced by lack of time, lack of co-operation by potential witnesses and the opposition of the court to a lengthy adjournment, to offer a case based not on evidence but on a legal technicality. Given the hostility of the deputy judge advocate, the legal adviser to the court, it was doomed to failure.

But, perhaps more importantly, the iniquity is evident in the events that both preceded and, to a lesser extent, succeeded the trial. In particular, it is evident in the scandalous decision to charge veterans with mostly spotless combat and disciplinary records with so serious an offence when the mitigating circumstances were so strong and when their actions could not have been further from the accepted definition of mutiny – open revolt against established authority.

As already noted, the efforts to organise 1,500 emergency reinforcements for Salerno on 14 September 1943 were an unco-ordinated muddle. Initially, General Alexander's 15th Army Group headquarters informed General Clark at Salerno and General Gale at Allied Force headquarters that 2,000 reinforcements were being sent from Philippeville that evening.[1] As replacements for units fighting at Salerno were being held in Philippeville, this made perfect sense. Yet, mysteriously, two hours later this instruction was cancelled and replaced by information that 1,500 men were to be sent from Tripoli the following morning.[2] Before receiving the second signal, Gale's staff appear to have second-guessed 15th Army Group headquarters' change of plan by informing the authorities at Tripoli to arrange for 1,500 reinforcements to be placed on stand-by.[3]

Given the time lapse between the sending and decoding of signals, it is difficult to pinpoint exactly who was reponsible for switching Tripoli for Philippeville. General Montgomery, who later discussed the matter with General Alexander, was not in any doubt. He blamed General Miller, Alexander's administrative chief, describing him as a 'dismal failure in Africa and Italy' and 'unfit' to be a major general in charge of administration. Furthermore, Montgomery confirmed that neither he nor Alexander were aware of the switch and would have prevented it if they had been. If confirmation was needed that the choice of Eighth Army veterans to reinforce units from another army was asking for trouble, the most revered British general of the Second World War has supplied it.[4]

Particularly inexcusable is the fact that the switch was unnecessary. A 15th Army Group instruction issued prior to the Salerno campaign stated that reinforcements for X Corps were located at Philippeville and that 4th Division troops were to be taken if base depots were exhausted.[5] On 14 September the infantry reinforcement depot at Philippeville contained more than 3,000 men,[6] while others were available from 4th Division units at Bougie. Furthermore, if time really was of the essence, then complete battalions from the American 3rd Division – destined for Salerno anyway – could have been transported from Sicily. In other words, there were other troops available and it was entirely superfluous to use a hotch-potch of Eighth Army veterans from Tripoli.

It is easy to sympathise with the Tripoli authorities, particularly the staff of 155 Camp, asked to supply 1,500 emergency reinforcements for Salerno. In charge of mainly Eighth Army men, having always returned them to their own units, here they were being asked to despatch them to a different army. It must have seemed the easy way out to inform the staff NCOs that normal routine was being kept to. 'I heard nothing official except the fact that they were going to their own units,' CSM Green told the court martial.[7] Here is irrefutable proof that the men were misled as to their destination. This deception stands out as the biggest single wrong done to the veterans and the fundamental cause of their refusal to join units at Salerno. Without it, even taking all other factors into account, it is unlikely that the mass disobedience would have occurred.

The partial breakdown of discipline at Salerno is a salutary lesson for all military administrators. The nature of war is such that individual soldiers are no more than cogs in a huge machine devoted to death and destruction. Their pride, principles, sensibility and very existence are often considered irrelevant when measured against that all-consuming monster, 'operational necessity'. But while the British soldier will doggedly march and fight in appalling conditions without respite, he retains a high sense of personal integrity which must not be transgressed. Explain to him what needs to be done and he will do it; deceive him and trouble is likely.

In this particular case, trouble was made inevitable by the fact that all those involved were Eighth Army men. At the time, this formation was unique in the British Army because of its unequalled record of success on the battlefield and the devoted relationship between its commander, General Montgomery, and his men. Before a major action, Montgomery would visit as many units as possible to talk to the troops about their particular task. He would also encourage his officers to tell their men more about an operation than would normally be the case, reasoning, rightly, that this would infuse a team spirit and a sense of purpose. As a result of this personal touch, and the successes that accrued, Montgomery developed a personality cult. He became, in every sense, an idol to which the undivided devotion of his men was directed. The prosecutor Lionel Daiches, during an interview with me in 1993, argued that the 'Montgomery cult' was central to the refusal to obey orders:

> When these men had to make a choice between loyalty to their country and loyalty to their units, it was the 'Monty cult' that swayed quite a number of them. He had fostered the feeling that the Eighth Army was an élite body of men, and many of its members could not bear to fight in any other. The probability is that these events could not have taken place with men from another army. The mutiny would never have happened had the whole thing been better handled. But once the cock-up started – given the force of the 'Montgomery cult' – there was set in chain a series of events which were inevitable. Therein lies the tragedy.

What gave the cult a practical orientation was the fact that members of the two divisions involved, particularly the 51st, had repeatedly been instructed to do everything in their power to ensure when separated that they always returned to their units. General Wimberley himself, the commander of the 51st, later confirmed that he had 'often' told men that if evacuated they should 'not allow themselves to get drafted to other divisions'.[8] By disobeying the order at Salerno, the men were attempting to obey an earlier imperative issued by their own officers.

Even if all the recuperated veterans sent on the ill-fated Salerno draft had been in A1 condition, fit and fully equipped to fight, the deception over their destination would still have given them cause for complaint. The fact that many were not only heightened their sense of grievance. Furthermore, it emphasises the extent to which the draft had degenerated into a farce by the time it left Tripoli. Sergeant Major Green's description – given in statements to Captain Murgatroyd – of his hurried attempts to detail the draft on the night of 14 September paints a picture of chaos and panic, where a desperate need to produce 1,500 men, any men, overrode normal procedure.

The result was that many of those sent were still recuperating from wounds and injuries, effectively unfit for battle, while still more, believing they were returning to their own units, joined of their own accord. We know of at least one man, Alexander McMichael – and he claims there were others – who was taken straight from a convalescent depot. In addition, the quality and quantity of kit issued was far below minimum requirements set out by GHQ Middle East. Some men did not even have rifles. Consequently, standard medical and equipment parades had to be cancelled because too many would have failed them.

When the men arrived at Salerno on 16 September they were given every reason to assume, rightly as it turned out, that they were *not* urgently required and that the existence of the beachhead was no longer in danger. Treated with indifference from the start, they were left in fields near the beach for two whole days before any were instructed to join front-line units. Over the next two days – 18 and 19 September – 1,200, including many 'rookies' and some X Corps men, went off. The recalcitrants, all Eighth Army veterans, do not appear to have been specifically ordered to move at this time, rather encouraged and then threatened. This failure by the transit camp officers to take decisive action when they first learnt that the men had a grievance can only have encouraged the men in their stand. General McCreery's speech in the afternoon of 19 September, in which he admitted that a 'cock-up' had been made, can only have further emboldened them. Every hour that passed without a definite order or their arrest must have convinced them that the authorities recognised the validity of their grievance and were unwilling to push matters to a head.

The composition of this group of 300 is interesting. According to the army psychiatrist Colonel Main, while it contained 'men of different calibre', including 'a few' anxious about 'future battle in strange company' and 'a few useless men who preferred idleness to discipline and service', the number in these two categories was 'few enough to have no directing influence on the others'. Instead, 'those with the highest divisional morale and a combative family spirit grouped themselves together in the decision to refuse all divisions but their own'. They believed, Main felt, 'that their actions were soldierly' and 'that a senior official would sooner of later support them'.[9]

From the moment of their arrest on the afternoon of 20 September, for refusing the same order for a third time, the men were treated by the authorities as if they had already been found guilty. The humiliation in the prisoner-of-war cage was followed by the deliberate rigours of the voyage back to North Africa, when the men were kept on deck and fed only hard tack. It was not until they reached 209 Prisoner-of-War Camp, and were put under the authority of the humane Lieutenant Everett, that conditions improved.

Taking into account all the circumstances that preceded the arrest of the men, it is impossible to justify the decision to try them for mutiny. A charge of disobeying the order of a superior officer would have been more than sufficient to deal with the 'crime' that was committed at Salerno. It may have appeared that the men combined to disobey an order, but their reasons for doing so, and the spirit in which they made their stand, in no way warranted a mutiny charge.

It is ironic, then, that the original charge preferred against the men in time for the taking of the summary of evidence on 29–30 September was the lesser one of disobedience. If that had not been later upgraded to mutiny, presumably on the recommendation of Lord Russell of Liverpool, then the events of 20 September 1943 would probably be no more than a footnote of history.

Once it had been decided to charge the men with mutiny – thus exposing them to the ultimate penalty, death – the onus was on the authorities to provide the time, personnel and co-operation necessary for the best possible defence to be put forward. Their failure to do so meant that irreparable damage had been done to the case for the defence even before the trial began.

The greatest single handicap imposed on the defence team was time. While the prosecution had five weeks to prepare their case, the 14 defending officers – five of them without legal qualification – were allowed just six days. Given the unprecedented number of defendants and the relatively small number of lawyers, this time allowance was hopelessly inadequate. To defend soldiers facing a capital charge properly, the defending officers should have taken individual statements which would have enabled them to pursue all possible defences. Each man's experience differed in some way, and to provide a detailed background to the events at Salerno it would have been necessary to take separate accounts; at a bare minimum, several hours would have been needed with each defendant. In the time available this simply was not possible, and the result was that, as Bill Murgatroyd admits, a number of crucial lines of enquiry were missed. The defending officers were never aware that the majority of the 1,500 reinforcements were raw recruits with no allegiance to any particular unit; nor did they know that General McCreery had spoken to the recalcitrants the day before their arrest, admitting that their arrival was the result of an administrative 'cock-up'.

Furthermore, there was not enough time to obtain sufficient evidence from other sources that would have put the soldiers' actions into context. As Murgatroyd recalls, the defence team were forced to rely on the desperate negative tactic of arguing that the prosecution had no case to answer, in effect 'driven into offering a case based on no evidence' because they 'did not have time to obtain evidence that would support any other form of defence'. Given the tenor of the tribunal, such legal niceties were never likely to be given the time of day.

It is tempting to ask the question: why did the defence not demand more time to prepare their case? In particular, why did they not insist on a lengthy adjournment at the beginning of the trial until they had gathered all the necessary evidence? When I interviewed Bill Murgatroyd in 1993, he told me that it was quickly obvious that 'the court was not going to give us an adjournment of more than a few hours at any one time', and that he did not know 'why we were not more forceful' with regard to this matter. Although not directly comparable, it is hard to imagine a defence team in a civil trial agreeing to commence without some of its evidence.

A possible explanation may lie in the fact that the senior defending officers were of the same rank as the junior court member and prosecutor. They seem to have felt that they did not have the 'authority' to oppose the will of their military superiors over the matter of an adjournment. The impossibility of them acting in a truly 'independent' manner, given the complication of their military rank, represents an inherent flaw in military trials.

A further factor in the unwillingness of the defending officers to demand more time may have been the belief that it would not do any good. Captain Evers' telegram of 26 October had destroyed the defence team's high hopes that 'friendly' witnesses at 155 Camp would confirm the defendants' claims that they had been misled, that their posting was contrary to all previous practice, and that many were sent unfit and underequipped. Sergeant Major Green, despite being called to Constantine as a potential prosecution witness, was prepared to appear for the defence and largely confirm these facts, but he alone was not considered sufficient to sway the court.

The contradiction between Green's eventual testimony in mitigation after the verdict, and Evers' failure to procure witnesses and documents that would have backed up Green's account, tends to indicate that the defence enquiries at Tripoli were deliberately frustrated by officers who had something to hide: an accurate account of the events of 14 September would have laid the blame for the many breaches of standard practice firmly at their door.

The trial itself contained a number of legal discrepancies. Firstly, the deliberately vague wording of the charge allowed the prosecution to claim, without offering any admissible evidence to support that claim, that the mutiny began before 20 September.

Second was the unwillingness of the president to grant an adjournment that would have enabled the defence to obtain all their witnesses. This led to at least one (ill) witness being abandoned and obviously contributed to the defence's decision to offer no evidence. The president, in particular, had no right to say that it was his 'duty' to see that the trial did not 'go on for weeks or months', and that the case would 'have to proceed without' a witness who was ill. Justice should not be held a hostage to time.[10]

Thirdly, the prosecution erroneously referred to the group that initially remained behind at the first transit area at Salerno as a 'baggage party'. Captain Lee, the chief prosecution witness, went along with this misnomer despite the fact that he was well aware that the reinforcements had no baggage and that the party was made up of the ill and the walking wounded. Lee himself had not fully recovered from a severe wound and was part of this group. If the court had been made aware of the fact that not all the reinforcements were 100 per cent fit, it can only have strengthened the case for the defence.

Fourthly, Major Money, the prosecutor, broke the fundamental court martial rule of the accused's right to silence by asking if Mulligan, Rae and DeLong had not been present at the fateful parade, 'how is it that although they had ample opportunity of saying so afterwards not one of them has opened his mouth to this day about it?'[11] In effect, he was arguing that, in the absence of other evidence, the silence of the three men was indicative of their presence and consequently their guilt. This was a deliberate infringement of court martial rule of procedure 60(B), which states that 'it is the duty of the court ... to prevent the prosecutor from commenting at any time on the failure of the accused ... to give evidence'. The rule goes on to say that the 'court should at once check a prosecutor if he infringes this rule, and should record upon the proceedings that they have done so.'[12] Needless to say, the court failed to do this.

Fifth comes the partisan nature of the deputy judge advocate. Rule of procedure 103(i) states that he should be 'careful to maintain an entirely impartial position'.[13] This, clearly, was not the case. He consistently made it plain that he opposed the idea of an adjournment, despite the fact that the defence did not have the evidence they required. During his direction on Quennell's submission of no case, he failed to mention which evidence had led him to infer combination between the DLI and non-DLI regiments; he also failed to point out that, contrary to the assertions of the prosecution, there was no admissible evidence of any mutinous behaviour before the parade on 20 September. But his greatest dereliction of duty came during his final summing up: first he made the bizarre point that disobeying one order on active service was worse than a general disobedience of all orders; then he repeated Major Money's earlier indiscretion by saying 'that nothing would have been easier, if a mistake had been made in respect of the identity of those men [Mulligan, Rae and DeLong], than for them to have gone into the witness box and given evidence about that matter'. The fact that they had not, Raphael said, 'entitled' the court to ask themselves 'why?'.[14] Once again, an illegitimate attempt to contradict the right of silence and reverse the burden of proof from the prosecution to the defence had been made. No surer confirmation of Raphael's determination to secure convictions is needed.

The unnecessarily harsh sentences meted out to the men are further proof that the trial was not a fair one. Certainly, there were no lack of guidelines for sentencing. The relevant *Manual of Military Law* stated that while 'provocation by a superior, or the existence of grievances, is no justification for mutiny', such circumstances should 'be allowed due weight in considering the question of punishment'.[15] *King's Regulations* advised the court when sentencing to take into account the 'nature and degree of the offence and the previous character of the accused', and that while sentences could 'vary according to the requirements of discipline', in general, and for a 'first offence', they should be 'light'.[16] Yet, despite the excellent evidence as to good character and the powerful mitigation in defence of the 'crime' – particularly Sergeant Major Green's testimony – the court still chose to sentence the three sergeants to death with *no recommendation to mercy*. A less justified penalty can rarely have been awarded in the history of military trials.

Furthermore, confirmation of the convictions and sentences should never have been allotted to General Gale because he, or a member of his staff, had been partially responsible for the administrative mix-up which led to Eighth Army veterans being sent to Salerno in the first place. As a result, his opinions could not have been 100 per cent impartial. In the same way, Lord Russell of Liverpool should not have been allowed to advise him on points of law raised by the defence because, as Quennell rightly pointed out in the petition, Russell 'had advised on the case before the trial'. The worst consequence of this was when he scandalously advised Gale that the convictions of Mulligan and Rae were safe in law when they patently were not.

The intervention of the adjutant general, Ronald Adam – who later described the case to Montgomery as 'one of the worst things that we have ever done'[17] – should have provided a relatively happy ending to this shoddy episode. That it did not is almost as unforgivable as the charge of mutiny itself.

It was as if the British authorities in North Africa could not bear to let the men off scot-free. Instead of being returned to their original units – in Britain preparing for D-Day – they were posted to unfamiliar battalions in Italy. Instead of being convinced that the suspensions were a genuine second chance, the privates and former lance corporals were lectured by an insensitive staff officer on the opportunity to 'retrieve their honour' with the proviso that any misdemeanours would mean a reimposition of sentence. 'Few understood that full reinstatement would be possible and some believed that a "suspension" meant only postponement and that they would eventually be called to serve the sentence,' wrote Colonel Main.[18]

Even more spiteful, the former sergeants and corporals were left for a month in a military prison under the impression that they would serve their full sentences before being told of the suspensions. This cruel act was as contradictory to the spirit in which Adam had ordered their release as the fateful speech about 'honour'.

Worse was to come. Guarded and generally treated like criminals during the journey back to Italy, it was freely known by all who came into contact with them that they were mutineers. This number included the members of their new units and, inevitably, many were victimised because of this. Being sent to Coventry, given the most dangerous tasks and denied leave and relief from the front line were just some of the indignities and dangers that many had to face. Allied with a belief that their sentences were bound to be reactivated, it is hardly surprising that so many deserted and went absent.

Without the tireless campaigning of former 51st Division commander General Wimberley, made aware of the trial by defending officer Captain Samwell, and, to a lesser extent, the intervention of General Montgomery, those who had their sentences reimposed would have languished in prisons for much longer than they did. Instead, Adam ordered a review of their sentences based on a psychiatric study of their motives for both disobeying the order at Salerno and later going absent after their sentences were suspended. Colonel Main's report was favourable in its conclusions and led directly to the release of most of the men in the summer of 1945.

Yet we should not imagine for a moment that release meant the end of the nightmare. Those alive today still bear the physical and mental scars of their experience, still harbour a bitter resentment at their treatment. Writing to his parents from Wormwood Scrubs in May 1945, Archie Newmarch managed to put his anger and disillusionment into words:

In the paper a few days ago I saw a piece about the pride of the British army, that a soldier liked pride. That's true, mam, the British army is built up on pride, but where did it get me and the other 192 men: seven years of the best. Wasn't we proud of our units, our division, wasn't we proud of the men we fought with and where we fought and what we fought for: liberty, freedom, peace? If that is what they call pride, liberty, freedom, peace, then god help England. My thoughts are not pretty for the injustice I was done. I hold a bitter grudge against the ones responsible for it, and until I am cleared of this charge and those who are responsible for this outrage are brought to justice, I will never fight again.[19]

Is it not about time that Newmarch, the handful of other mutineers still living and the families of those now dead are compensated for the injustice and suffering they have had to endure by the granting of a free pardon and the return of their campaign and gallantry medals? The new evidence contained in this book would seem to suggest so.

Open letter to the Secretary of State for Defence

Dear Secretary of State

In March 1982, following the screening of the BBC documentary *Mutiny*, your predecessor, John Nott, was asked by three Opposition MPs if he would 'consider recommending a pardon for, and the restoration of medals' to the more than 180 men found guilty of mutiny at Salerno in November 1943. Jerry Wiggin, Under-Secretary of State for the Armed Forces, provided a written answer, part of which flatly contradicted two claims made by the documentary: 'The existing Ministry of Defence records have been researched and there is no evidence that those who were found guilty of mutiny ... were not fit or were misled about their destination as vital reinforcements for the Salerno campaign ...' [Jerry Wiggin MP, Written Answer, 23 March 1982].

This book, the result of exhaustive research, contains new verbal and documentary evidence – including extracts from the court martial papers released in 1993 – that confirms these and other claims, and indicates that the men were victims of an injustice.

After being found guilty, the mutineers – all Eighth Army veterans of the North African and Sicilian campaigns – received sentences ranging from five years' penal servitude to death. The vast majority of these sentences were confirmed, and the men were about to begin long prison terms when the Adjutant General, Sir Ronald Adam, intervened. On a chance visit to Algeria, where the men were being held, he heard about the case – later describing it in a letter to General Montgomery as 'one of the worst things that we have ever done' – and immediately ordered the sentences to be suspended. This was done, but not in the spirit with which Adam had intended: told that the suspensions were a last chance to retrieve their honour and that any future misdemeanours would mean the immediate reimposition of their sentences, the men were once again posted to unfamiliar units in Italy. Notorious as mutineers, many were victimised by their new comrades and felt they were given unnecessarily dangerous tasks. Within weeks, almost half of them had either deserted or gone absent. On recapture their sentences were reactivated and they spent the rest of the war in prison. Most were released in the summer of 1945, as a consequence of a psychiatric report that cleared them of cowardice and concluded that their prime motive in refusing orders at Salerno was an excessive loyalty to their own units.

The lives of many, however, particularly those who felt driven to re-offend, were ruined. Stripped of their campaign and gallantry medals, broken in body and mind, they returned to only a semblance of normal civilian life. Ill health, nervous breakdowns, early retirements and marriage break-ups litter the intervening years.

Only by the granting of a free pardon, which it is in your power to recommend, can the handful of surviving mutineers and the families of others be released from the torment that has gripped them since 1943. Therefore I would ask you to read this book – which contains the many grounds on which I feel a pardon is justified – and then decide for yourself. The case, as you will find out, is not simply about deciding whether or not the men *technically* committed mutiny at Salerno, whether or not they seem guilty in the eyes of the law. It is about whether they were *morally* guilty of mutiny, and whether their treatment before, during and after the trial constitutes a miscarriage of justice.

You should bear in mind that, as established in the Court of Appeal in R v Foster [(1984) 2 All ER 679 at 687, (1985) QB 115 at 130] the 'effect of a free pardon' is 'to remove from the subject of the pardon "all pains, penalties and punishments whatsoever that from the same conviction may ensue", but not to eliminate the conviction itself'. In other words, unlike an acquittal or a quashed conviction, a pardon leaves unaffected the fact of the original verdict. As was successfully argued in the judicial review of the Derek Bentley case in 1993, 'the question in considering the grant of a free pardon is not whether' those convicted were 'innocent of the crime, but whether, in all the circumstances', they 'should be relieved of the punishment which was imposed'. [R v Secretary of State for the Home Office, *ex parte* Bentley, 24–25 July 1993.]

In addition, you should be aware that the Bentley judicial review established that the 'prerogative of mercy' is 'capable of being exercised in many different circumstances and over a wide range'. In other words, it is possible to award a conditional pardon which, in the case of the Salerno mutineers, could mean the return of all campaign and gallantry medals forfeited as a result of their alleged crimes.

Yours truly
Saul David   July 1995

Appendix

Author's note of appreciation

I would like to express my sincere gratitude to the following participants in the tragic events of 50 years ago, without whose assistance this book could not have been written.

Mutineers: Percy Aveyard, Hugh Fraser, Fred Jowett, Archie Newmarch, Edwin Scott, Robert Thompson, Ray Whitaker
Defence: William B Murgatroyd
Prosecution: Lionel H Daiches, QC
The Court: William B Harris, QC
Reinforcements: Albert G Lee, Alexander McMichael, Andy Scott
HMS *Charybdis*: Dennis Nicholls, Joe Michie, Eric Wilmot, John Eskdale
HMS *Euryalus*: Michael H Winter
HMS *Scylla*: Joe Robinson, Peter D Rayner
Others: Eric MacKenzie, Ronnie Serginson, Jack McNally, Lionel M Munby

Bibliography

Ahrenfeldt, Robert H, *Psychiatry in the British Army in the Second World War.* (Routledge & Kegan Paul, 1958)

Alexander of Tunis, Field Marshal Earl, *The Alexander Memoirs.* (Cassell, 1962)

Babington, Anthony, *For the Sake of Example: Capital Courts Martial 1914–18.* (Paladin, 1985)

Clark, Mark W, *Calculated Risk.* (Harper & Brothers, 1950)

Crew, F R E, *The Army Medical Services Campaigns.* (HMSO, 1956)

Ellis, John, *The Sharp End of War.* (David & Charles, 1980)

Hamilton, Nigel, *Monty – Master of the Battlefield 1942–1944.* (Hamish Hamilton, 1983)

Harris, John, *Scapegoat!: Famous Courts Martial.* (Severn House, 1988)

Hickey, Des and Smith, Gus, *Operation Avalanche: The Salerno Landings 1943.* (Heinemann, 1983)

Hughes, Robert, *Through The Waters: A Gunnery Officer in HMS Scylla 1942–43.* (William Kimber, 1956)

Jackson, W G F, *The Battle for Italy.* (Batsford, 1967)

James, Lawrence, *Mutiny: In the British and Commonwealth Forces, 1756–1956.* (Buchan & Enright, 1987)

Maloney, Brigadier C J C, *The Mediterranean and Middle East – Volume V.* (HMSO, 1973)

Morris, Eric, *Salerno: A Military Fiasco.* (Hutchinson, 1983)

Parliamentary Debates (Hansards), Fifth Series, Volume 410; Sixth Series, Volume 20

Patient, Alan, 'Mutiny at Salerno' in *The Listener,* 25 February 1982

Pond, Hugh, *Salerno.* (William Kimber, 1961)

Russell of Liverpool, Lord, *That Reminds Me.* (Cassell, 1959)

Samwell, Major H P, MC, *An Infantry Officer in the Eighth Army.* (Blackwood, 1945)

Stuart-Smith, James, 'Military Law: its history, administration and practice' in *Law Quarterly Review,* Volume 85, 1969, pp. 478–504

The Army Act 1881 with Amendments – 1935–9. (Eyre & Spottiswoode, 1939)

The Manual of Military Law, Seventh Edition (HMSO, 1929)

Wintringham, T H, *Mutiny.* (Stanly Nott, 1936)

The Secret Mutiny, BBC Radio, 19 February 1981

Mutiny, '40 Minutes', BBC 2, 24 February 1982

Newsnight, BBC 2, 24 February 1982

Chapter Notes and Sources

Abbreviations: Archives and Unpublished Documents

The Public Record Office, Kew, London: PRO, including papers from the
  Cabinet Office (CAB), the Prime Minister's Office (PREM) and the War
  Office (WO)
The Imperial War Museum, London (Department of Documents): IWM
Archie Newmarch (personal papers): AN
Dr Molly Main (family papers): MM
W B Murgatroyd (personal collection of trial defence documents): WBM

Chapter 1 – Operation *AVALANCHE*

1. Winston S Churchill, Mansion House Speech, 10 November 1942, *The
   Penguin Dictionary of Quotations* (1980), p. 111.
2. Brigadier C J C Maloney, *The Mediterranean and Middle East – Volume V*
   (HMSO, 1973), p. 223.
3. *Ibid.*, p. 260.
4. Signal from Lieutenant General Mark Clark to General Sir Harold
   Alexander, 1.10pm, 12 September, *Italian Campaign – Progress of Baytown
   and Avalanche*, WO 214 25, PRO.
5. *Minutes of Commander-in-Chief Meetings at Bizerte (with Alexander)*, 14 September 1943, WO 214 24, PRO.
6. *Administrative Instruction No 58*, 15th Army Group HQ, 'A' Branch War
   Diary, February–October 1943, WO 169 8463, PRO.
7. Signal from 15th Army Group Tactical HQ to Fifth Army HQ, 12.27pm,
   Cable In-Log, 1–30 September 1943, WO 204 106, PRO.
8. Signal from AFHQ to Tripoli District HQ, 1.25pm 14 September, AFHQ
   Cable Out-Log, 1–30 September 1943, WO 204 139, PRO.
9. Signal from 15th Army Group Tactical HQ to Fifth Army HQ, 2.45pm 14
   September, 15th Army Group Main HQ Operations Room Messages, WO
   169 8482, PRO.
10. Signal from 15th Army Group Tactical HQ to AFHQ, AFHQ Cable In-Log,
    1–30 September 1943, WO 204 106, PRO.
11. Signal from AFHQ to Tripolitania District HQ, 6pm 14 September, 15th
    Army Group Main HQ Operations Room Messages, WO 169 8482.
12. *Administrative Instruction No 58, op. cit.*
13. No 1 IRTD (Philippeville) War Diary, Sept 1943, WO 169 13836, PRO.
14. *Administrative Instruction No 58, op cit.*

15. 4th Division 'G' Branch War Diary, July-Dec 1943, WO 169 8699, PRO.
16. Signal from Tripolitania District HQ to AFHQ, 7.20 pm 14 Sept, 15th Army Gp Main HQ Ops Room Messages, WO 169 8482, PRO.
17. No 6 Advanced 02E War Diary, Jan–Dec 1943, WO 169 8413, PRO.
18. Letter from Gen Sir Ronald Adam to Gen Sir Bernard Montgomery, 14 April 1944, *The Papers of Field Marshal Viscount Montgomery of Alamein*, BLM 120, Reel 11, IWM.
19. Letter from Montgomery to Adam, 10 April 1944, *ibid.*
20. Mark W Clark, *Calculated Risk* (Harper & Brothers, 1950), p 207.
21. Signal from Alexander to Gen Dwight D Eisenhower, 6.06 pm 15 Sept, *Reports from General Alexander to General Eisenhower on the battle situation – 4 Sept to 3 Dec 1943*, WO 214 24, PRO.
22. Signal from Alexander to Churchill, 7.17 pm 15 Sept, *Telegrams relating to the progress of the build-up for Operations Avalanche and Baytown – Aug–Oct 1943*, PREM 3 345/4, PRO.
23. Signal from Fifth Army HQ to AFHQ, AFHQ Cable-In Log, *op cit.*

Chapter 2 – 'You're going back to your units'

1. Archie Newmarch, *Hijack to Mutiny*, unpublished personal account, pp 94–95, AN.
2. CSM R Green, *Proof of Evidence*: six statements made on 28 October 1943, WBM.
3. *Ibid.*
4. *Ibid.*
5. 155 Reinforcement and Transit Camp War Diary, May–Dec 1943, WO 169 13554, PRO.
6. Green, *Proof of Evidence*, *op cit.*
7. *Ibid.*
8. Green, Examination, 5th day of the trial, 2 Nov 1943, Court Martial Papers, WO 71 819, PRO.
9. *Notes on Divisional Commander's Conference*, 13 Sept 1943, 51st Division General Staff War Diary, Aug–Nov 1943, WO 169 8794, PRO.
10. Green, Examination, 5th day of the trial, *op cit.*
11. Green, *Proof of Evidence*, *op cit.*
12. Charles Daley, *The Secret Mutiny*, BBC Radio, 19 Feb 1981.
13. FAE Crew, *The Army Medical Services Campaigns* (HMSO, 1956) pp 70–1.
14. Newmarch, *Hijack to Mutiny*, *op cit.*
15. Lt Col TF Main, *General Matters in the Salerno Mutiny*, 9 Jan 1945, p 1, MM.
16. Green, *Proof of Evidence*, *op cit.*
17. *Ibid.*
18. *Ibid.*
19. Peter Paterson, *The Secret Mutiny*, *op cit.*
20. Hugh Fraser, *The Secret Mutiny*, *op cit.*
21. Letter from Peter Rayner to Alfred Morris MP, 6 April 1982.
22. Robert Hughes, *Through The Waters: A Gunnery Officer in HMS Scylla 1942–43* (William Kimber, 1956), p 191.
23. Green, *Proof of Evidence*, *op cit.*
24. William White, *The Secret Mutiny*, *op cit.*

Chapter 3 – 'We've been shanghai-ed'

1. Hughes, *Through The Waters, op cit*, p 187.
2. Main, *General Matters, op cit*, p 1.
3. *Ibid*, p 2.
4. *Ibid*.
5. Eric Morris, *Salerno: A military fiasco* (Hutchinson, 1983), p 294.
6. *Weekly Résumé*, 9–16 Sept 1943, War Cabinet Memoranda, WP (43) 403, Folios 10–11, CAB 66 41–41, PRO.
7. Clark, *Calculated Risk, op cit*, pp 208–9.
8. Maloney, *The Mediterranean and Middle East – Volume V, op cit*, p 289.
9. *Ibid*, p 504.
10. Main, *General Matters, op cit*, pp 2–3.
11. *Ibid*, p 3.
12. *Ibid*.
13. Maj Gen DN Wimberley, *Scottish Soldier* (unpublished memoirs), Volume 2, DH 12 9 79, p 209, IWM.
14. 5th Hampshires' War Diary, July–Dec 1943, WO 169 10224, PRO.
15. Letter from Montgomery to Gen Sir Alan Brooke, 14 Oct 1943, *The Montgomery Papers*, BLM 49, Reel 4, IWM.
16. Maj GG Ellison's written statement for the prosecution of the main points contained in Gen Sir Richard McCreery's address of 19 Sept 1943, Court Martial Papers, *op cit*; Des Hickey & Gus Smith, *Operation Avalanche: The Salerno Landings 1943* (Heinemann, 1983), pp 291–2; Hugh Pond, *Salerno* (William & Kimber, 1961), p 208.
17. Wimberley, *Scottish Soldier*, Vol 2, *op cit*, pp 209–10.
18. Main, *General Matters, op cit*, p 3.
19. *Ibid*.
20. Montgomery's speech to members of 51 Div, Messina, Sicily, 26 Sept 1943, 51 Div Gen Staff War Diary, *op cit*.
21. Montgomery's speech to officers before El Alamein, *Mutiny*, '40 Minutes', BBC 2, 24 Feb 1982.
22. Main, *General Matters, op cit*, p 1.
23. Wimberley, *Scottish Soldier*, Vol 2, *op cit*, p 209.
24. Maj RB Money's opening address, Day 2, 30 Oct 1943, Court Martial Papers, *op cit*.

Chapter 4 – Mutiny

1. Hickey & Smith, *Operation Avalanche*, pp 306–7, *op cit*.
2. Section 7, *The Army Act 1881 with Amendments – 1935–9* (Eyre & Spottiswoode, 1939).
3. Section 5, Chap III, *Manual of Military Law*, Seventh Edition (HMSO, 1929).
4. Examination and cross-examination of Capts Lee and Williams, Summary of Evidence, 29–30 Sept 1943, pp 10–17, Court Martial Papers, *op cit*; cross-examination of Lee and Williams, Days 2 and 3 of the trial, 30–31 Oct 1943, Court Martial Papers, *op cit*.
5. John McFarlane, *Mutiny*, '40 Minutes', *op cit*.
6. Wally Innes, *ibid*.

7. Lt AR Creed, examination and cross-examination, Day 3 of the trial, 31 Oct 1943, Court Martial Papers, *op cit.*
8. Capt JA Dallenger and Lt Creed, examination and cross-examination, Day 3 of the trial, *ibid.*
9. Capt Dallenger, *ibid.*
10. James West, letter published in the *Blackpool Evening Gazette*, Friday, March 1982.
11. Signal from Rear X Corps to Fifth Army, 15th Army Gp and AFHQ, recd 21 Sept, AFHQ Cable In-Log, *op cit.*
12. Signal from Maj Gen Charles Miller to Lt Gen Sir Humfrey Gale, recd 24 Sept, *ibid.*
13. Signal from AFHQ to 15th Army Gp HQ, 18 Sept 1943, *Return of Troops to UK for Overlord – Sept–Dec 1943*, WO 214 24, PRO.
14. Signal from Miller to Gale, recd 24 Sept, *op cit.*
15. Letter from Ld Russell of Liverpool to G1, AFHQ, 22 Dec 1943, Court Martial Papers, *op cit.*

Chapter 5 – Six days to prepare a defence

1. Newmarch, *Hijack to Mutiny*, *op cit*, p 105.
2. 30th Beds & Herts War Diary, Sept–Oct 1943, WO 169 10176, PRO.
3. Newmarch, *Hijack to Mutiny*, *op cit*, p 105.
4. Terry Corbett, *Mutiny*, 'Forty Minutes', *op cit.*
5. Corbett, letter published in *Reynold's News*, 8 Feb 1959.
6. Capt LH Daiches, Summary of Evidence, 29 Sept 1943, *op cit*, p 21.
7. Lee, *ibid*, pp 10–14.
8. 2nd Seaforths War Diary, Jan–Dec 1943, WO 169 10291, PRO.
9. 5th Hampshires War Diary, July–Dec 1943, WO 169 10229, PRO.
10. 7th Black Watch War Diary, Jan–Dec 1943, WO 169 10181, PRO.
11. 5th Camerons War Diary, Jan–Dec 1943, 10188; 1st Gordons War Diary, Jan–Dec 1943, WO 169 10215; 9th Durhams War Diary, Jan–Dec 1943, WO 169 10205, PRO.
12. Montgomery's Points for Alexander to consider at conference on 7 Oct 1943, *Italian Campaign – Progress of Baytown and Avalanche, op cit.*
13. Alexander's notes on his conference with Montgomery, 7 Oct 1943, *ibid.*
14. Mongomery's Diary, 27 Sept 1943, *The Montgomery Papers*, BLM 45, Reel 4, IWM.
15. Letter from Montgomery to Brooke, 14 Oct 1943, *The Montgomery Papers*, BLM 49, *op cit.*
16. Lord Russell of Liverpool, *That Reminds Me* (Cassell, 1959), p 164.
17. First amended version of the charge, tacked on to Summary of Evidence, 29–30 Oct 1943, Court Martial Papers, *op cit.*
18. List of defending officers and their defendants, 23 Oct 1943, WBM.
19. List of witnesses and documents required by the defence, *Statement of Agreement between the Prosecution and the Defence*, 24 Oct 1943, WBM.
20. *Ibid.*
21. 1/6th East Surreys War Diary, WO 169 10198.
22. Thumbnail sketches of the members of the Court, WBM.
23. Signal from Capt Evers in Tripoli to Capt Quennell in Constantine, sent 10

am, 26 Oct 1943, WBM.

24. Signal from Quennell in Constantine to Evers in Tripoli, 26 Oct 1943, WBM.
25. Green, *Proof of Evidence, op cit.*
26. Major HP Samwell MC, *An Infantry Officer in the Eighth Army* (Blackwood, 1945), p 140.
27. Amended mutiny charge, 28 Oct 1943, WBM.
28. Agenda for defending officers' meeting, 28 Oct 1943, WBM.

Chapter 6 – Court martial

1. Capt S Goldsmith's legal objection to the wording of the charge, Day 1 of the trial, 29 Oct 1943, Court Martial Papers, *op cit.*
2. Rule of Procedure 108, *Manual of Military Law,* Seventh Edition, *op cit,* p 682.
3. Maj GG Raphael's response to Goldsmith's objection, Day 1 of the trial, Court Martial Papers, *op cit.*
4. Rule of Procedure 103(f), *Manual of Military Law,* Seventh Edition, *op cit,* p 678.
5. Lt T Magnay's request for an adjournment, Day 1 of the trial, Court Martial Papers, *op cit.*
6. Maj RW Money's response to Magnay's request, *ibid.*
7. Magnay, *ibid.*
8. The court's response to Money's suggestion, *ibid.*
9. Rules of Procedure 15(A) and 104, *Manual of Military Law,* Seventh Edition, *op cit,* p 625 & p 679.
10. Interchange between Maj Gen A Galloway and Magnay, Day 1 of the trial, Court Martial Papers, *op cit.*
11. Interchange between Raphael, Galloway and Magnay, *ibid.*
12. Magnay's request for an adjournment and the court's response, *ibid.*
13. Capt HP Samwell's request for cigarettes for the accused and Galloway's response, *ibid.*
14. Magnay, Day 2 of the trial, 30 Oct 1943, Court Martial Papers, *op cit.*
15. Interchange between Money, Galloway and Magnay, *ibid.*
16. Money's opening address, *ibid.*
17. *Ibid.*
18. Examination of Capt AG Lee, *ibid.*
19. Capt H Quennell's request for an adjournment and the court's response, *ibid.*
20. RS Morton, *Scapegoats of a Desert Mutiny,* letter to the Daily Telegraph and Morning Post, 5 June 1961.
21. Quennell's 'character' statement, Day 3 of the trial, 31 Oct 1943, Court Martial Papers, *op cit.*
22. Raphael's ruling that Quennell's statement was 'not permissible', *ibid.*
23. Quennell's cross-examination of Lee, *ibid.*
24. Magnay's cross-examination of Lee, *ibid.*
25. Money's examination of Capt TW Williams, *ibid.*
26. Quennell's cross-examination of Williams, *ibid.*
27. Magnay's cross-examination of Williams, *ibid.*
28. Money's examination of Capt JA Dallenger, *ibid.*

29. Magnay's cross-examination of Dallenger, *ibid.*
30. Money's examination of Lt AR Creed, *ibid.*
31. Magnay's cross-examination of Creed, *ibid.*
32. Money's examination of Lt J Rees, *ibid.*
33. Magnay's cross-examination of Rees, *ibid.*
34. Money's examination of Sgt L Learmouth, *ibid.*
35. Quennell's cross-examination of Lt Rees, *ibid.*
36. Quennell's cross-examination of Lt EG Everett, *ibid.*
37. Magnay's submission of no case on behalf of Ptes J Mulligan and J Rae and Spr W DeLong, *ibid.*
38. Money's response to Magnay's submission, *ibid.*
39. Raphael's response to Magnay's submission, *ibid.*
40. The court's rejection of Magnay's submission, *ibid.*
41. Quennell's submission of no case on behalf of all the accused, *ibid.*

Chapter 7 – Guilty

1. Money's response to Quennell's submission, Day 4 of the trial, 1 Nov 1943, Court Martial Papers, *op cit.*
2. Raphael's response to Quennell's submission, *ibid.*
3. Magnay's closing speech, *ibid.*
4. Quennell's closing speech, *ibid.*
5. Capt GL Taylor's closing speech, *ibid.*
6. Capt WB Murgatroyd's closing speech, *ibid.*
7. Lt DRH Gardiner's closing speech, *ibid.*
8. Capt J Kailofer's closing speech, *ibid.*
9. Capt J Wheatley's closing speech, *ibid.*
10. Lt WJ Howat's closing speech, *ibid.*
11. Samwell's closing speech, *ibid.*
12. Lt FMH Edie's closing speech, *ibid.*
13. Capt Evers' closing speech, *ibid.*
14. Capt J Mitchell's closing speech, *ibid.*
15. Goldsmith's closing speech, *ibid.*
16. Lt H Hammonds' closing speech, *ibid.*
17. Raphael's summing-up speech, *ibid.*
18. Raphael's announcement of the verdict of not guilty for DeLong; Capt LH Daiches' announcement that 36 conduct sheets were missing; Gen Galloway grants Quennell's request for an adjournment; *ibid.*

Chapter 8 – 'Do not, please, be too hard on them!'

1. Mitchell's examination of Capt The Rev J Till, Day 5 of the trial, 2 Nov 1943, Court Martial Papers, *op cit.*
2. Murgatroyd's examination of CSM R Green, *ibid.*
3. Quennell's examination of Wheatley, *ibid.*
4. Quennell's examination of Kailofer, *ibid.*
5. Howat's examination of Pte G Kemp, *ibid.*

6. Samwell's examination of Howat, *ibid.*
7. Howat's examination of Samwell, *ibid.*
8. Howat's and Evers' examination of Mitchell, *ibid.*
9. Quennell's speech in mitigation, *ibid.*
10. Kailofer's speech in mitigation, *ibid.*
11. Wheatley's speech in mitigation, *ibid.*
12. Taylor's speech in mitigation, *ibid.*
13. Goldsmith's speech in mitigation, *ibid.*
14. Magnay's speech in mitigation, *ibid.*
15. Hammonds' speech in mitigation, *ibid.*
16. Murgatroyd's speech in mitigation, *ibid.*
17. Gardiner's speech in mitigation, *ibid.*
18. Evers' speech in mitigation, *ibid.*
19. Edie's speech in mitigation, *ibid.*
20. Howat's speech in mitigation, *ibid.*
21. Samwell's speech in mitigation, *ibid.*
22. Mitchell's speech in mitigation, *ibid.*
23. Galloway's closing words, *ibid.*

Chapter 9 – Sentenced to death

1. Letter from Maj WB Harris to his wife, 2 Nov 1943, author's original copy.
2. *The Humble Petition of all 181 men against conviction for mutiny*, Summary of Material Facts, pp 1–3, Court Martial Papers, *op cit.*
3. *The Humble Petition of all 181 men*, First Ground, pp 3–5, *ibid.*
4. *The Humble Petition of all 181 men*, Second Ground, pp 5–6, *ibid.*
5. *The Humble Petition of all 181 men*, Third Ground, p 6, *ibid.*
6. *The Humble Petition of all 181 men*, Appendix containing the appeal by the three sergeants against the death sentence, pp 6–7, *ibid.*
7. *Supplemental Petition of Ptes J Mulligan and R Rae of the Black Watch against conviction for mutiny*, Court Martial Papers, *op cit.*
8. Advice on Confirmation of Convictions and Sentences, Ld Russell of Liverpool to Lt Gen Gale, 8 Nov 1943, pp 1–3, Court Martial Papers, *op cit.*
9. *Ibid*, pp 3–4.
10. *Ibid*, p 4.
11. *Ibid*, p 4.
12. Gen Gale's decision on the confirmation of the verdicts and the sentences, 13 Nov 1943, Court Martial Papers, *op cit.*
13. *Ibid.*
14. *Ibid.*
15. Letter from Adam to Montgomery, 14 April 1944, *op cit.*
16. Newmarch, *Hijack to Mutiny*, *op cit*, p 114.
17. Main, *General Matters*, *op cit*, p 5.

Chapter 10 – Cannon-fodder

1. Main, *General Matters, op cit*, p 5.
2. Newmarch, *Hijack to Mutiny, op cit*, pp 117–18.
3. Main, *General Matters, op cit*, p 6.
4. Letter from Commonwealth War Graves Commission to A Newmarch, 4 April 1989, AN.
5. Innes, *Mutiny*, '40 Minutes', *op cit*.
6. Letter from Newmarch in 56th Military Prison, Brindisi, to his mother, 24 May 1944, AN.
7. Letter from Col, i/c Infantry & AEC Records York, to Mrs E Newmarch, 11 May 1944, AN.
8. McFarlane, *Mutiny*, '40 Minutes', *op cit*.
9. Russell of Liverpool, *That Reminds Me, op cit*, p 165.

Chapter 11 – 'One of the worst things that we have ever done'

1. Gen Sir Henry Wilson's response to the supplementary petition against sentence on behalf of all those convicted of mutiny, 15 Feb 1944, Court Martial Papers, *op cit*.
2. Ld Russell of Liverpool's memo concerning the supplementary petition against sentence, 22 Dec 1943, Court Martial Papers, *op cit*.
3. Maj GG Ellison's written statement for the prosecution of the main points contained in Gen McCreery's address of 19 Sept 1943, *op cit*.
4. Wimberley, *Scottish Soldier*, Vol 2, *op cit*, p 209.
5. *Ibid.*
6. *Ibid.*
7. Letter from Montgomery to Adam, 10 April 1944, *op cit*.
8. Letter from Adam to Montgomery, 14 April 1944, *op cit*.
9. Wimberley, *Scottish Soldier*, Vol 2, *op cit*, p 210.
10. *Ibid.*
11. McFarlane, *Mutiny*, '40 Minutes', *op cit*.
12. Letter from the War Office informing Mrs Aveyard that her son Percy had died from wounds received in action, dated 28 August 1943, AN.
13. Main, *General Matters, op cit*, pp 1–6.
14. Robert H Ahrenfeldt, *Psychiatry in the British Army in the Second World War*, (Routledge & Kegan Paul, 1958), pp 218–19.
15. Sir James Grigg MP, Written Answer, 17 April 1945, *Parliamentary Debates (Hansard)*, Fifth Series, Vol 410.
16. John McGovern MP reading out a letter from Mrs Edith Newmarch in the House of Commons on 20 April 1945, 'The 193 "Mutineers" of Salerno', article in the *Daily Express*, 21 April 1945.
17. Arthur Henderson MP's response to McGovern's reading of Mrs Newmarch's letter, *ibid*.
18. Letter from Grigg to Lt Comdr JG Braithwaite MP, 21 July 1944, AN.
19. Exchange between Henderson and McGovern, 'The 193 "Mutineers" of Salerno', *Daily Express, op cit*.

Chapter 12 – The human cost

1. Appendix XXXI (A), *King's Regulations* 1940, quoted in a letter from Miss LC Burrows of the Army Medal Office to A Newmarch, 13 March 1990, AN.
2. Jerry Wiggin MP, Written Answer, 23 March 1982, *Parliamentary Debates (Hansard)*, Sixth Series, Vol 20, pp 316–317.
3. Letter from Wiggin to James Hamilton MP, 15 March 1982, AN.
4. McFarlane, *The Secret Mutiny, op cit.*
5. Confrontation between Innes and Harris, *Newsnight*, BBC 2, 24 Feb 1982.

Chapter 13 – A pardonable offence

1. Signal from 15th Army Gp Tac HQ to Fifth Army HQ, 12.27 pm, 14 Sept 1943, *op cit.*
2. Signal from 15th Army Gp Tac HQ to Fifth Army HQ, 2.45 pm, 14 Sept 1943, *op cit.*
3. Signal from AFHQ to Trip Dist HQ, 1.25 pm, 14 Sept 1943, *op cit.*
4. Letter from Montgomery to Adam, 10 April 1944, *op cit.*
5. *Administration Instruction No 58, op cit.*
6. No 1 IRTD (Philippeville) War Diary, *op cit.*
7. Green, Day 5 of the trial, *op cit.*
8. Wimberley, *Scottish Soldier,* Vol 2, *op cit,* p 209.
9. Main, *General Matters, op cit,* p 3.
10. Galloway, Day 1 of the trial, *op cit.*
11. Money, Day 3 of the trial, *op cit.*
12. Rule of Procedure 60(B), *Manual of Military Law, op cit,* p 657.
13. Rule of Procedure 103(i), *ibid,* p 678.
14. Raphael, Day 4 of the trial, *op cit.*
15. Section 6, Chapter III, *Manual of Military Law, op cit.*
16. Sections (a) and (b), Para 681, *King's Regulations for the Army and the Royal Army Reserve: 1940,* Incorporating Amendments, 1945 (HMSO, 1945).
17. Letter from Adam to Montgomery, 14 April 1944, *op cit.*
18. Main, *General Matters, op cit,* p 5.
19. Letter from Archie Newmarch in Wormwood Scrubs to parents, 27 May 1945, AN.

Index